S0-AAC-247

ACKNOWLEDGEMENTS/DEDICATION

To Jesus Christ, my amazing Friend.

To Laura Ng, my amazing wife who loves Jesus.

To my amazing readers who love Jesus.

To my amazing theological vetters, Pastor Vic Torres and Pastor Tony Diuglio, who love to read about Jesus.

FOREWORD

I have been sharing Jesus for twenty-three years now, sixteen of those years on the missions' field. The first message I ever preached was in 1993 back in New York. It was a simple message about the storm the disciples found themselves in when crossing the Sea of Galilee. Many of the disciples were afraid they were going to drown in the open sea. There was nothing they could do to save themselves. When Jesus came to them, walking on the turbulent sea, they became even more afraid as they thought it was a spirit. But Peter, upon seeing Jesus walking on the restless waters, asked Jesus to bid him to come on to the sea also. Jesus answered Peter's question with one word, "Come!"

That single word 'Come' says it all. Jesus walked on water. That is why Peter could walk on water. Jesus did it first and we, who are in Jesus, can enjoy all that Jesus has done. Peter could never walk on water by his own strength. By his own works he would sink. He could never become like Jesus by his track record. All his performances and achievements as a professional fisherman were useless when it comes to walking on water. However, being in Jesus, he could walk on the restless waters. There is a whole different world under Jesus' feet. It's a fallen from grace world. But we are not part of that world. We are above it as we who are in Jesus can walk with Him on the waters. We can see and do the impossible when we rest upon the finished work of Jesus. We can find rest when there is restlessness all around us. Because Jesus did it for us, we can now rest in Him. Rest does not mean inactivity but a rest that can only be found in what Jesus has accomplished for us on the cross. Everything we do comes out of this rest in Jesus.

I am glad that you have chosen to 'Come' with me on this journey to see who Jesus really is. It is an amazing Grace journey. And when you see who Jesus is, you will finally see and know yourself. You do not need to strive to become because you already are. It is truly revolutionary. Actually, it should not come as a surprise as this book is all about Jesus and wherever He is, there will be a revolution. Welcome to the Jesus revolution!

We love him, because he first loved us.

1 John 4:19

The LOVE in rEVOLution is a reflection of how we see God's love for us. But one day we will see Love face to face and His name is Jesus.

Billy Ng

CONTENTS

To The Reader

This book is heavy on scripture and is intended as such. This book, after all, is a biblical study on Jesus and why He is Grace. The best way to read this book is to read the scripture in tandem with the explanations. That way, you get the full flavor of the message. While it is perfectly possible to skip all the scripture quoted, something will be lost along the way. For me personally, I find that even if I have read a particular passage of scripture a thousand times before, sometimes it is the thousand and one times that revelation finally occurs. I have used the King James Version (KJV) bible, as it is the only bible that is in the public domain and therefore, does not need permission to be quoted. I also find that the KJV gives plenty of fresh revelations, as it is direct, though sometimes quaint, in its prose. I hope that the scripture, while plenteous, would not detract but add to the message conveyed in this book.

This book has been divided into 40 chapters, with each chapter as independent as possible from each other. In some of the later chapters, I have interjected some short but personal missionary accounts into the introduction of the chapter. However, the sole message for each chapter is always Jesus and His grace. There is no grace without Jesus as Jesus is Grace. Almost every chapter presents a contrast or a parallel between the Old Testament and the New Testament. In the Old Testament, Jesus is hidden but in the New Testament, Jesus is revealed. At the end of each chapter, I hope that the Holy Spirit will reveal more of Jesus to you. By the end of the book, I hope the full revelation that Jesus is Grace will be evident to you. Grace is simply 'the unmerited gift or blessing brought to man by Jesus Christ'. The gift is Jesus Himself! Jesus is the unmerited gift of love from God to us.

In recent years, there has been a resurgence on the message of Grace or Jesus. At the same time, there has been a marked rise in criticisms against Grace. But Grace is not something new. Grace has always been shared and has always been criticized. Grace may have been poorly explained, resulting in its misunderstanding and subsequent criticisms. Acknowledging shortcomings in the teaching on grace, Jesus or Grace is still the only message worth sharing. If we do not share Jesus, what else do we share?

❧ 1 ❧

JESUS AND ONLY JESUS

The Bible is all about Jesus. Jesus is the center of the whole bible. As such, everything we read in the bible should be read through the lens of Jesus. If we do not read the bible through Jesus' lens, then by default we become the center of the bible. With 'us' as the center, most books in the bible then become How-to guides. We read the bible to discover how-to become better people, better leaders, better employees, better husbands and wives, better parents, better neighbors - the list goes on and on. We try to modify our behavior to reflect what we think Christian living should be like. We patch, we fix, we improve, we grow, we perform, we strive, we persevere, we clean, and we obey. When we feel or are told that our doing is insufficient, then we begin the whole works cycle again. We patch, we fix, we improve...and it goes on and on. It is mainly about us using the bible and our own efforts to better our own lives. While most of these efforts are very good and commendable, the emphasis is on us doing many good works.

However, if Jesus is the center of the bible, then another picture emerges. It is now Jesus who did all the good works. We begin to see that the bible is not primarily about us. It is about Jesus. But as Jesus is, so are we. As He is holy, so are we holy. As He is good, so are we good. As He is accepted, so are we accepted. As He is victorious, so are we victorious. As He is righteous, so are we righteous. And because of His finished work we become better people, leaders, employees, husbands and wives, parents and neighbors. In short, it is because of Jesus alone that we can become better people. We are brought into the picture only because of what Jesus did for us on the cross.

Many of us may actually agree that the bible is all about Jesus but practically, in our day-to-day lives, we walk our walk as though it all depended on us. At best, we compromise and arrive at a mixture of Jesus and our own works. It may be a 50-50 share or any wide-ranging scale depending on how much control we are willing to let go of and let Jesus be in charge of. We may be willing to let Jesus be the start but we will be in charge of today. And if by some superhuman effort, we let Jesus be in charge of today, we surely must control the end. Jesus can be Alpha but we will be Omega. Jesus may be the start of the bible but we will be the end of the bible.

Where did all these self-works come from? The genesis of all self-works came from Eve who was fooled by the devil to switch her focus from God to self. In *Genesis 3:5*, we read, *For God doth know that in the day ye eat thereof, then your eyes shall be opened, and ye shall be as gods, knowing good and evil.* Both Eve and Adam ate the fruit and they became as gods, knowing good and evil. Now that they were as gods, they no longer had any need for God. Now that they knew what was good and what was evil, they could decide for themselves, to do what they thought were good deeds and to avoid what they thought were bad deeds. Since they knew what to do, why was there a need for God? The devil subtly switched man's focus away from God, not to himself, but to man's own efforts and works. **The devil wanted man to know good and evil so as to draw man away from God.**

This holds true till today as we struggle to answer basic questions like whether the bible is about us and our works, a mixture, or all about Jesus. The bible is actually very clear about this simple question. In *Revelation 1:8,* we read, *I am Alpha and Omega, the beginning and the ending, saith the Lord, which is, and which was, and which is to come, the Almighty.* Jesus is the Alpha and the Omega. In English, we would say that He is A to Z or in

Hebrew, He is Aleph to Tav. He is the beginning and the ending of the bible. He was, He is, and He is to come. He is the first, He is the last, and He is everything in between. In addition, in *John 1:1-4*, it states that *In the beginning was the Word, and the Word was with God, and the Word was God. The same was in the beginning with God. All things were made by him; and without him was not anything made that was made. In him was life; and the life was the light of men.*

Without Jesus, there was not anything made that was made. Without Jesus, there would be nothing. Without Jesus, we would not exist. Jesus is life. And because of Jesus, we have life. He is the beginning, the middle and the end of the bible.

If we do not have this personal revelation of who Jesus is, then our whole Christian life revolves around our works and sacrifices. We tell our friends of our sacrifice for Jesus when we should actually tell our friends of Jesus' sacrifice for us. We proclaim our love for Jesus when the true proclamation should be of Jesus' love for us. We boast of all that we did for Jesus when actually, we should boast of all that Jesus had done for us.

And what did He do for us? He did the unthinkable. He died for us on the cross when we were yet His enemies. When we hated and despised Him, He loved us. For many of us, it is incomprehensible that Jesus could love us that much when we detested Him and wanted nothing to do with Him. It does not make sense. It is irrational and illogical. It is downright unnatural. In *Ephesians 3:17-19*, we read, *That Christ may dwell in your hearts by faith; that ye, being rooted and grounded in love, May be able to comprehend with all saints what is the breadth, and length, and depth, and height; And to know the love of Christ, which passeth knowledge, that ye might be filled with all the fulness of God.*

The fullness of God is the love of Jesus for us. We become full as we let Jesus love us. Jesus' love for us surpasses man's knowledge or wisdom. **Man cannot understand unconditional love without a revelation of Jesus.** As the cross had breadth, length, depth, and height so had His love for us. As the cross was rooted and grounded, so had His love for us. Jesus' love for us has weight and dimensions. We did not deserve such love but nonetheless, it was given to us freely. **And when we finally see Jesus and His amazing love for us, then and only then can we say how much we love Him back. We love Him because He first loved us.**

❧ 2 ❧

JESUS AND SHADOWS

The Old Testament is full of accounts about Jesus. At the start, Jesus Christ was promised. Then a picture of Jesus was shown. However, this picture of Jesus was not fully revealed. He was hidden or concealed. These 'hidden' accounts about Jesus were called 'shadows', 'types' or 'figures' in the bible. Shadows or types represent the form but is not the real person or thing. It is only an image of the real person or thing. It prefigures the real person that has not yet been fully revealed. Jesus Christ was kept a secret in the Old Testament but in the New Testament was made manifest. In the New Testament, the person of Jesus Christ was fully revealed. What was once hidden is now made known.

Frequently, only the Holy Spirit can reveal to us the true meaning of these shadows. Until the Holy Spirit's revelation, they remain mysteries. In *1 Corinthians 2:7-10*, we read, *But we speak the wisdom of God in a mystery, even the hidden wisdom, which God ordained before the world unto our glory: Which none of the princes of this world knew: for had they known it, they would not have crucified the Lord of glory. But as it is written, Eye hath not seen, nor ear heard, neither have entered into the heart of man, the things which God hath prepared for them that love him. But God hath revealed them unto us by his Spirit: for the Spirit searcheth all things, yea, the deep things of God.* Then again in *Romans 16:25-26, Now to him that is of power to stablish you according to my gospel, and the preaching of Jesus Christ, according to the revelation of the mystery, which was kept secret since the world began, But now is made manifest, and by the scriptures of the prophets, according to the commandment of the everlasting God, made known to all nations for the obedience of faith.* Also in *Colossians 1:26-27* which states, *Even the mystery which hath been hid from ages and from generations, but now is made manifest to his saints: To whom God would make known what is the riches of the glory of this mystery among the Gentiles; which is Christ in you, the hope of glory:*

The prophets in the Old Testament prophesied about the coming of Jesus but it was not fully revealed to them. In *1 Peter 1:10-13, Of which salvation the prophets have inquired and searched diligently, who prophesied of the grace that should come unto you: Searching what, or what manner of time the Spirit of Christ which was in them did signify, when it testified beforehand the sufferings of Christ, and the glory that should follow. Unto whom it was revealed, that not unto themselves, but unto us they did minister the things, which are now reported unto you by them that have preached the gospel unto you with the Holy Ghost sent down from heaven; which things the angels desire to look into. Wherefore gird up the loins of your mind, be sober, and hope to the end for the grace that is to be brought unto you at the revelation of Jesus Christ.* Even angels desired to know what was to come but it was not told to them as well. However, thanks to the Holy Spirit we now know more about the deep things of God, namely Jesus Christ. The Holy Spirit revealed Jesus Christ to us.

In *John 1:45*, we read, *Philip findeth Nathanael, and saith unto him, We have found him, of whom Moses in the law, and the prophets, did write, Jesus of Nazareth, the son of Joseph.* Again in *Acts 3:20-22, And he shall send Jesus Christ, which before was preached unto you: Whom the heaven must receive until the times of restitution of all things, which God hath spoken by the mouth of all his holy prophets since the world began. For Moses truly said unto the fathers, A prophet shall the Lord your God raise up unto you of your brethren, like unto me; him shall ye hear in all things whatsoever he shall say unto you.* Philip was the first disciple to see Jesus as the One whom Moses and the other prophets wrote and spoke about in the Old Testament. Then Jesus Himself reconfirmed this truth that Moses and the other prophets did indeed wrote about Him. *John 8:58* states that *Jesus said unto them, Verily, verily, I say unto you, Before Abraham was, I am.* Then in *Luke 24:44, And he said unto them, These are the words which I spake unto you, while I was yet with you, that all things must be fulfilled, which were written in the law of Moses, and in the prophets, and in the psalms, concerning me.* He mentioned that he existed before Abraham and that He was the One written about in the Psalms.

There are many examples of 'shadows' in the bible. For instance, the law that was given to Moses on Mount Sinai was a shadow of Jesus. *Hebrews 10:1* states, *For the law having a shadow of good things to come, and not the very image of the things, can never with those sacrifices which they offered year by year continually make the comers thereunto perfect.* When Jesus appeared, He fulfilled all the writings and prophecies of old.

Another example of a 'shadow' was the rock that Moses struck in the wilderness. This is clear from *1 Corinthians 10:4, And did all drink the same spiritual drink: for they drank of that spiritual Rock that followed them: and that Rock was Christ.* The real Rock was Jesus Himself who would be struck and crucified for us.

Also, in *1 Corinthians 15:21-22,* we read, *For since by man came death, by man came also the resurrection of the dead. For as in Adam all die, even so in Christ shall all be made alive.* Adam was called a figure or shadow of Jesus. We read this in *Romans 5:14-15, Nevertheless death reigned from Adam to Moses, even over them that had not sinned after the similitude of Adam's transgression, who is the figure of him that was to come. But not as the offence, so also is the free gift. For if through the offence of one many be dead, much more the grace of God, and the gift by grace, which is by one man, Jesus Christ, hath abounded unto many.* Through Adam, all men died but through Jesus all men lived. But not only did they live but they were made new and reigned as well.

The ark of Noah was also a shadow. *1 Peter 3:20-21* states, *Which sometime were disobedient, when once the longsuffering of God waited in the days of Noah, while the ark was a preparing, wherein few, that is, eight souls were saved by water. The like figure whereunto even baptism doth also now save us (not the putting away of the filth of the flesh, but the answer of a good conscience toward God,) by the resurrection of Jesus Christ.* The ark saved eight lives. The real ark is Jesus who saves all those who have faith in Him. Notice that in all cases, the real person is always more majestic and greater than its shadow. The grace of God is always much greater than the original sin.

The tabernacle was a shadow or figure. We read in *Hebrews 9:8-10, The Holy Ghost this signifying, that the way into the holiest of all was not yet made manifest, while as the first tabernacle was yet standing: Which was a figure for the time then present, in which were offered both gifts and sacrifices, that could not make him that did the service perfect, as pertaining to the conscience; Which stood only in meats and drinks, and divers washings, and carnal ordinances, imposed on them until the time of reformation.* The tabernacle in the Old Testament was a tent or building in which the Jews offered sacrifices unto God. All the objects and ordinances performed by the priests in the tabernacle pertain to Jesus Christ.

Even the high priest ministering in the tabernacle was a 'shadow'. The real High Priest is Jesus Christ. This is found in *Hebrews 8:1-5, Now of the things which we have spoken this is the sum: We have such an high priest, who is set on the right hand of the throne of the Majesty in the heavens; A minister of the sanctuary, and of the true tabernacle, which the Lord pitched, and not man. For every high priest is ordained to offer gifts and sacrifices: wherefore it is of necessity that this man have somewhat also to offer. For if he were on earth, he should not be a priest, seeing that there are priests that offer gifts according to the law: Who serve unto the example and shadow of heavenly things, as Moses was admonished of God when he was about to make the tabernacle: for, See, saith he, that thou make all things according to the pattern shewed to thee in the mount.*

There is another word in the bible that has the same meaning as 'shadow'. The word is 'veil'. A person's face can be concealed behind a veil. We can see the outline of the face but the features are not clear. This is found in *2 Corinthians 3:13-18* which states, *And not as Moses, which put a vail over his face, that the children of Israel could not stedfastly look to the end of that which is abolished: But their minds were blinded: for until this day remaineth the same vail untaken away in the reading of the old testament; which vail is done away in Christ. But even unto this day, when Moses is read, the vail is upon their heart. Nevertheless when it shall turn to the Lord, the vail shall be taken away. Now the Lord is that Spirit: and where the Spirit of the Lord is, there is liberty. But we all, with open face beholding as in a glass the glory of the Lord, are changed into the same image from glory to glory, even as by the Spirit of the Lord.*

Moses put a veil over his face so that the Israelites could not see his face properly. Moses' face represented the law. As the law was given, God provided for its abolishment. However, because of the veil, the Israelites could not see the coming of the end of the law and continued to trust and walk in it. Whenever the law was read, the veil was upon the peoples' hearts. They could not see clearly.

In *John 5:45*, we read, *Do not think that I will accuse you to the Father: there is one that accuseth you, even Moses, in whom ye trust.* We know that there is only one true accuser who is the devil, not Moses. In *Revelation 12:10, the accuser of our brethren is cast down, which accused them before our God day and night.* Nevertheless, all those who walk in the law are accused by the law. This veil can only be lifted and done away in Christ. When the Holy Spirit revealed Christ to us, we became free from the law. We begin to enjoy the liberty that Jesus brought. Now, we can look at Jesus' open face, who wears no veil, and marvel at our own glorious face reflected therein. We are glorious because He is glorious. Our faces bear the same image as His because He has made us become just like Him!

Therefore, we see that Jesus was hidden as a shadow or behind a veil in the Old Testament. Then He was revealed in the

New Testament. We will now examine the 'shadow' versus the 'real' in more detail. The real is always Jesus.

As you read the following chapters, let the Holy Spirit enter your spirit and soak you with fresh revelations of Jesus. I pray that each succeeding chapter will make you become more aware of how much you are loved and treasured by Jesus. I hope that a Jesus revolution will take place inside of you as He is revealed to you more and more.

↷ 3 ↶

JESUS AND THE ARK OF NOAH

To get to Noah, we have to start with his great grandfather Enoch. We start in *Genesis 5:21-27, And Enoch lived sixty and five years, and begat Methuselah: And Enoch walked with God after he begat Methuselah three hundred years, and begat sons and daughters: And all the days of Enoch were three hundred sixty and five years: And Enoch walked with God: and he was not; for God took him. And Methuselah lived an hundred eighty and seven years, and begat Lamech: And Methuselah lived after he begat Lamech seven hundred eighty and two years, and begat sons and daughters: And all the days of Methuselah were nine hundred sixty and nine years: and he died.* Enoch had a very close relationship with God and was one of the two people in the bible who did not die as God took him straight up to heaven. The other one who did not die was Elijah, who was taken up to heaven in a whirlwind.

Enoch had such a close walk with God that God revealed a secret to him. The secret was wrapped up in his son's name, Methuselah, which meant 'when he dies, it will come'. I am sure many people at that time asked the question, "What is coming when Methuselah dies?" The answer, of course, was the flood.

Man's actions and thoughts at that time had become so corrupt that God was going to destroy man from the face of the earth. Everything that God created was good. However, the good got corrupted. God never created badness or evil! *Genesis 6:5-8* states, *And God saw that the wickedness of man was great in the earth, and that every imagination of the thoughts of his heart was only evil continually. And it repented the Lord that he had made man on the earth, and it grieved him at his heart. And the Lord said, I will destroy man whom I have created from the face of the earth; both man, and beast, and the creeping thing, and the fowls of the air; for it repenteth me that I have made them. But Noah found grace in the eyes of the Lord.*

Note that it was man's actions and thoughts that were corrupt, not God's actions and thoughts. The works of men can never attain to God's holy and perfect standard. Yet men refused God, choosing to trust in their own works. Eventually, the works of men became so wicked and evil that there was a real possibility that if they were not stopped, the promised seed, Jesus Christ, would be threatened.

The timing of the coming worldwide flood was first revealed to Enoch. Enoch did not conceal this but exposed it through the name of his son, Methuselah. Every year that Methuselah lived was another year of grace. Another year for the people to come back to rest in God's goodness. But year after year, the people refused. Yet the flood was not sent. In fact, God showed His abundant grace to the evil world by allowing Methuselah to become the oldest man to ever live. He lived to an astonishing 969 years! (The next two were Jared who lived 962 years and Adam who lived 930 years). This amazing longevity of Methuselah permitted the world plenty of time to return to God. But none did except Noah.

A simple calculation confirms that Methuselah died in the same year when Noah, his grandson, was 600 years old. Methuselah was 187 years old when he had Lamech. Lamech was 182 years old when Noah was born. And Noah was 600 years old when the flood started. Adding up the numbers, we get $187+182+600=969$. That is the exact number of years that Methuselah lived. When Methuselah died, the flood waters were unleashed upon the earth.

We see this in *Genesis 5: 28-32, And Lamech lived an hundred eighty and two years, and begat a son: And he called his name Noah, saying, This same shall comfort us concerning our work and toil of our hands, because of the ground which the Lord hath cursed. And Lamech lived after he begat Noah five hundred ninety and five years, and begat sons and daughters: And all the days of Lamech were seven hundred seventy and seven years: and he died. And Noah was five hundred years old: and Noah begat Shem, Ham, and Japheth* and in *Genesis 7:6, And Noah was six hundred years old when the flood of waters was upon the earth.*

The ark took a maximum of 120 years to complete. *Genesis 6:3*, states, *And the Lord said, My spirit shall not always strive with man, for that he also is flesh: yet his days shall be an hundred and twenty years.* When God disclosed His plan to Noah, the countdown to the flood began. Somewhere in that period, the ark-building project began and completed. But what was really interesting was that God's promise to Noah to save his wife, his sons and their wives was given 20 years before his first son, Japheth, was even born!

The promise by God was 120 years before the flood. Noah was 500 years old when he had his first son. We see in *Genesis 5:32, And Noah was five hundred years old: and Noah begat Shem, Ham, and Japheth.* The flood came when he was 600. Therefore, God promised Noah that his sons and their wives would be saved at least 20 years before they were born. **The ark was given before the flood. The cure was given before the disease came. Salvation was given before there was sin. The Lamb was slain before the foundations of the earth were established.**

The design of the ark was precise and was revealed to Noah in advance. In *Genesis 6:14-19*, we read, *Make thee an ark of gopher wood; rooms shalt thou make in the ark, and shalt pitch it within and without with pitch. And this is the fashion which thou shalt make it of: The length of the ark shall be three hundred cubits, the breadth of it fifty cubits, and the height of it thirty cubits. A window shalt thou make to the ark, and in a cubit shalt thou finish it above; and the door of the ark shalt thou set in the side thereof; with lower, second, and third stories shalt thou make it. And, behold, I, even I, do bring a flood of waters upon the earth, to destroy all flesh, wherein is the breath of life, from under heaven; and everything that is in the earth shall die. But with thee will I establish my covenant; and thou shalt come into the ark, thou, and thy sons, and thy wife, and thy sons' wives with thee. And of every living thing of all flesh, two of every sort shalt thou bring into the ark, to keep them alive with thee; they shall be male and female.*

It was to be made of wood, with many rooms spread over three stories, with one window at the top and one door at the side, and to be completely covered with pitch or tar.

Genesis 7:1-4, 15-16 states, *And the Lord said unto Noah, Come thou and all thy house into the ark; for thee have I seen righteous before me in this generation. Of every clean beast thou shalt take to thee by sevens, the male and his female: and of beasts that are not clean by two, the male and his female. Of fowls also of the air by sevens, the male and the female; to keep seed alive upon the face of all the earth. For yet seven days, and I will cause it to rain upon the earth forty days and forty nights; and every living substance that I have made will I destroy from off the face of the earth. And they went in unto Noah into the ark, two and two of all flesh, wherein is the breath of life. And they that went in, went in male and female of all flesh, as God had commanded him: and the Lord shut him in.* Noah would bring his family into the ark as well as seven of every 'clean' animal and two of every 'unclean' animal. When the floods finally came, every living thing on the ground was destroyed except for Noah, his family, and the animals that were in the ark. But note that Noah did not earn grace. It was given to him freely.

In *1 Peter 3:20-22*, it is clear that the ark was a 'shadow' or 'figure' of something or someone. We read, *Which sometime were disobedient, when once the longsuffering of God waited in the days of Noah, while the ark was a preparing, wherein few, that is, eight souls were saved by water. The like figure whereunto even baptism doth also now save us (not the putting away of the filth of the flesh, but the answer of a good conscience toward God,) by the resurrection of Jesus Christ: Who is gone into heaven, and is on the right hand of God; angels and authorities and powers being made subject unto him.* That 'like figure' was Jesus Christ.

Knowing that Jesus is the true 'ark' changes the way we understand the flood. The ark's design was revealed in advance. Jesus was revealed to us in advance. He would be wounded for our transgressions and be bruised for our iniquities. He would bear our sins.

The ark was made of wood. The cross was made of wood. **Jesus on the cross and His later resurrection is always the answer.** Noah was invited by God to enter the ark. We are invited as well. The word used was 'Come' not 'Go'. It was an invitation not a command. For we are saved by grace not works. All those who entered the ark were secure and found the breath of life. All those who entered in Jesus are similarly secure for Jesus is the Breath of Life. *John 10:27-30* states, *My sheep hear my voice, and I know them, and they follow me: And I give unto them eternal life; and they shall never perish, neither shall any man pluck them out of my hand. My Father, which gave them me, is greater than all; and no man is able to pluck them out of my Father's hand. I and my Father are one.* No man would ever pluck us out of His hand. We have eternal salvation.

The ark had only one door. Jesus is the only door to salvation. *John 10:9* states, *I am the door: by me if any man enter in, he shall be saved, and shall go in and out, and find pasture.* There are no other doors or ways to salvation. God Himself shut the door of the ark. There was only one window located at the top of the ark. In *Colossians 3:1-3, If ye then be risen with Christ, seek those things which are above, where Christ sitteth on the right hand of God. Set your affection on things above, not on things on the earth. For ye are dead, and your life is hid with Christ in God.* At all times, our focus should be up at Jesus and His completed work. If we look at our own works and circumstances or at other people, we would sink. The ark was covered with pitch inside and outside. It was wholly covered. We are wholly covered and protected by Christ. We are hid in Christ. Our sins were covered, then taken away and no longer imputed to us. We see in *Romans 4:7-8, Saying, Blessed are they whose iniquities are forgiven, and whose sins are covered. Blessed is the man to whom the Lord will not impute sin.* There were many rooms in the ark. We read in

John 14:2-3, In my Father's house are many mansions: if it were not so, I would have told you. I go to prepare a place for you. And if I go and prepare a place for you, I will come again, and receive you unto myself; that where I am, there ye may be also. Jesus has prepared a room for each of us so that we can rest in His finished work.

When the rain and floods finally came, the ark was inundated with a deluge of water from above as well as from below. We read in *Genesis 7:11-12, 17, 23* that *In the six hundredth year of Noah's life, in the second month, the seventeenth day of the month, the same day were all the fountains of the great deep broken up, and the windows of heaven were opened. And the rain was upon the earth forty days and forty nights. And the flood was forty days upon the earth; and the waters increased, and bare up the ark, and it was lift up above the earth. And every living substance was destroyed which was upon the face of the ground, both man, and cattle, and the creeping things, and the fowl of the heaven; and they were destroyed from the earth: and Noah only remained alive, and they that were with him in the ark.*

The windows of heaven and the fountains of the great deep opened up at the same time. Such stormy ferocity had never been seen or would ever be seen again. All the fury of the storm was hurled at the ark. Far from capsizing, as the water got higher, the ark was lifted up above the waters. Only those who were in the ark survived the onslaught. They may fall from time to time due to the fury of the storm but they fell inside the ark, not outside. There were always safe and secure inside the ark as their feet rested on solid wood - the wood that would one day represent the cross on which we would rest upon. Grace lifted up the ark and continuously bore it up.

Similarly, God's wrath against our sins was hurled at Jesus Christ on the cross. **The judgment for our sins was put upon Jesus. For only the Lamb of God could take away the sins of the world. Only the perfection of Jesus could pay what we could never pay. We were redeemed with the precious blood of Christ, the lamb without blemish or spot.**

We read this in the following scriptures. *Colossians 3:6,*
For which things' sake the wrath of God cometh on the children of
disobedience:
Romans 1:18, 32, For the wrath of God is revealed from heaven
against all ungodliness and unrighteousness of men, who hold the
truth in unrighteousness; Who knowing the judgment of God, that
they which commit such things are worthy of death, not only do the
same, but have pleasure in them that do them.
John 1:29, The next day John seeth Jesus coming unto him, and
saith, Behold the Lamb of God, which taketh away the sin of the
world.
1 Peter 1:18-19, Forasmuch as ye know that ye were not
redeemed with corruptible things, as silver and gold, from your
vain conversation received by tradition from your fathers; But with
the precious blood of Christ, as of a lamb without blemish and
without spot:
2 Corinthians 5:21, For he hath made him to be sin for us, who
knew no sin; that we might be made the righteousness of God in
him.
　　　　We also read in *Isaiah 53:3-12, He is despised and rejected*
of men; a man of sorrows, and acquainted with grief: and we hid
as it were our faces from him; he was despised, and we esteemed
him not. Surely he hath borne our griefs, and carried our sorrows:
yet we did esteem him stricken, smitten of God, and afflicted. But
he was wounded for our transgressions, he was bruised for our
iniquities: the chastisement of our peace was upon him; and with
his stripes we are healed.
　　　　All we like sheep have gone astray; we have turned
everyone to his own way; and the Lord hath laid on him the
iniquity of us all. He was oppressed, and he was afflicted, yet he
opened not his mouth: he is brought as a lamb to the slaughter,
and as a sheep before her shearers is dumb, so he openeth not his
mouth. He was taken from prison and from judgment: and who
shall declare his generation? for he was cut off out of the land of
the living: for the transgression of my people was he stricken. And
he made his grave with the wicked, and with the rich in his death;
because he had done no violence, neither was any deceit in his

mouth. Yet it pleased the Lord to bruise him; he hath put him to grief: when thou shalt make his soul an offering for sin, he shall see his seed, he shall prolong his days, and the pleasure of the Lord shall prosper in his hand. He shall see of the travail of his soul, and shall be satisfied: by his knowledge shall my righteous servant justify many; for he shall bear their iniquities. Therefore will I divide him a portion with the great, and he shall divide the spoil with the strong; because he hath poured out his soul unto death: and he was numbered with the transgressors; and he bare the sin of many, and made intercession for the transgressors.

After the water's fusillade against the ark had subsided and assuaged, the ark came to rest upon the mountains of Ararat. We see in *Genesis 8:1-4, And God remembered Noah, and every living thing, and all the cattle that was with him in the ark: and God made a wind to pass over the earth, and the waters assuaged; The fountains also of the deep and the windows of heaven were stopped, and the rain from heaven was restrained; And the waters returned from off the earth continually: and after the end of the hundred and fifty days the waters were abated. And the ark rested in the seventh month, on the seventeenth day of the month, upon the mountains of Ararat.* The waters had done what they were supposed to do and there was nothing else left to be done. Therefore the ark rested.

Jesus Christ had a mission to do while He was here on earth. In *John 4:3, Jesus saith unto them, My meat is to do the will of him that sent me, and to finish his work.* His mission was to do the will of His Father. That was His meat that He ate from everyday. That was His purpose. But what was the will of His Father?

In *2 Peter 3:9*, it clearly states that *The Lord is not slack concerning his promise, as some men count slackness; but is longsuffering to us-ward, not willing that any should perish, but that all should come to repentance.* **The will of His Father was that none should perish but that all should come to repentance. Jesus' mission was to redeem each and every one of us. He could not rest until His mission was completed. He had to finish His work.** We see this in *John 19:30, When Jesus therefore* *had received the vinegar, he said, It is finished: and he bowed his head, and gave up the ghost.* When He finally hung on the cross for us, He cried victoriously, "It is finished" or in Greek "Tetelestai". It comes from the root word 'teleo' meaning fully accomplished. **Tetelestai means it is finished, it stands finished, and it will always be finished.** It was a victory cry, not an exhausted tired cry.

For example, when a merchant has paid his debt in full or has fully paid a price, he can say "Tetelestai". He does not have to pay anymore as it is fully paid. When the Israelites looked for a perfect sheep for the ritual offering, they would keep on looking until they found the unblemished one. Then they would say, "Tetelestai". There is no need to look further. When a servant had fully accomplished a job for his master, he can say, "Tetelestai". The work is completed. When the artist has finished his painting, he can also say, "Tetelestai". Nothing else can be added to the picture. It is truly finished!

In Genesis, God created the heavens and the earth. New things that did not exist before now existed. He created new things out of nothing. When God completed creation after six days, He rested from all His work of creation. In *Isaiah 40:28*, we read, *Hast thou not known? hast thou not heard, that the everlasting God, the Lord, the Creator of the ends of the earth, fainteth not, neither is weary?* It wasn't that He was tired or exhausted. He rested because everything that needed to be done was done. It was perfectly done and completely done, or 'Tetelestai'.

He even created rest so that no works could be added to the rest. In *Genesis 2:1-3*, we read, *Thus the heavens and the earth were finished, and all the host of them. And on the seventh day God ended his work which he had made; and he rested on the seventh day from all his work which he had made. And God blessed the seventh day, and sanctified it: because that in it he had rested from all his work which God created and made.* He saw all that He had made and it was very good.

Likewise, Jesus fulfilled his mission. The devil was defeated. The race is finished. The debt is paid in full. He came to redeem you and me. That work is now accomplished. He could finally rest. All prophecy was fulfilled. The law was fully satisfied. **All that was needed to redeem you and I was accomplished and stands accomplished and will always be accomplished.**

Therefore, He bowed His head and rested. During His ministry time, Jesus mentioned that He had no place to rest His head. That was because His work was not yet ended. He could only rest his head when sin was fully atoned for. This rest came before he died. **Only after He redeemed us did He die.** In *2 Corinthians 5:17, Therefore if any man be in Christ, he is a new creature: old things are passed away; behold, all things are become new.* Because of what He did, new creations that did not exist before now existed. By His death, He created new creatures. These new creations are people who have ceased from their own works and have chosen to enter into Jesus' rest. *Hebrews 4:8-10* states, *For if Jesus had given them rest, then would he not afterward have spoken of another day. There remaineth therefore a rest to the people of God. For he that is entered into his rest, he also hath ceased from his own works, as God did from his.*

Just like the ark, which rested on the mountains of Ararat, these new creations rested fully upon the finished work of Jesus Christ. Ararat actually means 'the curse is reversed'. The curse of sin is reversed. The old is dead and the new has taken its place. The new cannot become old again. The process is irreversible. And God saw these new creations that He had made and behold, it was very good. You and I, as new creations, are very good!

ࣞ 4 ࣞ

JESUS AND THE RAM

One of the earliest writings in the bible revealing Jesus is found in the account of Abraham. It is found in *Genesis 22:1-14, And it came to pass after these things, that God did tempt Abraham, and said unto him, Abraham: and he said, Behold, here I am. And he said, Take now thy son, thine only son Isaac, whom thou lovest, and get thee into the land of Moriah; and offer him there for a burnt offering upon one of the mountains which I will tell thee of. And Abraham rose up early in the morning, and saddled his ass, and took two of his young men with him, and Isaac his son, and clave the wood for the burnt offering, and rose up, and went unto the place of which God had told him. Then on the third day Abraham lifted up his eyes, and saw the place afar off.*

And Abraham said unto his young men, Abide ye here with the ass; and I and the lad will go yonder and worship, and come again to you, And Abraham took the wood of the burnt offering, and laid it upon Isaac his son; and he took the fire in his hand, and a knife; and they went both of them together. And Isaac spake unto Abraham his father, and said, My father: and he said, Here am I, my son. And he said, Behold the fire and the wood: but where is the lamb for a burnt offering? And Abraham said, My son, God will provide himself a lamb for a burnt offering: so they went both of them together.

And they came to the place which God had told him of; and Abraham built an altar there, and laid the wood in order, and bound Isaac his son, and laid him on the altar upon the wood. And Abraham stretched forth his hand, and took the knife to slay his son. And the angel of the Lord called unto him out of heaven, and said, Abraham, Abraham: and he said, Here am I. And he said, Lay not thine hand upon the lad, neither do thou anything unto him: for now I know that thou fearest God, seeing thou hast not withheld thy son, thine only son from me.

The focus of this scripture has usually been on Abraham's faith and obedience towards God. It goes something like this. When God tested Abraham in his old age, he obeyed instantly, without any questions or complaints. God asked Abraham to sacrifice Isaac, his only son, upon Mount Moriah. He was so eager to obey God that he went to bed early and woke up early. He then sharpened his knife before he piled the wood for the burnt offering upon his donkey. On the journey to the mountain, he bowed in obeisance and prayed earnestly for three days. Only when he reached the mountain did he dare lift up his eyes. He quickly prepared Isaac to become the sacrifice before being stopped by God. The lesson is that we must all become like Abraham, sacrificing all to a demanding God without hesitation. We must listen and then do whatever God calls us to do. And quickly as well for delay is of the devil! Only then will God be pleased with us.

If the bible is all about us, then the explanation above suffices. But since the bible is not about us, then there must be another explanation. In *Deuteronomy 12:31*, we read, *Thou shalt not do so unto the Lord thy God: for every abomination to the Lord, which he hateth, have they done unto their gods; for even their sons and their daughters they have burnt in the fire to their gods.* Child sacrifice is an abomination to God! Since God abhors child sacrifices, then God cannot have wanted Abraham to sacrifice Isaac. What God really wanted to show us through this scripture was that He would provide for us. However, we have to come to the point of laying down our works and to accept in exchange, His finished work and provision. **It is not about our sacrifice for God but it is about His sacrifice for us.**

Abraham made many mistakes, some mistakes repeatedly. Yet God unconditionally blessed Abraham based on God's covenant with Himself to bless him. Abraham's own works produced his first son, Ishmael. Abraham loved Ishmael. When Sarah wanted to send Ishmael away, he did not agree. In *Genesis 21:9-12*, we read, *And Sarah saw the son of Hagar the Egyptian, which she had born unto Abraham, mocking. Wherefore she said unto Abraham, Cast out this bondwoman and her son: for the son of this bondwoman shall not be heir with my son, even with Isaac. And the thing was very grievous in Abraham's sight because of his son. And God said unto Abraham, Let it not be grievous in thy sight because of the lad, and because of thy bondwoman; in all that Sarah hath said unto thee, hearken unto her voice; for in Isaac shall thy seed be called.* When God sided with Sarah, only then did Abraham consent and Ishmael was sent away. We know that God is a good God and not a cruel God. The reason God sided with Sarah was to remind Abraham that God Himself had provided him with a son, namely Isaac. Isaac was already born when Ishmael was sent away. There was no need for Abraham to do anything himself because God had provided for him by grace. Also, Ishmael had to be sent away as works cannot reside with grace in the same house. **Works reject grace and grace has no need for works.**

Isaac was born as the son of promise to Abraham when he was one hundred years old and Sarah was ninety. It was an impossible birth but God provided and therefore, Isaac was born.

It was all about God's provision and not about Abraham's works. And now God was testing Abraham's faith, not to see his obedience, but to see his faith in God's continued provision in the face of impossible circumstances. God did not want Isaac. God wanted Abraham to trust Him. He would provide the burnt offering sacrifice.

As Isaac was never meant to be the sacrifice, we cannot draw a parallel between him and Jesus. Yes, both were only sons of their fathers and they both rode on a donkey. Yes, there were three days mentioned and there were two servants/thieves in the story. Yes, Isaac carried the wood willingly up the hill just as Jesus carried the cross. Yes, he cried out to his father just like Jesus. Yes,

Mount Moriah is in the same area as the hill of Golgotha (it actually became the future site for God's temple). Yes, both were made fast to the wood. And yes, Isaac came back for his bride Rebekah just as Jesus would return for His bride, the church.

Incredible as these similarities are, there is one big difference - Jesus was to be the sacrifice but Isaac was not! In fact, if Isaac were to die there would be no Jesus. For the seed of Abraham, namely Isaac, would produce Jesus one day in the future.

To see Abraham's full self-works let us read from Genesis chapter 21 verses *27 and 31-34, And Abraham took sheep and oxen, and gave them unto Abimelech; and both of them made a covenant. Wherefore he called that place Beer-sheba; because there they sware both of them. Thus they made a covenant at Beer-sheba: then Abimelech rose up, and Phichol the chief captain of his host, and they returned into the land of the Philistines. And Abraham planted a grove in Beer-sheba, and called there on the name of the Lord, the everlasting God. And Abraham sojourned in the Philistines' land many days.*

Abraham was living in a Philistine town by the name of Gerar, in an area called Beersheba. He made a covenant with the Philistine king, Abimelech, and his general Phichol, concerning seven wells of water. Instead of fully trusting God's provision alone, Abraham entered into a covenant with the Philistines for protection and provision. Abraham then planted a grove of trees there. This is very strange as there is no record he had even planted a bush before. He ended up living there for thirty years.

God wanted Abraham to lay down all of the works of his hands and to trust in Him alone. He was to lay down the covenant with the Philistine king. He was to lay down the grove he had planted for a wood offering. We read this in *Nehemiah 10:34, And we cast the lots among the priests, the Levites, and the people, for the wood offering,* Abraham was to lay down Isaac also.

The wood for the burnt offering came from the grove he had planted. Abraham cut the wood for the burnt offering from the trees he had planted. Wood represents men's works in the bible. The wood for the burnt offering was laid in order like a list of our works. The last work that Abraham trusted in was in his son, Isaac. That was the pinnacle of self-works thus was laid on top of the pile of ordered wood. All of it had to be burnt up.

However, God had revealed to Abraham that He would provide the sacrifice. Abraham had to have faith that God would do as He promised. That was why Abraham could tell his two servants at the foot of the mountain that both he and Isaac would be back shortly after worshiping God at the altar. Then when Isaac asked about the lamb, Abraham answered that God Himself would provide the Offering. In *Genesis 22:8, And Abraham said, My son, God will provide himself a lamb for a burnt offering:* In the Hebrew language, the verse could also be read as *God will provide Himself a Lamb for a burnt offering – My Son!* Not Abraham to provide but God to provide! It was not Abraham's son but God's Son that was required.

Jesus was the Son. In *John 1:29,* we read, *Behold the Lamb of God, which taketh away the sin of the world.* Jesus was the Lamb of God. He was provided for us as the offering. He was the only One who could take away the sins of the world.

Abraham actually caught a fleeting glimpse of Jesus as he approached Mount Moriah. In *Genesis 22:4,* we read, *Then on the third day Abraham lifted up his eyes, and saw the place afar off* and in *John 8:56, Your father Abraham rejoiced to see my day: and he saw it, and was glad.* Abraham saw a 'figure' or 'shadow' of Jesus and rejoiced. He could not have understood the full significance of what he saw or what was to happen but he saw it and was filled with gladness.

Without Jesus, we would be judged based upon our works. With the sharpened knife pointing at our works, we would lie on the altar fully guilty and condemned. But the bible is not about us! It is not about Abraham or Isaac. The bible is about Jesus. God called to Abraham to lift up his eyes away from Isaac. The moment he turned from his own works, he saw a ram caught in a thicket by his horns. In *Genesis 22:13-14, And Abraham lifted up his eyes, and looked, and behold behind him a ram caught in a thicket by his horns: and Abraham went and took the ram, and offered him up for a burnt offering in the stead of his son. And Abraham called the name of that place Jehovah-jireh: as it is said to this day, In the mount of the Lord it shall be seen.* The ram is a male sheep.

In *Genesis 3:17-18,* we read, *And unto Adam he said, Because thou hast hearkened unto the voice of thy wife, and hast eaten of the tree, of which I commanded thee, saying, Thou shalt not eat of it: cursed is the ground for thy sake; in sorrow shalt thou eat of it all the days of thy life; Thorns also and thistles shall it bring forth to thee* and *Mark 15:17-18, And they clothed him with purple, and platted a crown of thorns, and put it about his head, And began to salute him, Hail, King of the Jews!* The thicket is a thorny bush. Thorns are a curse. The ram had its head caught in the thorns.

Jesus is the male sheep, his bloodied head wearing the crown of thorns, caught and ripped in the curse of our sins. He bore the curse on His head so we do not have to bear it. He was the substitute for us upon the altar. **He lived the life we could not live by fulfilling perfectly all the requirements of the law and died the death that was destined for us.**

Instead of our obedience, we should focus on His obedience. Instead of looking at ourselves and what we can do for Him, we should focus on Jesus and what He has done for us. Instead of our works for Him, let us focus on His work for us. Abraham did not call the place Abraham-jireh but Jehovah-jireh meaning God-Provider. Abraham provided nothing. He did not have to for God provided everything. In *1 John 2:2,* we read, *And he is the propitiation for our sins: and not for ours only, but also for the sins of the whole world.* God provided a propitiation or substitute for our sins. His name is Jesus.

God is not a demanding God. He is a supplying God. He did not demand a sacrifice from Abraham nor from you and me, but instead supplied us with a sacrifice. God would not have to supply anything if Abraham's or our sacrifice of works had been sufficiently good. However, no sacrifice from our part can ever meet God's standards. It always falls short. That is why He freely supplied us with what we did not have. He provided us with Jesus. **And Jesus is more than sufficient for us.**

⮞ 5 ⮜

JESUS AND THE ROCK

The purpose of God in bringing His people out of Egypt was so that He could have a relationship with them. He wanted to feast with His people and to show them His love. Then their services back to Him would be a rejoinder of such love and intimacy. The Promised Land was going to be a by-product of this loving relationship. We read in *Exodus 3:12, And he said, Certainly I will be with thee; and this shall be a token unto thee, that I have sent thee: When thou hast brought forth the people out of Egypt, ye shall serve God upon this mountain.* Then in *Exodus 5:1, And afterward Moses and Aaron went in, and told Pharaoh, Thus saith the Lord God of Israel, Let my people go, that they may hold a feast unto me in the wilderness.*

However, the Israelites did not understand that God wanted and desired this loving relationship. They wanted the new land, not God Himself. They craved for the blessings, not The Blessor. They looked at themselves and not at Him.

In *Exodus 17:1-4*, even after many miraculous works we find the same grievance - the absence of water at Maribah. We read, *And all the congregation of the children of Israel journeyed from the wilderness of Sin, after their journeys, according to the commandment of the Lord, and pitched in Rephidim: and there was no water for the people to drink. Wherefore the people did chide with Moses, and said, Give us water that we may drink. And*

Moses said unto them, Why chide ye with me? wherefore do ye tempt the Lord? And the people thirsted there for water; and the people murmured against Moses, and said, Wherefore is this that thou hast brought us up out of Egypt, to kill us and our children and our cattle with thirst? And Moses cried unto the Lord, saying, What shall I do unto this people? they be almost ready to stone me. The people challenged God's representative, Moses, quarreled with him, complained bitterly against him and almost stoned him. They distrusted God's motive for bringing them out of Egypt and even questioned God's presence.

A similar incident had occurred before. In *Exodus 15: 22-25*, we read, *So Moses brought Israel from the Red sea, and they went out into the wilderness of Shur; and they went three days in the wilderness, and found no water. And when they came to Marah, they could not drink of the waters of Marah, for they were bitter: therefore the name of it was called Marah. And the people murmured against Moses, saying, What shall we drink? And he cried unto the Lord; and the Lord shewed him a tree, which when he had cast into the waters, the waters were made sweet:* The answer to our problems is always Jesus. Here, the tree represents the cross which when Moses cast into the water transformed it. The cross changed everything! The waters became sweet because of Jesus.

So when the people murmured again, God's response was the same. As God's love for His people was unconditional of their love back for Him, He blessed them yet again. We see in *Exodus 17:5-7, And the Lord said unto Moses, Go on before the people, and take with thee of the elders of Israel; and thy rod, wherewith thou smotest the river, take in thine hand, and go. Behold, I will stand before thee there upon the rock in Horeb; and thou shalt smite the rock, and there shall come water out of it, that the people may drink. And Moses did so in the sight of the elders of Israel. And he called the name of the place Massah, and Meribah, because of the chiding of the children of Israel, and because they tempted the Lord, saying, Is the Lord among us, or not?*

Moses was to strike the rock and life-sustaining water would flow out of it. *Psalm 78:15-16* states, *He clave the rocks in the wilderness, and gave them drink as out of the great depths. He brought streams also out of the rock, and caused waters to run down like rivers.* And again in *Psalm 114:8, Which turned the rock into a standing water, the flint into a fountain of waters.* It would start as a trickle that would gather into a small pool. Then the fountains would be opened which would become streams. Streams would then become rivers that would follow them into the wilderness for many years to come. Furthermore, in Deuteronomy *32:13, He made him ride on the high places of the earth, that he might eat the increase of the fields; and he made him to suck honey out of the rock, and oil out of the flinty rock.* The water that followed them would taste like honey and oil.

What a picture of Grace! We see in *1 Corinthians 10:4, And did all drink the same spiritual drink: for they drank of that spiritual Rock that followed them: and that Rock was Christ.* We know that Jesus is the Living Water. In *John 4:10, 14, Jesus answered and said unto her, If thou knewest the gift of God, and who it is that saith to thee, Give me to drink; thou wouldest have asked of him, and he would have given thee living water. But whosoever drinketh of the water that I shall give him shall never thirst; but the water that I shall give him shall be in him a well of water springing up into everlasting life.* The Rock was Jesus who would be struck or crucified for us and from Him, a well of sweet, living water would flow out that would give us everlasting life. *Psalm 34:8* declares *O taste and see that the Lord is good: blessed is the man that trusteth in him.* One taste of Jesus goodness and we will be changed forever. He is our spiritual oasis of life and He is Grace.

But the Israelites did not appreciate Grace or Jesus. Thirty-eight years later, at Maribah-Kadesh, a similar event took place with a new generation of Israelites. In *Numbers 20:1-11*, we read, *Then came the children of Israel, even the whole congregation, into the desert of Zin in the first month: and the people abode in Kadesh; and Miriam died there, and was buried there. And there was no water for the congregation: and they gathered themselves together against Moses and against Aaron. And the people chode with Moses, and spake, saying, Would God that we had died when*

*our brethren died before the Lord! And why have ye brought up
the congregation of the Lord into this wilderness, that we and our
cattle should die there? And wherefore have ye made us to come
up out of Egypt, to bring us in unto this evil place? it is no place of
seed, or of figs, or of vines, or of pomegranates; neither is there
any water to drink. And Moses and Aaron went from the presence
of the assembly unto the door of the tabernacle of the
congregation, and they fell upon their faces: and the glory of the
Lord appeared unto them. And the Lord spake unto Moses, saying,
Take the rod, and gather thou the assembly together, thou, and
Aaron thy brother, and speak ye unto the rock before their eyes;
and it shall give forth his water, and thou shalt bring forth to them
water out of the rock: so thou shalt give the congregation and their
beasts drink. And Moses took the rod from before the Lord, as he
commanded him. And Moses and Aaron gathered the
congregation together before the rock, and he said unto them,
Hear now, ye rebels; must we fetch you water out of this rock?
And Moses lifted up his hand, and with his rod he smote the rock
twice: and the water came out abundantly, and the congregation
drank, and their beasts also.* By now, the life giving streams and
rivers had long dried up. In its place the hard unyielding law. Once
again, the people complained to Moses about the absence of water.

Same story, different circumstances! In those 38 years,
because of the people's insistence to trust in their own strength and
works, the law had been given to the people. The unconditional
love of God was now replaced by the people's conditional
obedience to the law.

God told Moses to speak to The Rock but he disobeyed
God. He spoke to the people instead and then hit the rock twice.
The Rock cannot be hit again, as Jesus' sacrifice was once and for
all time. To hit The Rock again would deny the sufficiency of
Jesus' once and for all time sacrifice. It implies the addition of our
works to what Jesus had already accomplished. Moses could have
just spoken to The Rock and it would have brought out life-giving
water. But Moses hit the rock in his own strength. Under the law,
his disobedience to God now had to be punished. In *Numbers
20:12, And the Lord spake unto Moses and Aaron, Because ye*

believed me not, to sanctify me in the eyes of the children of Israel, therefore ye shall not bring this congregation into the land which I have given them. The punishment was severe - Moses would not enter the Promised Land! He died in the land of Moab outside the Promised Land. Moses, who represented the Law, could not enter into the rest offered by the Promised Land. It fell on Joshua, a 'type' of Jesus to take the people in. Under the law, there would be no rest.

But God's grace is far greater than His anger. We see that in *Psalm 30:5, For his anger endureth but a moment; in his favour is life: weeping may endure for a night, but joy cometh in the morning.* Many years later, Moses was brought into the Promised Land. We read in *Luke 9:28-31, And it came to pass about an eight days after these sayings, he took Peter and John and James, and went up into a mountain to pray. And as he prayed, the fashion of his countenance was altered, and his raiment was white and glistering. And, behold, there talked with him two men, which were Moses and Elias: Who appeared in glory, and spake of his decease which he should accomplish at Jerusalem.*

Because of Jesus, Moses finally saw the land. As he stood with Elijah, who represented the prophets, they spoke to Jesus about the cross! **All the law and the writings of the prophets would be fulfilled at the cross.** The law, which kept Moses out of the land, would be ultimately fulfilled by Jesus Christ. The wrath and judgment of God, as written by the prophets, would ultimately be paid for by Jesus. What a joyous moment it must have been for both Moses and Elijah as they looked forward to the cross and its significance. It is the same for us. **Our joy is in Christ alone as we look back at the cross and its significance. Jesus did it all for us!**

❧ 6 ❧

JESUS AND THE SERPENT

In the book of Numbers, we come across another scripture depicting God's grace towards His people despite the law. We read in *Numbers 21:4-5, And they journeyed from mount Hor by the way of the Red sea, to compass the land of Edom: and the soul of the people was much discouraged because of the way. And the people spake against God, and against Moses, Wherefore have ye brought us up out of Egypt to die in the wilderness? for there is, no bread neither is there any water; and our soul loatheth this light bread.* Towards the end of their forty-year wandering in the desert, the people rebelled against God, once again. They complained about the manna, the light bread from heaven, completely missing the significance of this life changing bread. For it fed the angels as depicted in *Psalm 78:24-25, And had rained down manna upon them to eat, and had given them of the corn of heaven. Man did eat angels' food: he sent them meat to the full.*

And not only was this Bread good for angels, this Bread would give life to the whole earth. In *John 6:31-35, 48-51,* we see *Our fathers did eat manna in the desert; as it is written, He gave them bread from heaven to eat. Then Jesus said unto them, Verily, verily, I say unto you, Moses gave you not that bread from heaven; but my Father giveth you the true bread from heaven. For the bread of God is he which cometh down from heaven, and giveth life unto the world. Then said they unto him, Lord, evermore give us this bread. And Jesus said unto them, I am the bread of life: he that cometh to me shall never hunger; and he that believeth on me shall never thirst. I am that bread of life. Your fathers did eat manna in the wilderness, and are dead. This is the bread which cometh down from heaven, that a man may eat thereof, and not die. I am the living bread which came down from heaven: if any man eat of this bread, he shall live forever: and the bread that I will give is my flesh, which I will give for the life of the world.*

Jesus was the true bread from heaven. If we know Jesus we would live forever. However, the Israelites rejected the Bread. They hated it down to their souls or hearts. The resulting punishment was severe. We read in *Numbers 21:6, And the Lord sent fiery serpents among the people, and they bit the people; and much people of Israel died.* God lifted the cloud of glory that surrounded their camp and the fiery serpents which were kept at bay by grace were now allowed to attack the people. They suffered immensely from the bites before they died. Nothing could heal the stings. They died looking at their bites.

Before the law, there was no record of death for any Israelite in the wilderness. After the law, there was much death among the Israelites. Before the law, God blessed and protected the Israelites unconditionally. After the law, God's blessings and protection were conditional on their own works. And because of their works, God's protection was lifted. But because we believe on Jesus and His finished work on the cross, God protection over us would never be lifted! For God looks at Jesus, not us!

Numbers 21:7-9 states, Therefore the people came to Moses, and said, We have sinned, for we have spoken against the Lord, and against thee; pray unto the Lord, that he take away the serpents from us. And Moses prayed for the people. And the Lord said unto Moses, Make thee a fiery serpent, and set it upon a pole: and it shall come to pass, that every one that is bitten, when he looketh upon it, shall live. And Moses made a serpent of brass, and put it upon a pole, and it came to pass, that if a serpent had bitten any man, when he beheld the serpent of brass, he lived.

God asked Moses to make the image of a serpent in brass and then to set it upon a pole. The pole was needed so that every infected person could see it - even from afar. It was an ugly image representing the very creature that had bitten them in the first place. Moses must have wondered why God did not ask him to make an image of an eagle or a hawk. For eagles and hawks by nature would attack and kill serpents! But the image was to be a serpent. So it was made and hung upon a pole.

Whether the people took a fleeting glance at the serpent or stared at it for hours, the result was the same. There was no need for strong eyes. There was no need for perfect vision. The only need was a beholding of the brass serpent. Young men, old men, children, babies in mothers' arms, even blind men were instantaneously healed from their poisonous bites when they looked or faced the brass serpent. There was no need for sacrifices of animals. There was no need for long prayers. There was no need for prolonged counseling sessions. There was no need for expensive gifts of gold and precious stones for Moses. There was no need to look at their bites. There was no need for self-guilt. And there was no need for self-condemnation and judgment.

For they were not looking at an ugly serpent but Jesus Himself hanging on the cross! In *Isaiah 45:22*, we read, *Look unto me, and be ye saved, all the ends of the earth: for I am God, and there is none else.* And in *John 3:14-15, And as Moses lifted up the serpent in the wilderness, even so must the Son of man be lifted up: That whosoever believeth in him should not perish, but have eternal life.* **Look at Jesus and live!** Every sick person just had to look at Jesus. Every sinner just had to have saving faith in Jesus. Nothing more was required or needed. Jesus is all sufficient!

In *2 Corinthians 5:21*, we read, *For he hath made him to be sin for us, who knew no sin; that we might be made the righteousness of God in him.* Jesus who knew no sin was made sin for us and judged on the cross. Our sins were imputed upon Him. That is why it had to be the image of a serpent and not a real serpent that had to hang from the pole. The cure had the same form as that which caused the wound in the first place. And it was made from brass as brass denoted judgment in the Old Testament. *1 Corinthians 15:55-56* states, *O death, where is thy sting? O grave, where is thy victory? The sting of death is sin; and the strength of sin is the law.* Jesus Christ was judged as sin upon the cross for us and all those of us who would look upon Him would be healed from the sting of death brought about by sin.

The law of sin brings death. But Christ fulfilled the law condemning sin by His own flesh on the cross. *Romans 8:1-3* states, *There is therefore now no condemnation to them which are in Christ Jesus, who walk not after the flesh, but after the Spirit. For the law of the Spirit of life in Christ Jesus hath made me free from the law of sin and death. For what the law could not do, in that it was weak through the flesh, God sending his own Son in the likeness of sinful flesh, and for sin, condemned sin in the flesh.* **That is why there is now no condemnation for those of us who are in Jesus Christ. He is all we need!**

The account of the brass serpent did not end here. The Israelites actually carried it into the Promised Land and began to worship it as a god for many years until King Hezekiah eventually destroyed it. In *2 Kings 18:4, He removed the high places, and brake the images, and cut down the groves, and brake in pieces the brasen serpent that Moses had made: for unto those days the children of Israel did burn incense to it: and he called it Nehushtan.* Nehushtan meant 'just a piece of brass'. Just like us, the Israelites default setting was to worship their own works and achievements. They worshiped a lie. Instead of having their eyes turned toward Jesus, their eyes turned back to themselves and their achievements. *Romans 1:25* states, *Who changed the truth of God into a lie, and worshipped and served the creature more than the Creator, who is blessed forever.* Our own works should be broken into pieces and destroyed forever. For only when our eyes are upon Jesus can we be blessed forever.

❧ 7 ❧

JESUS AND JEWS

We know that the Old Testament was written by Jews for the Jewish nation. It is a Jewish book. For example, the first five books of the Old Testament are often referred to as the Torah or 'instructions for life'. But most of us, myself included, are gentiles (non-Jews). So how do we fit into the picture? Is the Old Testament applicable to us as gentiles? But let's start with an even simpler question – was Abraham a Jew?

In *Genesis 11:31-32, 12:1-2,* we read, *And Terah took Abram his son, and Lot the son of Haran his son's son, and Sarai his daughter in law, his son Abram's wife; and they went forth with them from Ur of the Chaldees, to go into the land of Canaan; and they came unto Haran, and dwelt there. And the days of Terah were two hundred and five years: and Terah died in Haran. Now the Lord had said unto Abram, Get thee out of thy country, and from thy kindred, and from thy father's house, unto a land that I will shew thee: And I will make of thee a great nation, and I will bless thee, and make thy name great; and thou shalt be a blessing.* Abraham was originally from the city of Ur in the Chaldees. That made Abraham a Chaldean. But when Abraham obeyed God and left his homeland for a new land, God created an entirely new nation. In *Genesis 14:13, And there came one that had escaped, and told Abram the Hebrew.* This new nation would become the Hebrew nation, with Abraham as the patriarch. Abraham started out as a Chaldean and then became a Hebrew. His son, Isaac, was a Hebrew. But God changed the name of his grandson, Jacob, to Israel. Hence, all of Jacob's descendants became known as Israelites. Later on, the Israelites became divided into two kingdoms. The Northern kingdom maintained themselves as Israelites while the southern kingdom became the kingdom of Judah or 'Jews'. Therefore, all Jews are Israelites, and all Israelites are Hebrews. Practically, the terms Hebrews, Israelites, and Jews are used interchangeably and I have used these terms as such.

So, Abraham was a Hebrew but we can call him an Israelite or a Jew as well. In fact, anyone who can trace his/her roots back to Abraham is considered a Hebrew, Israelite or more commonly, a Jew. It does not matter what his/her beliefs are or what he/she does for a living. An atheist Jew, a Jew practicing another religion, or a Jew who does not even know that he is a Jew is still a Jew. A Jew is always a Jew. For example, a Jew who believes in Jesus Christ is called a Messianic Jew.

On the other hand, a gentile is always a gentile unless he/she converts to Judaism or the religion of the Jews. But the conversion process must be under the Jewish law known as Halakha. Just believing in Judaism and following all the teachings of Judaism does not make a person become a Jew. Gentiles who convert to Judaism are called proselytes in the bible. Some proselytes are Jews and some are not. It all depends on Halakha. A gentile who does not come under Halakha is never a Jew.

When Abraham left Ur for an unknown new land, God promised to bless Abraham unconditionally. He would be the father of a great nation; his name would be remembered; he would be blessed with land and many children; and most importantly, from his loins would come The Seed, Jesus Christ!

Abraham would have plentiful seeds, as numerous as the stars in the heaven or the sand on the seashore. The sand on the seashore referred to Abraham's genetic seed, the Israelites; while the stars in the heaven referred to Abraham's spiritual seed, the gentiles. But there was also a singular seed mentioned that would possess the gate of His enemies and that would bless the whole earth. In *Genesis 22:17-18*, we read of this singular seed. *That in*

*blessing I will bless thee, and in multiplying I will multiply thy seed
as the stars of the heaven, and as the sand which is upon the sea
shore; and thy seed shall possess the gate of his enemies; And in
thy seed shall all the nations of the earth be blessed; because thou
hast obeyed my voice.* The Promised Seed was none other than
Jesus Christ, and confirmed in *Galatians 3:16, Now to Abraham
and his seed were the promises made. He saith not, And to seeds,
as of many; but as of one, And to thy seed, which is Christ.* This
singular Seed was promised as far back as in the Garden of Eden.
We see in *Genesis 3:15, And I will put enmity between thee and the
woman, and between thy seed and her seed; it shall bruise thy
head, and thou shalt bruise his heel.*

     Abraham found these unconditional promises or grace too
staggering to believe and asked for a confirmation from God. God
decided to make a covenant with Abraham. We call this the
Abrahamic Covenant. A covenant is an agreement between two or
more parties and involved a ceremony. In *Jeremiah 34:18-19, And
I will give the men that have transgressed my covenant, which have
not performed the words of the covenant which they had made
before me, when they cut the calf in twain, and passed between the
parts thereof, The princes of Judah, and the princes of Jerusalem,
the eunuchs, and the priests, and all the people of the land, which
passed between the parts of the calf.*

     In this case, it involved three animals and two birds. A
heifer, a she goat, and a ram were killed, split in half and laid in
two rows with a path in between the bloody carcasses. The
turtledove and the pigeon were not split but laid on the ground. To
seal the agreement or covenant, the parties of the covenant would
walk in between the split halves, on the blood of the animals, as if
saying 'May this be done to me if I do not honor the covenant!' It
was that serious. Some fowls, representing Satan and his demons,
came immediately to steal the carcasses away, to prevent the
sealing of this covenant, but Abraham drove them away. And then
a wonderful but strange thing happened. God put Abraham to
sleep. You may ask. "If Abraham was sleeping, how would the
covenant be sealed?" The answer came when night fell. We read in
Genesis 15:7-18, And he said unto him, I am the Lord that

brought thee out of Ur of the Chaldees, to give thee this land to inherit it. And he said, Lord God, whereby shall I know that I shall inherit it? And he said unto him, Take me an heifer of three years old, and a she goat of three years old, and a ram of three years old, and a turtledove, and a young pigeon. And he took unto him all these, and divided them in the midst, and laid each piece one against another: but the birds divided he not. And when the fowls came down upon the carcases, Abram drove them away. And when the sun was going down, a deep sleep fell upon Abram; and, lo, an horror of great darkness fell upon him. And he said unto Abram, Know of a surety that thy seed shall be a stranger in a land that is not theirs, and shall serve them; and they shall afflict them four hundred years; And also that nation, whom they shall serve, will I judge: and afterward shall they come out with great substance. And thou shalt go to thy fathers in peace; thou shalt be buried in a good old age. But in the fourth generation they shall come hither again: for the iniquity of the Amorites is not yet full.

And it came to pass, that, when the sun went down, and it was dark, behold a smoking furnace, and a burning lamp that passed between those pieces. In the same day the Lord made a covenant with Abram, saying, Unto thy seed have I given this land, from the river of Egypt unto the great river, the river Euphrates.

A smoking furnace, representing the Father, and a burning lamp, representing Jesus, walked between the pieces. The turtledove and the pigeon, representing the Holy Spirit, were already on the ground. Thus, the covenant was made between God the Father, God the Son, and God the Holy Spirit as they walked between the carcasses. God alone sealed the covenant. Nothing was required of Abraham. All the promises would be fulfilled by God alone, by His grace. It was unconditional upon Abraham and his works. We read in *Hebrews 6:13-14, For when God made promise to Abraham, because he could swear by no greater, he sware by himself, Saying, Surely blessing I will bless thee, and multiplying I will multiply thee.* God swore by Himself because He could swear by none greater that all of His promises would be fulfilled by Himself.

Through all the mistakes that Abraham made, God continued to bless him as the covenant was unconditional upon Abraham's works. It was based only upon God's goodness and His word to honor His covenant. In *Genesis 12:10-17, And there was a famine in the land: and Abram went down into Egypt to sojourn there; for the famine was grievous in the land. And it came to pass, when he was come near to enter into Egypt, that he said unto Sarai his wife, Behold now, I know that thou art a fair woman to look upon: Therefore it shall come to pass, when the Egyptians shall see thee, that they shall say, This is his wife: and they will kill me, but they will save thee alive. Say, I pray thee, thou art my sister: that it may be well with me for thy sake; and my soul shall live because of thee. And it came to pass, that, when Abram was come into Egypt, the Egyptians beheld the woman that she was very fair. The princes also of Pharaoh saw her, and commended her before Pharaoh: and the woman was taken into Pharaoh's house. And he entreated Abram well for her sake: and he had sheep, and oxen, and he asses, and menservants, and maidservants, and she asses, and camels. And the Lord plagued Pharaoh and his house with great plagues because of Sarai Abram's wife.*

We see Abraham going to Egypt, instead of to God, looking for food; Abraham telling Sarah his wife to lie for him, and then lying to Pharaoh for personal gain. If the blessings of God had been based on Abraham's works, he would have been punished greatly. But it was not. We read that God plagued Pharaoh instead! It is all very unfair until we realize that the covenant was not conditional upon Abraham. Abraham lied and cheated but God blessed him! **God did not bless Abraham for his cheating and lying but God blessed him because He Himself was faithful regardless of Abraham's works.**

When Sarah cajoled her husband to sleep with her handmaid Hagar, Abraham quickly acquiesced. We read in *Genesis 16:1-4, 11-12, Now Sarai Abram's wife bare him no children: and she had an handmaid, an Egyptian, whose name was Hagar. And Sarai said unto Abram, Behold now, the Lord hath restrained me from bearing: I pray thee, go in unto my maid; it*

*may be that I may obtain children by her. And Abram hearkened to
the voice of Sarai. And Sarai Abram's wife took Hagar her maid
the Egyptian, after Abram had dwelt ten years in the land of
Canaan, and gave her to her husband Abram to be his wife. And he
went in unto Hagar, and she conceived: and when she saw that she
had conceived, her mistress was despised in her eyes. And the
angel of the Lord said unto her, Behold, thou art with child, and
shalt bear a son, and shalt call his name Ishmael; because the
Lord hath heard thy affliction. And he will be a wild man; his hand
will be against every man, and every man's hand against him; and
he shall dwell in the presence of all his brethren.*

The result was Ishmael, a wild man who would be against
every man and every man would be against him. There are
consequences for our actions but Abraham was never punished for
his actions. Then Abraham lied and cheated again, this time with
the king of Gerar by the name of Abimelech. We see in *Genesis
20:1-3, 9-16, And Abraham journeyed from thence toward the
south country, and dwelled between Kadesh and Shur, and
sojourned in Gerar. And Abraham said of Sarah his wife, She is my
sister: and Abimelech king of Gerar sent, and took Sarah. But God
came to Abimelech in a dream by night, and said to him, Behold,
thou art but a dead man, for the woman which thou hast taken; for
she is a man's wife.*

*Then Abimelech called Abraham, and said unto him, What
hast thou done unto us? and what have I offended thee, that thou
hast brought on me and on my kingdom a great sin? thou hast
done deeds unto me that ought not to be done. And Abimelech said
unto Abraham, What sawest thou, that thou hast done this thing?
And Abraham said, Because I thought, Surely the fear of God is
not in this place; and they will slay me for my wife's sake. And yet
indeed she is my sister; she is the daughter of my father, but not
the daughter of my mother; and she became my wife. And it came
to pass, when God caused me to wander from my father's house,
that I said unto her, This is thy kindness which thou shalt shew
unto me; at every place whither we shall come, say of me, He is my
brother. And Abimelech took sheep, and oxen, and menservants,
and womenservants, and gave them unto Abraham, and restored*

*him Sarah his wife. And Abimelech said, Behold, my land is before
thee: dwell where it pleaseth thee. And unto Sarah he said, Behold,
I have given thy brother a thousand pieces of silver: behold, he is
to thee a covering of the eyes, unto all that are with thee, and with
all other: thus she was reproved.*

He did many deeds to Abimelech that ought not to have
been done. But once again Abraham was not rebuked. He was not
rewarded for his nefarious actions but rather, blessed by God
unconditionally. He was given more servants, more livestock, and
more treasures. Despite Abraham's continued works and mistakes,
God continued to fulfill His promises to him based upon His
Goodness. At last, Abraham, in his old age, was blessed with Isaac.

Isaac was the son of promise. Abraham and Sarah had Isaac
after the Holy Spirit breathed upon them. Their names were Abram
and Sarai before but after the breath of God, 'ruacH', came upon
them; their names were changed to AbraHam and SaraH. We read
this in *Genesis 17:5-6, 15-16, Neither shall thy name any more be
called Abram, but thy name shall be Abraham; for a father of
many nations have I made thee. And I will make thee exceeding
fruitful, and I will make nations of thee, and kings shall come out
of thee. And God said unto Abraham, As for Sarai thy wife, thou
shalt not call her name Sarai, but Sarah shall her name be. And I
will bless her, and give thee a son also of her: yea, I will bless her,
and she shall be a mother of nations; kings of people shall be of
her.* And from Isaac would one day come the Promised Seed, Jesus
Christ.

Because of God's unconditional promise to Abraham, he
remained blessed for the rest of his life. But what about us,
gentiles? Do we get to enjoy these blessings intended for Abraham
and his descendants, the Jews? The answer is a resounding YES.

An agricultural example is used in the bible to illustrate
this. It is called grafting. The normal and natural grafting process is
very simple. A scion or a young shoot is cut from a productive
tree. This scion is then grafted onto a wild or a non-producing tree.
The in-grafted limb now produces fruit according to its nature, not
its old non-productive host. Therefore, a tree that produces no fruit
would now start bearing fruit. But Paul described the process in

reverse to show us the Grace that God has for us. In the natural, the process as described by Paul is impossible. But because of Jesus, it becomes possible!

The olive tree symbolized the Jewish nation. We see in *Romans 11:17, And if some of the branches be broken off, and thou, being a wild olive tree, wert graffed in among them, and with them partakest of the root and fatness of the olive tree.* The roots of the tree represented the unconditional promises of God to Abraham. It is called the fatness or the goodness of the tree. But on this Jewish tree, some of the branches are broken off. These are the Jews who have rejected the unconditional love of God. They are the civil and ecclesiastical rulers, the Pharisees, the Sadducees, and the priests for they teach about the conditional love and acceptance of God thus laying heavy and grievous burdens upon the people. We call them legalists today.

We, the gentiles, are called wild olive trees with wild branches. We are non-productive. So God takes us unproductive branches and grafts us into the goodness of His tree. We can now partake of the root and the fatness of the olive tree. **All the unconditional blessings of Abraham now come to us because of what Jesus Christ did for us. He hung on the cross to redeem us from the curse of the law.** In *Galatians 3:13-15, 28-29,* we read that *Christ hath redeemed us from the curse of the law, being made a curse for us: for it is written, Cursed is every one that hangeth on a tree: That the blessing of Abraham might come on the Gentiles through Jesus Christ; that we might receive the promise of the Spirit through faith.* He was made a curse for us so that we would enjoy His blessings. Because we are now spiritually grafted in, we who cannot be Jews physically by blood are now counted as Abraham's seed and heirs according to the promise. We become children of the promise just like Isaac. And as children of the promise, we get to enjoy all the blessings of God freely. *Galatians 3: 28-29* states that *There is neither Jew nor Greek, there is neither bond nor free, there is neither male nor female: for ye are all one in Christ Jesus. And if ye be Christ's, then are ye Abraham's seed, and heirs according to the promise.* We become heirs because of Jesus!

❧ 8 ❧

JESUS AND THE FINGER OF GOD

There was sin, but no law, before Moses. When Adam sinned against God by disobeying a direct command, the result was sin followed by death. Sin brought consequences. In this case, sin brought spiritual and physical death to all mankind. Death began to reign. But the sin was not imputed or charged to mankind as there was no law yet. In *Romans 5:13-14*, we read, *For until the law sin was in the world: but sin is not imputed when there is no law. Nevertheless death reigned from Adam to Moses, even over them that had not sinned after the similitude of Adam's transgression, who is the figure of him that was to come.* **Since there was no law, man could not be punished for sinning. Man was responsible for the sin but was not punished for the sin.**

Men died because Adam died! **But God did not held the people's sins against them until the law was given. Then and only then were men punished for their actions according to the law.** In *Genesis 3:22-24, And the Lord God said, Behold, the man is become as one of us, to know good and evil: and now, lest he put forth his hand, and take also of the tree of life, and eat, and live forever: Therefore the Lord God sent him forth from the garden of Eden, to till the ground from whence he was taken.* The only reason why Adam and Eve were driven out of the garden of Eden was so that they would not eat from the tree of life and live forever. They never ate from that tree before because death came after their sin, not before. It was not punishment that drove them out but love for mankind because God had a better plan for sinful man - a real Tree of Life!

Similarly, when Cain intentionally killed Abel, he lost the right to be a 'tiller of the ground'. He also started fearing death at the hands of his other brothers, sisters, nephews, and nieces who would take revenge on the killing. The consequence of Cain's sin was that he left Eden to live in the land of Nod. If the law had existed back then, Cain would have been punished with death. In Leviticus *24:17* we read, *And he that killeth any man shall surely be put to death.* In fact, all of Adam and Eve's children would have been judged and put to death for breaking the law of incest had the law existed. **Sin brought many evils and consequences but was not imputed upon mankind until after the law came.**

The law was given to Moses many thousands of years later after Adam but only, as we shall see, because of the pride of the Israelites. Three months after leaving Egypt, Moses made his first trip up Mount Sinai. Moses made multiple trips up Mount Sinai after this first ascent.

We read in *Exodus 19:1-8, In the third month, when the children of Israel were gone forth out of the land of Egypt, the same day came they into the wilderness of Sinai. For they were departed from Rephidim, and were come to the desert of Sinai, and had pitched in the wilderness; and there Israel camped before the mount. And Moses went up unto God, and the Lord called unto him out of the mountain, saying, Thus shalt thou say to the house of Jacob, and tell the children of Israel; Ye have seen what I did unto the Egyptians, and how I bare you on eagles' wings, and brought you unto myself. Now therefore, if ye will obey my voice indeed, and keep my covenant, then ye shall be a peculiar treasure unto me above all people: for all the earth is mine: And ye shall be unto me a kingdom of priests, and an holy nation. These are the words which thou shalt speak unto the children of Israel. And Moses came and called for the elders of the people, and laid before their faces all these words which the Lord commanded him. And all the people answered together, and said, All that the Lord hath spoken we will do. And Moses returned the words of the people unto the Lord.*

On this first trip, God spoke to Moses and reminded him that it was He that that did all the miracles back in Egypt, it was He that bore them, it was He that brought them out to Himself. It was all God's goodness and faithfulness in keeping the covenant that He made with Himself when Abraham was put into a deep sleep. It was a reminder of the unconditional love of God for His people. They were to be His peculiar treasure. They were to be a kingdom of priests and they were to be a Holy nation. They would be holy because He was holy. Because of His Holiness and Goodness, His people were to enjoy Him. God alone would provide and care for His people.

But when Moses went down Mount Sinai and conveyed what God had said, the people replied with pride that whatever God had commanded they would be well able to do. They rejected the unconditional love of God that He had offered to them freely. Not realizing the absolute holiness of God, the people thought they could obey and do and thus, achieve holiness. **It was a sad day indeed as the people exchanged an unconditional covenant for a conditional one. One that they would have to fulfill. One that required their own works. One that would ultimately judge, condemn, and kill them. 'All that the Lord has spoken we will do' reigns as some of the proudest, yet saddest, words recorded in the whole bible.**

Even before Moses went up the mountain again to report back to God what the people had said, God heard these proud words. In *Deuteronomy 5:28-29*, we read, *And the Lord heard the voice of your words, when ye spake unto me; and the Lord said unto me, I have heard the voice of the words of this people, which they have spoken unto thee: they have well said all that they have spoken. O that there were such an heart in them, that they would fear me, and keep all my commandments always, that it might be well with them, and with their children forever!* How it must have hurt Him to have His unconditional love freely given to be rejected! Although the peoples' words sounded good, God knew that they were incapable of fulfilling it, as God knew their hearts and their flesh.

Everything changed after that! We read in *Exodus 19:9-25,
And the Lord said unto Moses, Lo, I come unto thee in a thick
cloud, that the people may hear when I speak with thee, and
believe thee forever. And Moses told the words of the people unto
the Lord. And the Lord said unto Moses, Go unto the people, and
sanctify them to day and tomorrow, and let them wash their
clothes, And be ready against the third day: for the third day the
Lord will come down in the sight of all the people upon mount
Sinai. And thou shalt set bounds unto the people round about,
saying, Take heed to yourselves, that ye go not up into the mount,
or touch the border of it: whosoever toucheth the mount shall be
surely put to death: There shall not an hand touch it, but he shall
surely be stoned, or shot through; whether it be beast or man, it
shall not live: when the trumpet soundeth long, they shall come up
to the mount.*

*And Moses went down from the mount unto the people, and
sanctified the people; and they washed their clothes. And he said
unto the people, Be ready against the third day: come not at your
wives. And it came to pass on the third day in the morning, that
there were thunders and lightnings, and a thick cloud upon the
mount, and the voice of the trumpet exceeding loud; so that all the
people that was in the camp trembled. And Moses brought forth the
people out of the camp to meet with God; and they stood at the
nether part of the mount. And mount Sinai was altogether on a
smoke, because the Lord descended upon it in fire: and the smoke
thereof ascended as the smoke of a furnace, and the whole mount
quaked greatly. And when the voice of the trumpet sounded long,
and waxed louder and louder, Moses spake, and God answered
him by a voice.*

*And the Lord came down upon mount Sinai, on the top of
the mount: and the Lord called Moses up to the top of the mount;
and Moses went up. And the Lord said unto Moses, Go down,
charge the people, lest they break through unto the Lord to gaze,
and many of them perish. And let the priests also, which come near
to the Lord, sanctify themselves, lest the Lord break forth upon
them. And Moses said unto the Lord, The people cannot come up to
mount Sinai: for thou chargedst us, saying, Set bounds about the*

*mount, and sanctify it. And the Lord said unto him, Away, get thee
down, and thou shalt come up, thou, and Aaron with thee: but let
not the priests and the people break through to come up unto the
Lord, lest he break forth upon them. So Moses went down unto the
people, and spake unto them.*

The people were now to wash their clothes and had to be
sanctified. While God kept them clean and holy before, now the
people had to do it for themselves. They were told that they could
not go up the mountain or even touch the bottom or the border of
it. As none of them could wash themselves clean or be self-
sanctified, no matter how much scrubbing they did, none of them
could approach God. Their judgment for touching the mountain
would be stoning or being shot through with an arrow or dart. Even
their wandering animals would be stoned or shot dead. None of
them could draw near to God and live.

When God came down upon Mount Sinai, the awesome
holiness of God was displayed for all to see. It was nothing like
anyone had ever seen. There were thunders and lightnings, fire and
smoke, blackness and darkness, tempests and earthquakes, thick
clouds and loud trumpets before God's voice spoke through. He
charged Moses and the people to not come close; otherwise they
would perish or die. There were no records of death for any
Israelite on their journey from Egypt to Sinai because they were
bound with an unconditional covenant. All of that was about to
change.

The holiness of God was so intense that the whole
mountain shook. In *Hebrews 12:20-21, (For they could not endure
that which was commanded, And if so much as a beast touch the
mountain, it shall be stoned, or thrust through with a dart: And so
terrible was the sight, that Moses said, I exceedingly fear and
quake:)* The people shook in fear. Even Moses shook with fear.
Man saw his impending doom before the law was given.

While none of them, including Moses, could see God's face
they all heard His voice as He gave them the Ten Commandments
orally. This was the start of the covenant of death or the
ministration of death. The people then charged Moses to be the
mediator between God and them as they were afraid that they

would die if God were to speak to them directly. Moses replied that God was now out to prove them by their works.

We read of this account in *Exodus 20:1-22, And God spake all these words, saying, I am the Lord thy God, which have brought thee out of the land of Egypt, out of the house of bondage. Thou shalt have no other gods before me. Thou shalt not make unto thee any graven image, or any likeness of anything that is in heaven above, or that is in the earth beneath, or that is in the water under the earth: Thou shalt not bow down thyself to them, nor serve them: for I the Lord thy God am a jealous God, visiting the iniquity of the fathers upon the children unto the third and fourth generation of them that hate me; And shewing mercy unto thousands of them that love me, and keep my commandments. Thou shalt not take the name of the Lord thy God in vain; for the Lord will not hold him guiltless that taketh his name in vain. Remember the sabbath day, to keep it holy. Six days shalt thou labour, and do all thy work: But the seventh day is the sabbath of the Lord thy God: in it thou shalt not do any work, thou, nor thy son, nor thy daughter, thy manservant, nor thy maidservant, nor thy cattle, nor thy stranger that is within thy gates: For in six days the Lord made heaven and earth, the sea, and all that in them is, and rested the seventh day: wherefore the Lord blessed the sabbath day, and hallowed it. Honour thy father and thy mother: that thy days may be long upon the land which the Lord thy God giveth thee. Thou shalt not kill. Thou shalt not commit adultery. Thou shalt not steal. Thou shalt not bear false witness against thy neighbour. Thou shalt not covet thy neighbour's house, thou shalt not covet thy neighbour's wife, nor his manservant, nor his maidservant, nor his ox, nor his ass, nor any thing that is thy neighbour's.*

And all the people saw the thunderings, and the lightnings, and the noise of the trumpet, and the mountain smoking: and when the people saw it, they removed, and stood afar off. And they said unto Moses, Speak thou with us, and we will hear: but let not God speak with us, lest we die. And Moses said unto the people, Fear not: for God is come to prove you, and that his fear may be before your faces, that ye sin not.

Moses then went up the mountain again and received additional statutes as recorded in Exodus at the end of chapter 20 until chapter 23. Moses brought all these additional statutes before the people orally. The people answered again with one voice, 'All the words which the Lord has said we will do'. This covenant, called the Mosaic Covenant because of Moses, was now ratified. An altar was built together with twelve pillars. Burnt and peace offerings were sacrificed. The blood of the sacrificed animals was then sprinkled on the altar. Moses who had by now recorded all the Ten Commandments plus the additional statutes in a book, called the book of the covenant, now read from it. The people reaffirmed their obedience to the laws written therein. Blood was then sprinkled upon the people and the book before partaking of a covenant meal together.

Then Moses was called to go up Mount Sinai again. This time he would be up there for forty days and nights. During this time he received instructions on how to build the tabernacle. At the end of the forty days, Moses was given two tablets of stone written on both sides by the finger of God. It seemed that only the Ten Commandments were written on the tablets. All the other statutes and judgments given by God were written in the book of the law or covenant. This book of the law was stored in the side of the ark of the covenant. Together they constituted the law of God, which the Israelites vowed to follow. We say that the law is now both codified and written down. The Israelites vowed to follow all of the laws, not some of the laws. 'All' included the Ten Commandments as well as the additional statutes and ordinances. They were not separate laws but a corporate whole.

This is found in the following scriptures: *Exodus 24:3-8, 12-18, And Moses came and told the people all the words of the Lord, and all the judgments: and all the people answered with one voice, and said, All the words which the Lord hath said will we do. And Moses wrote all the words of the Lord, and rose up early in the morning, and builded an altar under the hill, and twelve pillars, according to the twelve tribes of Israel. And he sent young men of the children of Israel, which offered burnt offerings, and sacrificed peace offerings of oxen unto the Lord. And Moses took*

*half of the blood, and put it in basons; and half of the blood he
sprinkled on the altar. And he took the book of the covenant, and
read in the audience of the people: and they said, All that the Lord
hath said will we do, and be obedient. And Moses took the blood,
and sprinkled it on the people, and said, Behold the blood of the
covenant, which the Lord hath made with you concerning all these
words.*

*And the Lord said unto Moses, Come up to me into the
mount, and be there: and I will give thee tables of stone, and a law,
and commandments which I have written; that thou mayest teach
them. And Moses rose up, and his minister Joshua: and Moses
went up into the mount of God. And he said unto the elders, Tarry
ye here for us, until we come again unto you: and, behold, Aaron
and Hur are with you: if any man have any matters to do, let him
come unto them. And Moses went up into the mount, and a cloud
covered the mount. And the glory of the Lord abode upon mount
Sinai, and the cloud covered it six days: and the seventh day he
called unto Moses out of the midst of the cloud. And the sight of the
glory of the Lord was like devouring fire on the top of the mount in
the eyes of the children of Israel. And Moses went into the midst of
the cloud, and gat him up into the mount: and Moses was in the
mount forty days and forty nights.*

*Exodus 31:18, And he gave unto Moses, when he had made an end
of communing with him upon mount Sinai, two tables of testimony,
tables of stone, written with the finger of God.*

*Exodus 32:15-16, And Moses turned, and went down from the
mount, and the two tables of the testimony were in his hand: the
tables were written on both their sides; on the one side and on the
other were they written. And the tables were the work of God, and
the writing was the writing of God, graven upon the tables.*

*Deuteronomy 4:13-14, And he declared unto you his covenant,
which he commanded you to perform, even ten commandments;
and he wrote them upon two tables of stone. And the Lord
commanded me at that time to teach you statutes and judgments,
that ye might do them in the land whither ye go over to possess it.*

*Deuteronomy 31:24-26, And it came to pass, when Moses had
made an end of writing the words of this law in a book, until they*

were finished, That Moses commanded the Levites, which bare the
ark of the covenant of the Lord, saying, Take this book of the law,
and put it in the side of the ark of the covenant of the Lord your
God, that it may be there for a witness against thee.

The Mosaic law was conditional upon the behavior and
performance of the Israelites. They would be blessed if they
obeyed the law. On the other hand, they would be cursed and
punished if they disobeyed. Now that the law had been given,
sin would be imputed upon them. God could now hold the
peoples' sins against them. The law is as inflexible as an old
wineskin. It is unbending, unyielding, and rigid. It is as grim and as
stern as the stone it was written on. Punishment for breaking the
law would be meted out to all transgressors without exception.

We see in *Romans 7:12, Wherefore the law is holy, and the*
commandment holy, and just, and good. **The law was holy, just,**
and good. It came from God Himself! In fact, it was so holy,
just, and good that it was perfect. But this perfect law was
given to imperfect people to uphold. It had tragic results.

When the Israelites saw that Moses still had not come down
from Mount Sinai, they asked Aaron (Moses elder brother) to
make them a god. With the golden earrings from the people, he
fashioned a golden calf. Then Aaron made a proclamation that
there would be a feast to the Lord, as represented by the golden
calf, the next day. 'The Lord' in the verse literally means
YAHWEH, the true God of Israel, not a substitute god. In doing
so, he broke the first two commandments that the people had
recently sworn to uphold and obey. The punishment was death for
about three thousand men. The law brought death upon mankind as
sin was now charged to them. They were blotted out of God's
book.

We read this in *Exodus 32:1-10, 26-28, 30-33, And when*
the people saw that Moses delayed to come down out of the mount,
the people gathered themselves together unto Aaron, and said unto
him, Up, make us gods, which shall go before us; for as for this
Moses, the man that brought us up out of the land of Egypt, we wot
not what is become of him. And Aaron said unto them, Break off
the golden earrings, which are in the ears of your wives, of your

sons, and of your daughters, and bring them unto me. And all the people brake off the golden earrings which were in their ears, and brought them unto Aaron. And he received them at their hand, and fashioned it with a graving tool, after he had made it a molten calf: and they said, These be thy gods, O Israel, which brought thee up out of the land of Egypt. And when Aaron saw it, he built an altar before it; and Aaron made proclamation, and said, Tomorrow is a feast to the Lord. And they rose up early on the morrow, and offered burnt offerings, and brought peace offerings; and the people sat down to eat and to drink, and rose up to play. And the Lord said unto Moses, Go, get thee down; for thy people, which thou broughtest out of the land of Egypt, have corrupted themselves: They have turned aside quickly out of the way which I commanded them: they have made them a molten calf, and have worshipped it, and have sacrificed thereunto, and said, These be thy gods, O Israel, which have brought thee up out of the land of Egypt. And the Lord said unto Moses, I have seen this people, and, behold, it is a stiffnecked people: Now therefore let me alone, that my wrath may wax hot against them, and that I may consume them: and I will make of thee a great nation.

Then Moses stood in the gate of the camp, and said, Who is on the Lord's side? let him come unto me. And all the sons of Levi gathered themselves together unto him. And he said unto them, Thus saith the Lord God of Israel, Put every man his sword by his side, and go in and out from gate to gate throughout the camp, and slay every man his brother, and every man his companion, and every man his neighbour. And the children of Levi did according to the word of Moses: and there fell of the people that day about three thousand men.

And it came to pass on the morrow, that Moses said unto the people, Ye have sinned a great sin: and now I will go up unto the Lord; peradventure I shall make an atonement for your sin. And Moses returned unto the Lord, and said, Oh, this people have sinned a great sin, and have made them gods of gold. Yet now, if thou wilt forgive their sin; and if not, blot me, I pray thee, out of thy book which thou hast written. And the Lord said unto Moses, Whosoever hath sinned against me, him will I blot out of my book.

But the finger of God that wrote the tablets of stone in the Old Testament did not stop writing. With His finger, He wrote out the curses of the law and wrote in grace and love. With His finger, He wrote us into the book of life once again.

In *John 8:3-12*, we read, *And the scribes and Pharisees brought unto him a woman taken in adultery; and when they had set her in the midst, They say unto him, Master, this woman was taken in adultery, in the very act. Now Moses in the law commanded us, that such should be stoned: but what sayest thou? This they said, tempting him, that they might have to accuse him. But Jesus stooped down, and with his finger wrote on the ground, as though he heard them not. So when they continued asking him, he lifted up himself, and said unto them, He that is without sin among you, let him first cast a stone at her. And again he stooped down, and wrote on the ground. And they which heard it, being convicted by their own conscience, went out one by one, beginning at the eldest, even unto the last: and Jesus was left alone, and the woman standing in the midst. When Jesus had lifted up himself, and saw none but the woman, he said unto her, Woman, where are those thine accusers? hath no man condemned thee? She said, No man, Lord. And Jesus said unto her, Neither do I condemn thee: go, and sin no more. Then spake Jesus again unto them, saying, I am the light of the world: he that followeth me shall not walk in darkness, but shall have the light of life.*

Under the law, written by the finger of God, a woman caught in the act of adultery either by her husband or by other witnesses was immediately put to death. *Leviticus 20:10* states, *And the man that committeth adultery with another man's wife, even he that committeth adultery with his neighbour's wife, the adulterer and the adulteress shall surely be put to death.* Both the adulterer and the adulteress would be stoned to death outside the city walls. The woman caught in the act is never brought before the priest, as the law is very clear as to the punishment. In *Deuteronomy 22:22-24, If a man be found lying with a woman married to an husband, then they shall both of them die, both the man that lay with the woman, and the woman: so shalt thou put away evil from Israel. If a damsel that is a virgin be betrothed unto an husband, and a man find her in the city, and lie with her; Then ye shall bring them both out unto the gate of that city, and ye shall stone them with stones that they die; the damsel, because she cried not, being in the city; and the man, because he hath humbled his neighbour's wife: so thou shalt put away evil from among you.*

But if the woman is suspected but not caught in the act, then the law states that the woman is to be brought before the priest to undergo a water ordeal or test. This water ordeal or test is found in *Numbers 5:11-31, And the Lord spake unto Moses, saying, Speak unto the children of Israel, and say unto them, If any man's wife go aside, and commit a trespass against him, And a man lie with her carnally, and it be hid from the eyes of her husband, and be kept close, and she be defiled, and there be no witness against her, neither she be taken with the manner; And the spirit of jealousy come upon him, and he be jealous of his wife, and she be defiled: or if the spirit of jealousy come upon him, and he be jealous of his wife, and she be not defiled:*

Then shall the man bring his wife unto the priest, and he shall bring her offering for her, the tenth part of an ephah of barley meal; he shall pour no oil upon it, nor put frankincense thereon; for it is an offering of jealousy, an offering of memorial, bringing iniquity to remembrance. And the priest shall bring her near, and set her before the Lord: And the priest shall take holy water in an earthen vessel; and of the dust that is in the floor of the tabernacle the priest shall take, and put it into the water: And the priest shall set the woman before the Lord, and uncover the woman's head, and put the offering of memorial in her hands, which is the jealousy offering: and the priest shall have in his hand the bitter water that causeth the curse: And the priest shall charge her by an oath, and say unto the woman, If no man have lain with thee, and if thou hast not gone aside to uncleanness with another instead of thy husband, be thou free from this bitter water that causeth the curse: But if thou hast gone aside to another instead of thy husband, and if thou be defiled, and some man have lain with thee beside thine husband: Then the priest shall charge the woman with an oath of cursing, and the priest shall say unto the woman, The Lord make thee a curse and an oath among thy people, when the Lord doth make thy thigh to rot, and thy belly to swell; And this water that causeth the curse shall go into thy bowels, to make thy belly to swell, and thy thigh to rot: And the woman shall say, Amen, amen.

And the priest shall write these curses in a book, and he shall blot them out with the bitter water: And he shall cause the woman to drink the bitter water that causeth the curse: and the water that causeth the curse shall enter into her, and become bitter.

Then the priest shall take the jealousy offering out of the woman's hand, and shall wave the offering before the Lord, and offer it upon the altar: And the priest shall take an handful of the offering, even the memorial thereof, and burn it upon the altar, and afterward shall cause the woman to drink the water. And when he hath made her to drink the water, then it shall come to pass, that, if she be defiled, and have done trespass against her husband, that the water that causeth the curse shall enter into her, and become bitter, and her belly shall swell, and her thigh shall rot: and the woman shall be a curse among her people. And if the woman be not defiled, but be clean; then she shall be free, and shall conceive seed. This is the law of jealousies, when a wife goeth aside to another instead of her husband, and is defiled; Or when the spirit of jealousy cometh upon him, and he be jealous over his wife, and shall set the woman before the Lord, and the priest shall execute upon her all this law. Then shall the man be guiltless from iniquity, and this woman shall bear her iniquity.

If a woman were suspected of adultery, the priest performing the water ordeal would mix water from the laver (basin where the priest washes) with the dust from the temple floor. Then the curse of the sin of adultery would be written on a scroll or in a book. With the ink still wet, the priest would pour the premixed water onto the curse. The water would blot out the curse. This water, now mixed with the ink from the curse, would be recollected and the accused made to drink it. It was called bitter water. If the woman were guilty she would be cursed. With the passing of time, her belly would swell and her thigh would rot. If she were innocent, nothing would happen to her.

In *Exodus 32:20*, we read, *And he took the calf which they had made, and burnt it in the fire, and ground it to powder, and strawed it upon the water, and made the children of Israel drink of it.* Moses actually demonstrated this process when he burnt the golden calf, ground it to powder, mixed the gold powder with water and made the guilty Israelites drink the mixture. As we saw before, it brought death shortly after.

Back to the scripture on the woman caught in adultery, the Pharisees and scribes had been very jealous of Jesus. Many people now believed Jesus as the Son of God. The law keepers and legalists were losing power and control. When Jesus said He was the Living Water, even more people believed in Him. We read in *John 7:30-32, 37-38,40 Then they sought to take him: but no man laid hands on him, because his hour was not yet come. And many of the people believed on him, and said, When Christ cometh, will he do more miracles than these which this man hath done? The Pharisees heard that the people murmured such things concerning him; and the Pharisees and the chief priests sent officers to take him. In the last day, that great day of the feast, Jesus stood and cried, saying, If any man thirst, let him come unto me, and drink. He that believeth on me, as the scripture hath said, out of his belly shall flow rivers of living water. Many of the people therefore, when they heard this saying, said, Of a truth this is the Prophet.*

The Pharisees and scribes then hatched a plan to discredit Jesus and His teachings. It was to be a brilliant plan. But it did not turn out the way they had anticipated.

The scribes and Pharisees who took the woman to Jesus for trial knew the law very well. They were both law keepers and law interpreters. If the woman were caught in the act of adultery as they claimed, both the woman and the man would have been taken outside the city gates and be stoned to death according to the law. There would be no necessity for a priestly trial.

Since the woman was taken to Jesus, and there was no other guilty man or witnesses in this incident, she could not have been caught in the act of adultery. My conclusion is that the woman was not guilty but brought before Jesus to tempt Him. She was the bait used by the Pharisees and scribes to discredit Jesus.

The temptation or test of Jesus was simple. If the woman was guilty as stated, Jesus who did not break any law must insist on stoning. This would nullify His teachings on grace and mercy. If He released her from stoning, then He would have broken the law. Thus, He cannot be the spotless Lamb of God. Jesus had to be spotless. That was the reason for Jesus' birth from a virgin, circumcision, and offerings at the temple. Jesus did not break a single law. He kept it all and thus fulfilled it.

But if the woman was not guilty of adultery in the first place and Jesus had her stoned, then He would be proven not to be the Son of God. The Son of God would have known that she was innocent. There was only one right decision and that was for Jesus to have known that the woman was innocent in the first place and to then release her from the guilty charge.

But before He released her, Jesus showed the Pharisees and scribes the exact fulfillment of the law as described in Numbers. He wrote on the dust in the temple with His finger. What did He wrote? In my opinion, He wrote exactly what the Old Testament priest wrote – the curse of the sin, but not the sin of adultery but the sin of bearing false witness.

All the Pharisees and scribes saw the writing. When Jesus asked them to stone the woman, they could not do it, as they would have innocent blood on their hands making them in turn liable for murder. Then Jesus did the unthinkable. He wrote again and blotted out His first set of writing. When the law was given to Moses, men were blotted out. Now sin was blotted out and men were written in. Jesus had just finished a lesson on Living Water. Now the Living Water mixed His finger with the dust of the temple and blotted out the sin that He first wrote on the floor. Their sins He would remember no more! What was called bitter water is now sweet water. What was once a curse was a curse no more. In *Colossians 2:14,* we read, *Blotting out the handwriting of ordinances that was against us, which was contrary to us, and took it out of the way, nailing it to his cross.* **Jesus blotted out the law and the commandments, took it out of the way, and nailed it to the cross.**

As their sin of bearing false witness was exposed and then blotted out by Grace, the Pharisees and scribes could not face Jesus and skulked away. When Jesus stood up, the woman was told by Grace or Jesus that she was not condemned but that she should go and sin no more; meaning that going to 'bed' with the Pharisees again and again would have its consequences. As Jesus had not died on the cross yet, sin still had dominion over the woman.

We see in *John 1:17, For the law was given by Moses, but grace and truth came by Jesus Christ.* In original Greek, the contrast is even more evident:

For the law…………..through Moses……… was given,
Grace and the Truth….through Jesus Christ… came.

The cold, hard, unyielding, lifeless law was given to Moses but Grace, Truth, warmth, compassion, love, and life came by Jesus Christ. Grace and Truth are not two separate words but one word that represents Jesus. In Grace, there would be no shame and condemnation. That is the Truth. *Romans 8:1* state that *There is therefore now no condemnation to them which are in Christ Jesus, who walk not after the flesh, but after the Spirit.* The Light of the World had taken out the darkness and had replaced it with the light of life. **The Light exposes our cleanliness and our beauty, not our shame. The Light displays our sinless nature and our perfection in Christ for all to see. The darkness that hides our sins and ugliness has been replaced. We are now immaculate and unsoiled. The law that was given by Moses written with the finger of God was blotted out by the same finger of Grace and Truth, Jesus Christ.**

❧ 9 ☙

JESUS AND THE VEIL

The law was glorious but it was a transient, passing glory. The moment it was given, it was already on its way out. After spending forty days and forty nights on Mount Sinai, Moses was given the tablets of stone wherein were written the Ten Commandments. But when Moses saw that the people could not even keep the very first commandment, which they earlier vowed to, he became enraged, threw the tablets onto the ground and broke them. We see this in *Exodus 32:19, And it came to pass, as soon as he came nigh unto the camp, that he saw the calf, and the dancing: and Moses' anger waxed hot, and he cast the tables out of his hands, and brake them beneath the mount.*

God then instructed Moses to hew out another two tablets and that He would replicate what was written on the first set of tablets. God supplied the first two tablets. The second set of tablets was hewed out by Moses. Moses spent another forty days and nights with God whereby more ordinances were given to him. We read in *Exodus 34:1, 27-28, And the Lord said unto Moses, Hew thee two tables of stone like unto the first: and I will write upon these tables the words that were in the first tables, which thou brakest. And the Lord said unto Moses, Write thou these words: for after the tenor of these words I have made a covenant with thee and with Israel. And he was there with the Lord forty days and forty nights; he did neither eat bread, nor drink water. **And he*** *wrote upon the tables the words of the covenant, the ten commandments.*

Note that the 'he' in the last sentence is preceded by 'And' meaning a break from the previous sentence. 'He' in this case meant God, not Moses. Moses did not write the second set of tablets neither did he had the tools to do so. God said He would do it and He did. It was God who wrote all the commandments upon the tablets. The tablets that God wrote were then put into the ark. However, Moses recorded the additional statues and judgments in the book of the law or covenant. This book was placed in the side of the ark, not in the ark as the tablets. As mentioned before, together they constitute the law of God.

We see this in *Deuteronomy 10:1-5, At that time the Lord said unto me, Hew thee two tables of stone like unto the first, and come up unto me into the mount, and make thee an ark of wood. And I will write on the tables the words that were in the first tables which thou brakest, and thou shalt put them in the ark. And I made an ark of shittim wood, and hewed two tables of stone like unto the first, and went up into the mount, having the two tables in mine hand. And he wrote on the tables, according to the first writing, the ten commandments, which the Lord spake unto you in the mount out of the midst of the fire in the day of the assembly: and the Lord gave them unto me. And I turned myself and came down from the mount, and put the tables in the ark which I had made; and there they be, as the Lord commanded me* and in *Deuteronomy 31:26, Take this book of the law, and put it in the side of the ark of the covenant of the Lord your God, that it may be there for a witness against thee.*

By the way, if you have ever wondered what stone the law was written on, the answer is blue sapphire. The Ten Commandments and the other statutes were written on stones of blue sapphire. In *Exodus 24:9-12, Then went up Moses, and Aaron, Nadab, and Abihu, and seventy of the elders of Israel: And they saw the God of Israel: and there was under his feet as it were a paved work of a sapphire stone, and as it were the body of heaven in his clearness. And upon the nobles of the children of Israel he laid not his hand: also they saw God, and did eat and drink. And*

the Lord said unto Moses, Come up to me into the mount, and be
there: and I will give thee tables of stone, and a law, and
commandments which I have written; that thou mayest teach them.

When Moses and the elders went up Mount Sinai to receive
the first two stone tablets, they clearly saw the feet of God standing
upon sapphire stone. Then when God told Moses that He would
give him the law written on the tablets of stone, the original
Hebrew meaning meant tablets of *the* stone aforementioned,
meaning the sapphire stone that God had been standing on.

This blue color was also commemorated in the blue ribbon,
which is found on the fringe or the border of Israelites' garments.
This is seen in *Numbers 15:37-40, And the Lord spake unto Moses,*
saying, Speak unto the children of Israel, and bid them that they
make them fringes in the borders of their garments throughout
their generations, and that they put upon the fringe of the borders
a ribband of blue: And it shall be unto you for a fringe, that ye may
look upon it, and remember all the commandments of the Lord,
and do them; and that ye seek not after your own heart and your
own eyes, after which ye use to go a whoring: That ye may
remember, and do all my commandments, and be holy unto your
God. When they looked upon the blue fringe, they would
remember the blue sapphire stone on which the Ten
Commandments were written.

When Moses came down the mountain with the new blue
tablets, his face shone from the time spent in the glory of the Lord.
Whatever comes from God is glorious. The law came from God
and was glorious. But that glory was to be done away. So when
Moses talked with the Israelites, he wore a veil to cover the fact
that the glory of the law was fading. But when Moses went in
before the Lord to speak with Him, He would take the veil off,
until he came out. Then he would put the veil on again so that the
Israelites could not see the end of that which was being abolished.
The law was 'being' made obsolete even as it was given.

Because of the veil, the Israelites could not see clearly.
They thought that Moses face was and would always remain
glorious because of the law. They could not see the glory fading
away behind the veil. Till this day, the same veil covers the Old

Testament and the hearts of many people. What they think is glorious has actually vanished. In its place something much more glorious has appeared. Jesus Christ has appeared and He is the only one who can tear down the veil that had blinded so many people. He is the only one who can set us free from the veil of the law. He is the only one who can give us liberty.

We read this in the following scriptures: *Exodus 34: 29-35, And it came to pass, when Moses came down from mount Sinai with the two tables of testimony in Moses' hand, when he came down from the mount, that Moses wist not that the skin of his face shone while he talked with him. And when Aaron and all the children of Israel saw Moses, behold, the skin of his face shone; and they were afraid to come nigh him. And Moses called unto them; and Aaron and all the rulers of the congregation returned unto him: and Moses talked with them. And afterward all the children of Israel came nigh: and he gave them in commandment all that the Lord had spoken with him in mount Sinai. And till Moses had done speaking with them, he put a vail on his face. But when Moses went in before the Lord to speak with him, he took the vail off, until he came out. And he came out, and spake unto the children of Israel that which he was commanded. And the children of Israel saw the face of Moses, that the skin of Moses' face shone: and Moses put the vail upon his face again, until he went in to speak with him.*
2 Corinthians 3:6-18, Who also hath made us able ministers of the new testament; not of the letter, but of the spirit: for the letter killeth, but the spirit giveth life. But if the ministration of death, written and engraven in stones, was glorious, so that the children of Israel could not stedfastly behold the face of Moses for the glory of his countenance; which glory was to be done away: How shall not the ministration of the spirit be rather glorious? For if the ministration of condemnation be glory, much more doth the ministration of righteousness exceed in glory. For even that which was made glorious had no glory in this respect, by reason of the glory that excelleth. For if that which is done away was glorious, much more that which remaineth is glorious. Seeing then that we have such hope, we use great plainness of speech: And not as

*Moses, which put a vail over his face, that the children of Israel
could not stedfastly look to the end of that which is abolished: But
their minds were blinded: for until this day remaineth the same
vail untaken away in the reading of the old testament; which vail is
done away in Christ. But even unto this day, when Moses is read,
the vail is upon their heart. Nevertheless when it shall turn to the
Lord, the vail shall be taken away. Now the Lord is that Spirit: and
where the Spirit of the Lord is, there is liberty. But we all, with
open face beholding as in a glass the glory of the Lord, are
changed into the same image from glory to glory, even as by the
Spirit of the Lord.*

**The law was a transient glory when it was given, meant
to be replaced. But the people could not see that it was meant
to be succeeded by Jesus. What was to be supplanted was held
on to and taught as though it was the real thing.** The prophet
Isaiah likened the law to tables full of vomit and filthiness. We see
this in *Isaiah 28:8-20, For all tables are full of vomit and
filthiness, so that there is no place clean. Whom shall he teach
knowledge? and whom shall he make to understand doctrine? them
that are weaned from the milk, and drawn from the breasts. For
precept must be upon precept, precept upon precept; line upon
line, line upon line; here a little, and there a little: For with
stammering lips and another tongue will he speak to this people.
To whom he said, This is the rest wherewith ye may cause the
weary to rest; and this is the refreshing: yet they would not hear.*

*But the word of the Lord was unto them precept upon
precept, precept upon precept; line upon line, line upon line; here
a little, and there a little; that they might go, and fall backward,
and be broken, and snared, and taken. Wherefore hear the word of
the Lord, ye scornful men, that rule this people which is in
Jerusalem. Because ye have said, We have made a covenant with
death, and with hell are we at agreement; when the overflowing
scourge shall pass through, it shall not come unto us: for we have
made lies our refuge, and under falsehood have we hid ourselves:*

*Therefore thus saith the Lord God, Behold, I lay in Zion for
a foundation, a stone, a tried stone, a precious corner stone, a sure
foundation: he that believeth shall not make haste. Judgment also*

will I lay to the line, and righteousness to the plummet: and the hail shall sweep away the refuge of lies, and the waters shall overflow the hiding place. And your covenant with death shall be disannulled, and your agreement with hell shall not stand; when the overflowing scourge shall pass through, then ye shall be trodden down by it. From the time that it goeth forth it shall take you: for morning by morning shall it pass over, by day and by night: and it shall be a vexation only to understand the report. For the bed is shorter than that a man can stretch himself on it: and the covering narrower than that he can wrap himself in it.

Because of its sole emphasis on self-works, the Pharisees and scribes would teach the people the law precept upon precept, line upon line, and to do a little here and a little there. They taught that doing the law would bring the people rest. They taught the people that they would be refreshed if they followed the law line by line and precept by precept. Because of the veil upon their hearts, they could not see the utter futility of their own efforts in keeping the law. **As the people tried to do the law line by line and precept by precept, God judged them back line by line and precept by precept. As the people strictly followed the law, God judged them back strictly with the law.** He used the line and the plummet to judge them. It was strict and exact. In *James 2:10*, we read, *For whosoever shall keep the whole law, and yet offend in one point, he is guilty of all.* Breaking one line or one precept of the law meant breaking the whole law. **For whosoever shall keep the whole law, and yet offend in one point, he is guilty of all.** Because of their inability to follow the whole law, the people fell backward; broken, snared, and taken in by the trap of the law.

Therefore, the people labored to find rest that never came. Their bed was always too short and their coverings too narrow. No matter how hard they tried to follow the law, some parts of them would be exposed. They were in a bed of lies and falsehood. There was no refuge and rest under the law. The law was like a covenant made with death and hell. Small wonder then when we read in *Nehemiah 8:9, For all the people wept, when they heard the words of the law.* They did not weep for joy. They wept because they saw their own sins, failures and mistakes. As more of the law was read more of their own unworthiness was exposed. The law brought guilt, condemnation, death, and hell for the people.

However, there is wonderful news coming! God had laid in Zion a foundation stone, a tried stone, a precious cornerstone, a sure foundation. This foundation and cornerstone is Jesus Christ. As the law or the ministration of death was glorious in the Old Testament, Jesus Christ or the ministration of the Spirit would be so much more glorious in the New Testament. There is no veil in Jesus Christ. His glory shines plainly for all to see and He shines forever. It never fades or passes away. It is permanent unlike the passing glory of the law. Jesus is the same yesterday, today, and forevermore. One look at His excellent glory and everything pales in comparison. The law became a shadow immediately. The darkness went when the light shone on it. The shadow disappeared when The Light shone on it. Sin was removed when Light came in. The bondage disappeared when Liberty appeared. The deception disappeared when The Truth appeared. **The law disappeared when Grace appeared.** All serfdom was overturned at the appearance of Jesus.

When we place our faith in Jesus, we walk out of darkness permanently. We walk in the light of life forever because of Jesus. If we make a mistake and sin, we still walk in the light. We are saved by Grace and maintained by Grace. We do not walk out of the light into darkness when we sin and then walk back into the light again when we feel we have not sinned. Either we are in the light or we are not. There is no walking in and out of the light. We do not become sinners again as Jesus became sin for us. God is light and in Him is no darkness at all. When we walk as children of light, we always remain in the light because the blood of Christ continuously cleanses us from all our sins. That is why we can never be called sinners again.

Note that Grace prevents us from sinning ever again in our spirit but at the same time, it does not guarantee us that we will never ever sin again in our mind or body. This will be covered in detail in a later chapter. What Grace does is to guarantee us right standing with God, in spite of our sin. When we are in the light and sin, then we are known as saints that sinned. At the same time, because of Jesus, we are considered as never having sinned at all.

But if we have no faith in Jesus, meaning we walk in darkness, then when we sin we are known as sinners that sinned. Many times sinners are not even aware of sin as the darkness masks their sin. **Saints walk in the light even if they sin and sinners walk in darkness even if they do not or are unaware of their sin. The righteous are righteous because of Jesus and not because of their works. The sinners are sinners because they do not have Jesus. It is also not because of their works. The only sin that sinners are ultimately guilty of is the sin of not believing in Jesus. All other sins were dealt with at the cross.** So whether a righteous man sins or a sinner acts righteously is all to no avail. For it is not about us but it is all about Jesus. He is the One who keeps us from falling and he is the One who presents us faultless before God. **It is not good or bad works that separate light from darkness. Only Jesus separates light from darkness. Jesus is Light and without Jesus, there is darkness.**

We read about this in the following scriptures: *John 8:12, 32, 36, Then spake Jesus again unto them, saying, I am the light of the world: he that followeth me shall not walk in darkness, but shall have the light of life.   And ye shall know the truth, and the truth shall make you free.   If the Son therefore shall make you free, ye shall be free indeed.*
2 Corinthians 4:6, For God, who commanded the light to shine out of darkness, hath shined in our hearts, to give the light of the knowledge of the glory of God in the face of Jesus Christ.
Ephesians 5:8, For ye were sometimes darkness, but now are ye light in the Lord: walk as children of light:
Luke 1:79, To give light to them that sit in darkness and in the shadow of death, to guide our feet into the way of peace.
1 John 1:5-7, This then is the message which we have heard of him, and declare unto you, that God is light, and in him is no darkness at all. If we say that we have fellowship with him, and walk in darkness, we lie, and do not the truth: But if we walk in the light, as he is in the light, we have fellowship one with another, and the blood of Jesus Christ his Son cleanseth us from all sin.

1 Peter 2:9, But ye are a chosen generation, a royal priesthood, an holy nation, a peculiar people; that ye should shew forth the praises of him who hath called you out of darkness into his marvellous light:
Colossians 1:12-14, Giving thanks unto the Father, which hath made us meet to be partakers of the inheritance of the saints in light: Who hath delivered us from the power of darkness, and hath translated us into the kingdom of his dear Son: In whom we have redemption through his blood, even the forgiveness of sin.
Jude 24-25, Now unto him that is able to keep you from falling, and to present you faultless before the presence of his glory with exceeding joy, To the only wise God our Saviour, be glory and majesty, dominion and power, both now and ever. Amen.

And for all those of us who are in Jesus, His glory becomes our glory as we look upon Him. Just like us looking at a mirror, we see ourselves glorious because of His glory. As we look on His face, we see our face. And because His glory never fades our glory never fades. In *1 Corinthians 1:30-31*, we read, *But of him are ye in Christ Jesus, who of God is made unto us wisdom, and righteousness, and sanctification, and redemption: That, according as it is written, He that glorieth, let him glory in the Lord.* In Jesus, without any works on our part, we have redemption, righteousness, and sanctification. As Jesus has the completeness of the Godhead in Him, we are also complete in Him. In *Colossians 2:9-10, For in him dwelleth all the fulness of the Godhead bodily. And ye are complete in him, which is the head of all principality and power.* In Him, we have everything. Jesus is sufficient for me. Jesus is sufficient for you. He is all glory.

❧ 10 ❧

JESUS AND HALAKHA

Halakha or Jewish law derives itself from three sources. The first source comes from the first five books of the bible, also called the Torah or mitzvot d'oraita. There are 613 laws in the Torah (to see the list, please refer to Appendix A). Many of these laws cannot be followed today as modern day Israel does not have a temple/tabernacle. The second source for the laws arose after the destruction of the temple by the Romans in 70AD. The rabbis rose to prominence, after the destruction of Jerusalem and the temple, and greatly expanded the Torah. The rabbis trace their origins back to the Pharisees. The law was now expanded to include laws that prevented accidentally violating the first set of laws. Laws for public welfare were added as well. This is generally known as mitzvot d'rabbanan. All these additional laws are collectively known as the Talmud and in print, are about 6,200 pages long. The last source came from customs of the people now made into law, or generally called minhag. The law, as a whole, is significant in volume and there are disagreements among the Jews as to which laws are accepted and which are not.

Many Christians do not fully understand the significance of the law or the death it brings. Firstly, Halakha is a Jewish law for Jews. Gentiles were never under Halakha but later, adopted all or some parts of it. We see this quite clearly in the early church in Galatia when the law wormed its way into grace resulting in a mix.

This mixture was never meant to be. In *Acts 13:37-39, 42-48*, we read, *But he, whom God raised again, saw no corruption. Be it known unto you therefore, men and brethren, that through this man is preached unto you the forgiveness of sins: And by him all that believe are justified from all things, from which ye could not be justified by the law of Moses.*

And when the Jews were gone out of the synagogue, the Gentiles besought that these words might be preached to them the next sabbath. Now when the congregation was broken up, many of the Jews and religious proselytes followed Paul and Barnabas: who, speaking to them, persuaded them to continue in the grace of God. And the next sabbath day came almost the whole city together to hear the word of God. But when the Jews saw the multitudes, they were filled with envy, and spake against those things which were spoken by Paul, contradicting and blaspheming. Then Paul and Barnabas waxed bold, and said, It was necessary that the word of God should first have been spoken to you: but seeing ye put it from you, and judge yourselves unworthy of everlasting life, lo, we turn to the Gentiles. For so hath the Lord commanded us, saying, I have set thee to be a light of the Gentiles, that thou shouldest be for salvation unto the ends of the earth. And when the Gentiles heard this, they were glad, and glorified the word of the Lord: and as many as were ordained to eternal life believed.

Paul declared that it was only through Jesus Christ that people would be justified, not through Halakha. This was such good news that almost all the gentiles in the whole city showed up the following week to hear more about Jesus. They received Jesus gladly and were ordained to eternal life. But the Pharisees did not like losing their status as interpreters of the law to the message of grace brought by Paul. They quarreled and disputed strongly with Paul that the law was necessary for salvation.

We read in *Acts 15:1-2, 7-12, And certain men which came down from Judaea taught the brethren, and said, Except ye be circumcised after the manner of Moses, ye cannot be saved. When therefore Paul and Barnabas had no small dissension and disputation with them, they determined that Paul and Barnabas, and certain other of them, should go up to Jerusalem unto the apostles and elders about this question.   And when there had been much disputing, Peter rose up, and said unto them, Men and brethren, ye know how that a good while ago God made choice among us, that the Gentiles by my mouth should hear the word of the gospel, and believe. And God, which knoweth the hearts, bare them witness, giving them the Holy Ghost, even as he did unto us; And put no difference between us and them, purifying their hearts by faith. Now therefore why tempt ye God, to put a yoke upon the neck of the disciples, which neither our fathers nor we were able to bear? But we believe that through the grace of the Lord Jesus Christ we shall be saved, even as they. Then all the multitude kept silence, and gave audience to Barnabas and Paul, declaring what miracles and wonders God had wrought among the Gentiles by them.*

Peter was now dragged into the argument. He sided with Paul and asked the Pharisees why they would want to put a yoke around these new believers and disciples as they themselves, as Jews, could not carry that heavy yoke of the law. Then he declared that it was the grace of God, Jesus Christ, who saved both gentiles and Jews.

We often forget that the apostles believed firmly that it was all about Jesus and what He did on the cross that mattered. However, because of the Pharisees insistence on the importance of the law, the law began to creep into the early church. A mixture of law and grace ensued. Even today, for many people, they think that the law consists of some good morals and some good behavior. Therefore, it seems harmless enough. But as we saw above, the law is a huge body of works, not a few harmless rules that we live by. The law is actually man's effort and works to earn God's approval and acceptance. It is man saying, "Through my goodness, You God, have to accept me! Whatever you ask, God, we can do because we are good enough! We know good from evil and since we can do it all, we need no help from You. And definitely, we have no need or want of a Savior because we can save ourselves!"

These people are deceived into thinking that through their own works they can merit or earn God's approval. **They**

underestimate God's absolute holiness. When God descended upon Mount Sinai, He said that every man and animal would be put to instantaneous death by stoning or shooting through with an arrow/dart should they even touch the mountain. Man's sinful flesh cannot come into contact with God's holiness and live. God is infinitely holy and man is not. No number of rules, no matter how large and expansive, can begin to adequately describe God's holiness.

Why then was the law given to the Jews since it was impossible for them to keep all of it? And even if it was possible, which it is not, it would still be inadequate! The answer is simple. It is found in *Galatians 3:16-28, Now to Abraham and his seed were the promises made. He saith not, And to seeds, as of many; but as of one, And to thy seed, which is Christ. And this I say, that the covenant, that was confirmed before of God in Christ, the law, which was four hundred and thirty years after, cannot disannul, that it should make the promise of none effect.18 For if the inheritance be of the law, it is no more of promise: but God gave it to Abraham by promise.*

Wherefore then serveth the law? It was added because of transgressions, till the seed should come to whom the promise was made; and it was ordained by angels in the hand of a mediator. Now a mediator is not a mediator of one, but God is one. Is the law then against the promises of God? God forbid: for if there had been a law given which could have given life, verily righteousness should have been by the law.

But the scripture hath concluded all under sin, that the promise by faith of Jesus Christ might be given to them that believe. But before faith came, we were kept under the law, shut up unto the faith which should afterwards be revealed. Wherefore the law was our schoolmaster to bring us unto Christ, that we might be justified by faith. But after that faith is come, we are no longer under a schoolmaster. For ye are all the children of God by faith in Christ Jesus. For as many of you as have been baptized into Christ have put on Christ. There is neither Jew nor Greek, there is neither bond nor free, there is neither male nor female: for ye are all one in Christ Jesus.

The law was given to them to bring them to Christ. The original word for schoolmaster as used here is 'paidagogos', meaning a slave or servant who is in charge of a young boy to supervise, control, and discipline him. The slave, like the law, is strict, rigid, exacting, stringent, and punctilious to the young boy. The slave actually does not teach or educate the boy as a teacher would. Instead, the slave watches the young boy every minute, looming over and meting out punishment whenever the boy does wrong. As a paidagogos, the law would continue to discipline Israel until the appearing of the Promised Seed, Jesus Christ. Till then, the law would discipline and punish them continuously. Just like the slave, the law does not and was not meant to educate or teach them anything. It does not even lift a finger to help. It was meant to show them that they would always lack and would never meet the standard as required by God. The law would point out all of their shortcomings and pound into them their inadequacy. The pain of all these punishments was to drive them and show them their absolute need for Jesus. The law was added after the Abrahamic Covenant and it would last for a period of time. From Exodus to Malachi and into the pre-cross sections of the New Testament, it was all about the law. But as John the Baptist put it, 'prepare ye the way of the Lord'. The way of the Lord is Jesus, not the law.

The law was given by Moses but Grace and Truth came by Jesus Christ. *John 1:17* states clearly, *For the law was given by Moses, but grace and truth came by Jesus Christ*. Without Jesus, there would be no hope for them. **Without Jesus nobody, Jew or gentile, would become a child of God. With faith in Jesus, anybody can become a child of God. For Jesus imputes righteousness and perfection to those who have faith in Him**.

Still, many Christians not realizing the insidious nature of the law attempt to haphazardly follow and dabble with it. Women may not wear pants but they will eat pork. Men may not wear women's clothing but they will borrow with interest, thus causing the lender to sin. Others pray to God but violate the Sabbath. Some try to eat kosher meat but do not cook it kosher. They recite grace before and after a meal of lobsters, oysters and shrimp cooked with cheese, using non-kosher utensils. They abstain from eating insects but wonder why John the Baptist sinned and ate insects. To them it is a harmless game but James tells us clearly that the law has to be kept completely. Failing to do that would bring grave results. In *James 2:10-11, For whosoever shall keep the whole law, and yet offend in one point, he is guilty of all. For he that said, Do not commit adultery, said also, Do not kill. Now if thou commit no adultery, yet if thou kill, thou art become a transgressor of the law.* The law is a whole and whoever misses one is guilty of all. Yet people follow it randomly, chaotically, casually, and aimlessly. They are actually living as though Jesus had not come or is not needed, even if He came.

In an attempt to organize this haphazard behavior, Christian scholars then came up with an arbitrary system to divide the law into three categories; namely, moral, civil, and ceremonial. Moral laws dealt with timeless truths covering human ethical behavior; civil laws covered legal aspects like economics, property, and criminal justices; while ceremonial laws encompassed priestly activities, sacrifices, and festivals. According to this system, Christians only have to follow the moral laws and can ignore the rest. The biggest fault of this division of the law was that there was no hint of any such distinctions in the Old Testament. This is manmade and man's decision to chop up verses into categories. The distinctions themselves cause problems. For example, is the Sabbath moral or ceremonial? Since the Sabbath was part of the worship system it could be ceremonial but as it is part of the Ten Commandments, it could be moral as well. Furthermore, if it is moral and we are to follow it, then why aren't we as Christians following it?

We shake our heads in unbelief when the law commands the wife of one of two men fighting to have her hand cut off after she had grabbed her husband's adversary by his testicles. We see this in *Deuteronomy 25:11-12, When men strive together one with another, and the wife of the one draweth near for to deliver her husband out of the hand of him that smiteth him, and putteth forth her hand, and taketh him by the secrets: Then thou shalt cut off her hand, thine eye shall not pity her.*

Then we read in *Numbers 15:31-36, Because he hath despised the word of the Lord, and hath broken his commandment, that soul shall utterly be cut off; his iniquity shall be upon him. And while the children of Israel were in the wilderness, they found a man that gathered sticks upon the sabbath day. And they that found him gathering sticks brought him unto Moses and Aaron, and unto all the congregation. And they put him in ward, because it was not declared what should be done to him. And the Lord said unto Moses, The man shall be surely put to death: all the congregation shall stone him with stones without the camp. And all the congregation brought him without the camp, and stoned him with stones, and he died; as the Lord commanded Moses.* A man gathering sticks on the Sabbath, presumably for cooking, was taken outside the camp and stoned to death. If that is the punishment for not following the moral law, then we should all likewise be executed for not obeying the Sabbath. We should all be dead or at the very least, walk about with amputated limbs.

In *Leviticus 19:18-19,* we read about the moral law of loving our neighbor as ourselves. *Thou shalt not avenge, nor bear any grudge against the children of thy people, but thou shalt love thy neighbour as thyself: I am the Lord. Ye shall keep my statutes. Thou shalt not let thy cattle gender with a diverse kind: thou shalt not sow thy field with mingled seed: neither shall a garment mingled of linen and woollen come upon thee.* We want to follow this because Jesus mentioned it but this verse is immediately followed by the commandment that we must keep all of God's statutes, including the moral law of not letting bulls sire with cows of different breeds; not sowing two different seeds in the same field; and to not wear a garment that has a mixture of linen and wool. All of these involve the moral separation of something holy from another that is not. Yet none of us really follow these moral laws. Also, we do not realize who exactly are our 'neighbors'.

Precisely for that reason, all of us are guilty of breaking some or all of the law and deserve to die. Under the law, the entire world is guilty before God. By the law, none of us are justified or made righteous in the sight of God. Because by the law, we know that we have sinned and deserve to be punished. In *Romans 4:15,* we read, *Because the law worketh wrath: for where no law is, there is no transgression.* Sin became a transgression when the law was given. It was a standard to measure violations. If there were no law, we would still know that we have sinned but we would not be punished for it. Sin cannot be charged if there is no law to define it. In *Romans 5:13,* we read, *For until the law sin was in the world: but sin is not imputed when there is no law.* Sin cannot be imputed when there is no law. So, the tougher the law, the more aware we become of our sinful nature and the more punishment we deserve. *1 Corinthians 15:56* states that *The sting of death is sin; and the strength of sin is the law.* More law meant more knowledge of sin, which meant more guilt and punishment. The law punishes us for our sins but cannot remove the desire to sin from us. It simply condemns all of us.

When we come under the law or a mixture, we come under the curse of the law. We see this in *Nehemiah 10:29, They clave to their brethren, their nobles, and entered into a curse, and into an oath, to walk in God's law, which was given by Moses the servant of God, and to observe and do all the commandments of the Lord our Lord, and his judgments and his statutes.* And again in *Galatians 3:10-12, For as many as are of the works of the law are under the curse: for it is written, Cursed is every one that continueth not in all things which are written in the book of the law to do them. But that no man is justified by the law in the sight of God, it is evident: for, The just shall live by faith. And the law is not of faith: but, The man that doeth them shall live in them.*

The law demands continued and perfect obedience to the book of the law but does not teach or help us at all. For many of us, we do not even know what is written in the book of the law far less follow and do all that is written in it. In God's sight, none of us can become justified by the law. *Romans 3:19-20* states, *Now we know that what things soever the law saith, it saith to them who are under the law: that every mouth may be stopped, and all the world may become guilty before God. Therefore by the deeds of the law there shall no flesh be justified in his sight: for by the law is the knowledge of sin.*

Paul wrote insightfully about this curse of the law in *Romans 7:7-25, What shall we say then? Is the law sin? God forbid. Nay, I had not known sin, but by the law: for I had not known lust, except the law had said, Thou shalt not covet. But sin, taking occasion by the commandment, wrought in me all manner of concupiscence. For without the law sin was dead. For I was alive without the law once: but when the commandment came, sin revived, and I died. And the commandment, which was ordained to life, I found to be unto death. For sin, taking occasion by the commandment, deceived me, and by it slew me.*

Wherefore the law is holy, and the commandment holy, and just, and good. Was then that which is good made death unto me? God forbid. But sin, that it might appear sin, working death in me by that which is good; that sin by the commandment might become exceeding sinful. For we know that the law is spiritual: but I am carnal, sold under sin. For that which I do I allow not: for what I would, that do I not; but what I hate, that do I. If then I do that which I would not, I consent unto the law that it is good. Now then it is no more I that do it, but sin that dwelleth in me. For I know that in me (that is, in my flesh,) dwelleth no good thing: for to will is present with me; but how to perform that which is good I find not. For the good that I would I do not: but the evil which I would not, that I do. Now if I do that I would not, it is no more I that do it, but sin that dwelleth in me. I find then a law, that, when I would do good, evil is present with me. For I delight in the law of God after the inward man: But I see another law in my members, warring against the law of my mind, and bringing me into captivity to the law of sin which is in my members. O wretched man that I am! who shall deliver me from the body of this death? I thank God through Jesus Christ our Lord. So then with the mind I myself serve the law of God; but with the flesh the law of sin.

Without the law, sin was dead. With the law, sin revived and the war began. Paul stated unequivocally that the law was holy, just, and good. But the law was spiritual, while we are still living in the flesh and carnal in nature. Our spirit rejoices at the holy, just, and good law but our flesh cannot live by it. Our spirit wants to do what is holy but our flesh wants to sin. This resulting war between the spirit and the flesh is fought out in our mind. The end result is captivity to the law of sin. Sin wins every time where our flesh is concerned. We are just not strong enough to defeat sin with our carnal bodies. It is impossible. And sin brings death.

So what is the solution? Who shall deliver us from this death? Paul gave us the answer as well. **The law cannot give us life and has no power to make us holy. Only Jesus Christ our Lord can give us life and make us holy!** *Galatians 3:13* states that *Christ hath redeemed us from the curse of the law, being made a curse for us: for it is written, Cursed is every one that hangeth on a tree:* Christ has redeemed us from the curse of the law and the death that it brought. He took the curse upon Himself when He hung on the cross for us. What we could not do, He came to do.

The law continuously showed us where we erred but does not help us not to err. The law demanded holiness but only showed us our sinful nature. The law threatened us continuously but never once revealed love and understanding. The law exposes our sins but does not help us not to sin. By the works of the law, no flesh will be justified. It does not teach us anything. Living under the law, we have nothing to boast about. We read in *Romans 3:27-28, Where is boasting then? It is excluded. By what law? of works? Nay: but by the law of faith. Therefore we conclude that a man is justified by faith without the deeds of the law.*

But we can boast about our teacher, Jesus! Because of Him, the law decayed, waxed old, and was taken away. *Hebrews 8:12-13* states, *For I will be merciful to their unrighteousness, and their sins and their iniquities will I remember no more. In that he saith, A new covenant, he hath made the first old. Now that which decayeth and waxeth old is ready to vanish away.*

We read in *Galatians 2:16, 19, 21, Knowing that a man is not justified by the works of the law, but by the faith of Jesus Christ, even we have believed in Jesus Christ, that we might be justified by the faith of Christ, and not by the works of the law: for by the works of the law shall no flesh be justified. For I through the law am dead to the law, that I might live unto God. I do not frustrate the grace of God: for if righteousness come by the law, then Christ is dead in vain.* **We are justified because of our faith**

in Jesus. We are righteous because of Jesus. God did not get soft on sin for the punishment for sin fell on Jesus. Jesus is the Grace of God. We live because of Jesus. Because of Jesus, all our sins and iniquities are not only taken away but also remembered no more.

In *Matthew 11:28-30,* it says *Come unto me, all ye that labour and are heavy laden, and I will give you rest. Take my yoke upon you, and learn of me; for I am meek and lowly in heart: and ye shall find rest unto your souls. 30 For my yoke is easy, and my burden is light.* Because of Jesus, the heavy burden of the law of works and labor was lifted and we can now rest in Him.

Furthermore, in *Matthew 5:17-18,* we read, *Think not that I am come to destroy the law, or the prophets: I am not come to destroy, but to fulfil.* Jesus did not destroy the law but fulfilled it. The law was only for a period of time. Then it passed away. Because of Jesus the law died. *Romans 7:4-6* states, *Wherefore, my brethren, ye also are become dead to the law by the body of Christ; that ye should be married to another, even to him who is raised from the dead, that we should bring forth fruit unto God. For when we were in the flesh, the motions of sins, which were by the law, did work in our members to bring forth fruit unto death. But now we are delivered from the law, that being dead wherein we were held; that we should serve in newness of spirit, and not in the oldness of the letter.*

But *Romans 8:1-16* puts it best, *There is therefore now no condemnation to them which are in Christ Jesus, who walk not after the flesh, but after the Spirit. For the law of the Spirit of life in Christ Jesus hath made me free from the law of sin and death. For what the law could not do, in that it was weak through the flesh, God sending his own Son in the likeness of sinful flesh, and for sin, condemned sin in the flesh: That the righteousness of the law might be fulfilled in us, who walk not after the flesh, but after the Spirit. For they that are after the flesh do mind the things of the flesh; but they that are after the Spirit the things of the Spirit. For to be carnally minded is death; but to be spiritually minded is life and peace. Because the carnal mind is enmity against God: for it is not subject to the law of God, neither indeed can be. So then they that are in the flesh cannot please God. But ye are not in the flesh, but in the Spirit, if so be that the Spirit of God dwell in you. Now if any man have not the Spirit of Christ, he is none of his. And if Christ be in you, the body is dead because of sin; but the Spirit is life because of righteousness. But if the Spirit of him that raised up Jesus from the dead dwell in you, he that raised up Christ from the dead shall also quicken your mortal bodies by his Spirit that dwelleth in you. Therefore, brethren, we are debtors, not to the flesh, to live after the flesh. For if ye live after the flesh, ye shall die: but if ye through the Spirit do mortify the deeds of the body, ye shall live.*

For as many as are led by the Spirit of God, they are the sons of God. For ye have not received the spirit of bondage again to fear; but ye have received the Spirit of adoption, whereby we cry, Abba, Father. The Spirit itself beareth witness with our spirit, that we are the children of God:

Because of Jesus, we are no longer condemned. Because of Jesus, our spirit now lives eternally and cannot sin and does not want to sin. Because of Jesus, our spirit now becomes greater than our flesh. **The sin that our flesh could not fight against was condemned by Jesus who was made in the likeness of sinful flesh. The spirit of bondage was broken and we are freed. We are made new in our spirit. The battle that we could not win was won by Jesus.** The battle in our mind ceases as the war is won. *Romans 6:14* states that *For sin shall not have dominion over you: for ye are not under the law, but under grace.* Sin has no dominion over us as we are now under Grace! It is simply not in our nature to sin anymore. We no longer walk after the flesh but after the Spirit.

All of us who have faith in Jesus received the Spirit of adoption and God became our Father, Abba. Because of Jesus, we become the children of God. Not only did God become our Father but his name is Father! *John 12:28* states, *Father, glorify thy name. Then came there a voice from heaven, saying, I have both glorified it, and will glorify it again.* Our God's name is Father. My father's name is Father. **Your father's name is Father**. It is a glorious name indeed.

❧ 11 ❧

JESUS AND POMEGRANATES

Someone once stated that the pomegranate represented the law, as there were 613 seeds in a pomegranate corresponding to the 613 commandments of the Torah. Therefore, when Adam and Eve bit into the forbidden fruit in the Garden of Eden, they must have bitten into a pomegranate for they ate of the law and sin was revealed. A quick check of the number of seeds in a pomegranate shows that pomegranates do not have 613 seeds. Also, it is possible to sin without the law. With the law, sin could be imputed and punishment meted out. As Adam and Eve were not punished, they could not have eaten the 'law' or pomegranate.

Pomegranates feature prominently throughout the Old Testament. When the spies went into the Promised Land, which was flowing with milk and honey, they did not come out with any milk or honey. In *Numbers 13:23-27, And they came unto the brook of Eshcol, and cut down from thence a branch with one cluster of grapes, and they bare it between two upon a staff; and they brought of the pomegranates, and of the figs. The place was called the brook Eshcol, because of the cluster of grapes which the children of Israel cut down from thence. And they returned from searching of the land after forty days. And they went and came to Moses, and to Aaron, and to all the congregation of the children of Israel, unto the wilderness of Paran, to Kadesh; and brought back word unto them, and unto all the congregation, and shewed them the fruit of the land. And they told him, and said, We came unto the land whither thou sentest us, and surely it floweth with milk and honey; and this is the fruit of it.* Instead, they carried between two of them a cluster of grapes hung on a staff. Beside the grapes on the vine hanging on a stick, they carried out with them pomegranates and figs. The fruit of the new land was then shown to all the Israelites.

The Israelites failed to see that the fruit of their new life would be Jesus, as represented by the vine and grapes hanging on a piece of wood between two men. They were symbolically carrying Jesus to the entire world. Not only for the Jews, as represented by the figs, but to the gentiles as well. The other fruit that they carried out were the pomegranates, representing the blood of Christ and His righteousness. There are twelve sections in a pomegranate, representing the twelve tribes of Israel. In addition, the many seeds in a pomegranate may depict the many believers caught up by faith in Jesus. Opening up a pomegranate may splatter one with red juice signifying the blood of Jesus poured out for us. The pomegranate reminds us that we can only be righteous through the blood sacrifice of Jesus.

Pomegranates are also featured on the hem of the high priest garment. We see in *Exodus 28:33-35, And beneath upon the hem of it thou shalt make pomegranates of blue, and of purple, and of scarlet, round about the hem thereof; and bells of gold between them round about: A golden bell and a pomegranate, a golden bell and a pomegranate, upon the hem of the robe round about. And it shall be upon Aaron to minister: and his sound shall be heard when he goeth in unto the holy place before the Lord, and when he cometh out, that he die not.* Stitched into the hem would be a golden bell and then a pomegranate, another bell followed by another pomegranate, all around the garment. Bells are to be heard although they could be harsh, loud, and strident. Golden bells, however, make soft and gentle sounds as if to make a kingly announcement. Paired up together, the tongues of the bells announce Jesus over and over again. Round and round they would pronounce the name of Jesus. If the bells were to stop, we would die just like Aaron would die when he ministered in the Holy

Place. Without Jesus, there would be no life. With Jesus, there would be new life.

Note that the oral tradition of a rope tied around Aaron's ankle to pull out his dead body from the Holy of Holies is not found in the bible. In *Leviticus 16:23, And Aaron shall come into the tabernacle of the congregation, and shall put off the linen garments, which he put on when he went into the holy place, and shall leave them there.* Aaron put on the garment when he ministered in the Holy Place, not the Holiest Place, and he took off the garment when he had finished ministering. Even if the tradition of the rope were true, Aaron would still be anchored to the people and in their ability to pull him out or their ability to keep the law. However, under the new covenant, our anchor is to Jesus not people. *Hebrews 6:19-20* states that *Which hope we have as an anchor of the soul, both sure and stedfast, and which entereth into that within the veil; Whither the forerunner is for us entered, even Jesus, made an high priest for ever after the order of Melchisedec.* Our High Priest, Jesus Christ, takes us into the throne room of God and makes us sit with Him on the throne. Unlike Aaron, none of us who knows Christ need fear death, as He is our righteousness.

Pomegranates are also prominently displayed on the top of the two brass pillars that guarded the entrance to Solomon's temple. We read in *1 Kings 7:13-22, And king Solomon sent and fetched Hiram out of Tyre. He was a widow's son of the tribe of Naphtali, and his father was a man of Tyre, a worker in brass: and he was filled with wisdom, and understanding, and cunning to work all works in brass. And he came to king Solomon, and wrought all his work. For he cast two pillars of brass, of eighteen cubits high apiece: and a line of twelve cubits did compass either of them about.*

And he made two chapiters of molten brass, to set upon the tops of the pillars: the height of the one chapiter was five cubits, and the height of the other chapiter was five cubits: And nets of checker work, and wreaths of chain work, for the chapiters which were upon the top of the pillars; seven for the one chapiter, and seven for the other chapiter. And he made the pillars, and two rows round about upon the one network, to cover the chapiters that were upon the top, with pomegranates: and so did he for the other chapter. And the chapiters that were upon the top of the pillars were of lily work in the porch, four cubits. And the chapiters upon the two pillars had pomegranates also above, over against the belly which was by the network: and the pomegranates were two hundred in rows round about upon the other chapiter.

And he set up the pillars in the porch of the temple: and he set up the right pillar, and called the name thereof Jachin: and he set up the left pillar, and he called the name thereof Boaz. And upon the top of the pillars was lily work: so was the work of the pillars finished.

Seen from a distance, the chapiters covered with small pomegranates; the nets of checker work; the wreaths of chain work; and the lily or lotus work resemble a giant pomegranate sitting atop each pillar. The pillars do not support any load but stand by themselves at the only entrance door to the temple.

The door of the temple faces east. Looking out from the temple, the right pillar stands south while the left pillar stands north. The right pillar known as Jachin, means 'He will establish'. The left pillar known as Boaz means 'In Him is strength'. The two pillars together show that God will establish a Coming King whose strength will be in God! Only through this King can one enter the temple to the Holy of Holies.

The first or right pillar 'establishes' Solomon as the legal or royal right to the Coming King. However, one of Solomon's descendants, Jehoiachin also known as Coniah, became cursed to never have his descendants to become king ever again. We see this in *2 Samuel 7:12-17, And when thy days be fulfilled, and thou shalt sleep with thy fathers, I will set up thy seed after thee, which shall proceed out of thy bowels, and I will establish his kingdom. He shall build an house for my name, and I will stablish the throne of his kingdom for ever. I will be his father, and he shall be my son. If he commit iniquity, I will chasten him with the rod of men, and with the stripes of the children of men: But my mercy shall not depart away from him, as I took it from Saul, whom I put away before thee. And thine house and thy kingdom shall be established for ever before thee: thy throne shall be established for ever.*

According to all these words, and according to all this vision, so did Nathan speak unto David. And again in *2 Kings 24:8-15, Jehoiachin was eighteen years old when he began to reign, and he reigned in Jerusalem three months. And his mother's name was Nehushta, the daughter of Elnathan of Jerusalem. And he did that which was evil in the sight of the Lord, according to all that his father had done. At that time the servants of Nebuchadnezzar king of Babylon came up against Jerusalem, and the city was besieged. And Nebuchadnezzar king of Babylon came against the city, and his servants did besiege it.*

And Jehoiachin the king of Judah went out to the king of Babylon, he, and his mother, and his servants, and his princes, and his officers: and the king of Babylon took him in the eighth year of his reign. And he carried out thence all the treasures of the house of the Lord, and the treasures of the king's house, and cut in pieces all the vessels of gold which Solomon king of Israel had made in the temple of the Lord, as the Lord had said. And he carried away all Jerusalem, and all the princes, and all the mighty men of valour, even ten thousand captives, and all the craftsmen and smiths: none remained, save the poorest sort of the people of the land. And he carried away Jehoiachin to Babylon, and the king's mother, and the king's wives, and his officers, and the mighty of the land, those carried he into captivity from Jerusalem to Babylon. Also, in *Jeremiah 22:28, Is this man Coniah a despised broken idol? is he a vessel wherein is no pleasure? wherefore are they cast out, he and his seed, and are cast into a land which they know not?*

Jehoiachin and his descendants lost the biological right to father a king. Therefore, Solomon had the legal or royal right, but due to Jehoiachin, not the biological right to the Coming King. From Jehoiachin came Joseph, husband of Mary. Jesus could never be king if He was only from the loins of Joseph. Joseph had the legal right but not the biological right to Jesus.

The second or left pillar shows that David, who trusted in God's 'strength' to defeat his enemies, would have the biological right to the Coming King. *Jeremiah 23:5-6* states, *Behold, the days come, saith the Lord, that I will raise unto David a righteous*

Branch, and a King shall reign and prosper, and shall execute
judgment and justice in the earth. In his days Judah shall be
saved, and Israel shall dwell safely: and this is his name whereby
he shall be called, THE Lord OUR RIGHTEOUSNESS.

David had lost the legal right due to his many sins.
However, David had many sons besides Solomon. One of his many
sons was Nathan. Nathan's descendants ended with Heli who had
daughters, one of whom was Mary. We read this in *Luke 3:23, 31,*
And Jesus himself began to be about thirty years of age, being (as
was supposed) the son of Joseph, which was the son of Heli, ...
which was the son of Nathan, which was the son of David. Mary
had the biological right but not the legal right to Jesus.

Then in *Matthew 1:18,* we see *Now the birth of Jesus*
Christ was on this wise: When as his mother Mary was espoused to
Joseph, before they came together, she was found with child of the
Holy Ghost. It was only when Joseph and Mary were considered
legally married that Jesus was born of the virgin, Mary. **Jesus was**
the Coming King, having both the biological right and the legal
right to become the King. He was the Coming King as described
by the two pillars of pomegranates. He is the only entranceway to
the Father. It is by Him and though Him that we have access to the
most Holy Place. His name is Jesus and He would save His people
from their sins.

๛ 12 ๛

JESUS AND THE TOWER OF THEBEZ

In *Joshua 24:3-13*, God once again showed the Israelites that all the blessings that they enjoyed were because of His goodness alone. We read, *And I took your father Abraham from the other side of the flood, and led him throughout all the land of Canaan, and multiplied his seed, and gave him Isaac. And I gave unto Isaac Jacob and Esau: and I gave unto Esau mount Seir, to possess it; but Jacob and his children went down into Egypt. I sent Moses also and Aaron, and I plagued Egypt, according to that which I did among them: and afterward I brought you out. And I brought your fathers out of Egypt: and ye came unto the sea; and the Egyptians pursued after your fathers with chariots and horsemen unto the Red sea. And when they cried unto the Lord, he put darkness between you and the Egyptians, and brought the sea upon them, and covered them; and your eyes have seen what I have done in Egypt: and ye dwelt in the wilderness a long season.*

And I brought you into the land of the Amorites, which dwelt on the other side Jordan; and they fought with you: and I gave them into your hand, that ye might possess their land; and I destroyed them from before you. Then Balak the son of Zippor, king of Moab, arose and warred against Israel, and sent and called Balaam the son of Beor to curse you: But I would not hearken unto Balaam; therefore he blessed you still: so I delivered you out of his hand. And ye went over Jordan, and came unto

Jericho: and the men of Jericho fought against you, the Amorites, and the Perizzites, and the Canaanites, and the Hittites, and the Girgashites, the Hivites, and the Jebusites; and I delivered them into your hand. And I sent the hornet before you, which drave them out from before you, even the two kings of the Amorites; but not with thy sword, nor with thy bow. And I have given you a land for which ye did not labour, and cities which ye built not, and ye dwell in them; of the vineyards and oliveyards which ye planted not do ye eat.

In each case, God Himself did it all for us. He led, He multiplied, He gave, He brought, He covered, He protected, He delivered and He destroyed our enemies. God reiterated that He gave us the land that we did not work for, He gave us cities to stay in that we did not built, and He gave us fruits to enjoy that we did not plant.

Then Joshua in verses 14-15, like us, with a thankful heart, acknowledged the goodness of God and responded, *Now therefore fear the Lord, and serve him in sincerity and in truth: and put away the gods which your fathers served on the other side of the flood, and in Egypt; and serve ye the Lord. And if it seem evil unto you to serve the Lord, choose you this day whom ye will serve; whether the gods which your fathers served that were on the other side of the flood, or the gods of the Amorites, in whose land ye dwell: but as for me and my house, we will serve the Lord.*

This desire to serve on Joshua's part came as a response to God's great love towards him and his household first. He listed all of God's goodness towards him first, before committing his whole household to serve the Lord. It is a delight to serve God when we know that we are His delight first. But the rest of the people reversed this order yet again. They listed their strength, not to forsake God, first. We see this in *Joshua 24:16-18, 21, 24, And the people answered and said, God forbid that we should forsake the Lord, to serve other gods; For the Lord our God, he it is that brought us up and our fathers out of the land of Egypt, from the house of bondage, and which did those great signs in our sight, and preserved us in all the way wherein we went, and among all the people through whom we passed: And the Lord drave out from*

before us all the people, even the Amorites which dwelt in the land:
therefore will we also serve the Lord; for he is our God. And the
people said unto Joshua, Nay; but we will serve the Lord. And the
people said unto Joshua, The Lord our God will we serve, and his
voice will we obey.

The people answered haughtily in their own strength -
"Who do you think we are? We can do it. We will serve the Lord
and we will obey His voice. As if we would forsake God and serve
other gods! We are better than that! How can you even think that
we will not be able to do this simple thing? Of course we will
always serve our God. After all, how can we forget God who has
done great wonders for us?" However, Joshua saw their self-
serving pride immediately and made a curious statement. In *Joshua
24:19-20,* we read, *And Joshua said unto the people, Ye cannot
serve the Lord: for he is an holy God; he is a jealous God; he will
not forgive your transgressions nor your sins. If ye forsake the
Lord, and serve strange gods, then he will turn and do you hurt,
and consume you, after that he hath done you good.*

It was curious because only five verses earlier Joshua was
exhorting the people to serve the Lord. Now he is saying that the
people cannot serve the Lord! The explanation is simple. **We
cannot serve God from our own strength. Sooner or later, our
own strength will fail. We can only serve God from His
strength.** However, the people were adamant that they could do in
their own strength whatever God called them to do. In *Joshua
24:22-27,* we read, *And Joshua said unto the people, Ye are
witnesses against yourselves that ye have chosen you the Lord, to
serve him. And they said, We are witnesses. Now therefore put
away, said he, the strange gods which are among you, and incline
your heart unto the Lord God of Israel. So Joshua made a
covenant with the people that day, and set them a statute and an
ordinance in Shechem. And Joshua wrote these words in the book
of the law of God, and took a great stone, and set it up there under
an oak, that was by the sanctuary of the Lord. And Joshua said
unto all the people, Behold, this stone shall be a witness unto us;
for it hath heard all the words of the Lord which he spake unto us:
it shall be therefore a witness unto you, lest ye deny your God.*

Their words were duly recorded in the book of the law. A monument, in the form of a great stone, marked their intentions. This stone, which recorded the will of the people, was then either buried or set up as an altar under an oak tree in Shechem. This oak tree seemed to be the same oak tree mentioned in Genesis 12:6 where God first gave His unconditional promise to Abraham after he left his homeland. Then, it was the will of God. Now, it was the will of the people.

About 250 years later, in Judges Chapter 8:30-31, we find Gideon at the end of his life. Gideon (aka Jerubbaal meaning 'one who has cast down the altar of Baal') had many wives and possibly, many concubines. One of his concubines was from Schechem who had a son called Abimelech. Abimelech was one of the seventy sons of Gideon and he wanted to be king over all Israel. After Gideon passed away, the children of Israel started serving another god by the name of Baal-berith. We take up the story in *Judges 9:1-5, And Abimelech the son of Jerubbaal went to Shechem unto his mother's brethren, and communed with them, and with all the family of the house of his mother's father, saying, Speak, I pray you, in the ears of all the men of Shechem, Whether is better for you, either that all the sons of Jerubbaal, which are threescore and ten persons, reign over you, or that one reign over you? remember also that I am your bone and your flesh. And his mother's brethren spake of him in the ears of all the men of Shechem all these words: and their hearts inclined to follow Abimelech; for they said, He is our brother. And they gave him threescore and ten pieces of silver out of the house of Baal-berith, wherewith Abimelech hired vain and light persons, which followed him. And he went unto his father's house at Ophrah, and slew his brethren the sons of Jerubbaal, being threescore and ten persons, upon one stone: notwithstanding yet Jotham the youngest son of Jerubbaal was left; for he hid himself.*

Abimelech wanted to be king. He went to Shechem and convinced his relatives on his mother's side to pay for his murderous scheme to kill all his brothers. The money came from the temple of Baal-berith. With this money, he hired men and succeeded in killing all of his brothers (except one). He would become the first king in the Promised Land. In *Judges 9:6, And all the men of Shechem gathered together, and all the house of Millo, and went, and made Abimelech king, by the plain of the pillar that was in Shechem.*

This coronation ceremony would have had little significance but that it was held by the very tree that Joshua recorded the vows of the people, in stone, to never forsake the Lord. The stone would now bear witness to their intentions. As the people now worshipped Baal-berith, they suffered the curse of breaking the law.

In *Judges 9:45-49*, we read, *And Abimelech fought against the city all that day; and he took the city, and slew the people that was therein, and beat down the city, and sowed it with salt. And when all the men of the tower of Shechem heard that, they entered into an hold of the house of the god Berith. And it was told Abimelech, that all the men of the tower of Shechem were gathered together. And Abimelech gat him up to mount Zalmon, he and all the people that were with him; and Abimelech took an axe in his hand, and cut down a bough from the trees, and took it, and laid it on his shoulder, and said unto the people that were with him, What ye have seen me do, make haste, and do as I have done. And all the people likewise cut down every man his bough, and followed Abimelech, and put them to the hold, and set the hold on fire upon them; so that all the men of the tower of Shechem died also, about a thousand men and women.*

During Abimelech's reign, he was betrayed, the people who betrayed him were slaughtered, and Shechem was ultimately demolished and sowed with salt to prevent future growth. The last stand in the strong tower of Shechem was futile as it was burnt to the ground and another thousand people perished.

The curse of breaking the law spread, finally reaching the city of Thebez. Death was all around as the surviving people rushed into the strong tower of Thebez. We see in *Judges 9:50-52, Then went Abimelech to Thebez, and encamped against Thebez, and took it. But there was a strong tower within the city, and thither fled all the men and women, and all they of the city, and shut it to them, and gat them up to the top of the tower. And*

Abimelech came unto the tower, and fought against it, and went hard unto the door of the tower to burn it with fire.

The account would have ended no different from the one in Shechem except that this was a very different tower. Thebez in Hebrew means 'brightness' or 'whiteness of white linen'. We know Jesus dressed in white linen. And in *Proverbs 18:10,* we know that *The name of the Lord is a strong tower: the righteous runneth into it, and is safe.* Who is the name of the Lord? None other than Jesus Christ Himself who is the strong tower that the inhabitants of Thebez ran into. They were shut in as Noah and his family was shut in the ark. The people did not even try to defend the door but instead went straight to the top of the tower.

In the tabernacle, there were three partitions. The first was the Outer Court, then the Inner Court, and the last part was the Holy of Holies where the Ark of the Covenant was. We know that the Ark stands as a symbol of Jesus. Hence, the people of Thebez went into Jesus Christ and rested in His presence at the top of the tower. There was no need to do anything as Jesus covered them in His grace. Notice that Abimelech fought against the tower, not the people, but to no avail. **The consuming fire of breaking the law stopped when the people trusted fully in Jesus Christ and not in their own strength to fight against the enemy.**

The devil is still outside today threatening to burn us alive and urging us to fight back with all our might. The moment we trust in our own strength, the devil will penetrate our defenses and kill us. **But no devil, no demon, and certainly no person can ever separate us from the protective love of God when we rest in Jesus.**

The story ended when an ordinary woman, not a warrior, dropped a stone over the top of the tower that crushed Abimelech's skull. In *Judges 9:53-54, And a certain woman cast a piece of a millstone upon Abimelech's head, and all to brake his skull. Then he called hastily unto the young man his armourbearer, and said unto him, Draw thy sword, and slay me, that men say not of me, A woman slew him. And his young man thrust him through, and he died.* To cover his shame, Abimelech asked his aide to kill him. Nobody remembered the aide. However, the ordinary woman was remembered forever as recorded in *2 Samuel 11:21, Who smote Abimelech the son of Jerubbesheth? did not a woman cast a piece of a millstone upon him from the wall, that he died in Thebez?* An ordinary woman resting in the power of Jesus can crush an enemy king's head!

In *Genesis 3:15,* it says *And I will put enmity between thee and the woman, and between thy seed and her seed; it shall bruise thy head, and thou shalt bruise his heel.* The seed of the woman, Jesus Christ, the corner stone, has crushed the devil's head. The devil was put under Jesus' heel at the cross. **Because of Jesus completed work on the cross, the devil is completely bruised, crushed, squashed, mashed and vanquished forever. He has absolutely no power over us.**

❧ 13 ❧

JESUS AND THE CENSUS

In the Abrahamic Covenant, God promised to innumerably multiply Abraham's descendants. We read in *Hebrews 11:11-12, Through faith also Sara herself received strength to conceive seed, and was delivered of a child when she was past age, because she judged him faithful who had promised. Therefore sprang there even of one, and him as good as dead, so many as the stars of the sky in multitude, and as the sand which is by the sea shore innumerable.* It was to be an effortless process. The blessings would be so great that it would be uncountable. Abraham would be the genetic father of all the Jews that would be as countless as the sand upon the seashore. He was also to be the spiritual father to all the gentiles grafted in by Jesus. This would be a far greater number than the Jews. These gentiles would be like the stars in the sky in multitude. Whatever God has promised, it would keep on growing and multiplying.

After the law was given, the Abrahamic Covenant was set aside, now superseded by the Mosaic Covenant. Note that the Abrahamic Covenant has not been replaced or abolished but still exists to this day. The Mosaic Covenant was based on men's efforts and works. Every action taken by men, contrary to the law, now resulted in a subtraction. The effortless growth ceased; to be replaced by attenuation and detraction. Everything became a struggle and everything had a price attached to it. The innumerable now became 'numerable'.

We have the first census commanded right after the instruction on how to build the altar of burnt offering. We read in *Exodus 30:11-16, And the Lord spake unto Moses, saying, When thou takest the sum of the children of Israel after their number, then shall they give every man a ransom for his soul unto the Lord, when thou numberest them; that there be no plague among them, when thou numberest them. This they shall give, every one that passeth among them that are numbered, half a shekel after the shekel of the sanctuary: (a shekel is twenty gerahs:) an half shekel shall be the offering of the Lord. Every one that passeth among them that are numbered, from twenty years old and above, shall give an offering unto the Lord. The rich shall not give more, and the poor shall not give less than half a shekel, when they give an offering unto the Lord, to make an atonement for your souls. And thou shalt take the atonement money of the children of Israel, and shalt appoint it for the service of the tabernacle of the congregation; that it may be a memorial unto the children of Israel before the Lord, to make an atonement for your souls.* Because of the law, sin was now imputed upon the people. Every man was to give a ransom of half a shekel for his sin. The law demanded that the people pay the price. It was an atonement for their souls. When they paid the ransom, God would spare them from the plague attached to taking a census.

In the book of Numbers, the Israelites were numbered again twice. This time it was for military service. In *Numbers 1:2-3, Take ye the sum of all the congregation of the children of Israel, after their families, by the house of their fathers, with the number of their names, every male by their polls; From twenty years old and upward, all that are able to go forth to war in Israel: thou and Aaron shall number them by their armies.* And again in *Numbers 26:1-4, And it came to pass after the plague, that the Lord spake unto Moses and unto Eleazar the son of Aaron the priest, saying, Take the sum of all the congregation of the children of Israel, from twenty years old and upward, throughout their father's house, all that are able to go to war in Israel. And Moses and Eleazar the priest spake with them in the plains of Moab by Jordan near Jericho, saying,   Take the sum of the people, from twenty years old and upward; as the Lord commanded Moses and the children of Israel, which went forth out of the land of Egypt.* In war, they would die and their numbers attenuated. There would be attrition and a diminution of the Jews due to the law.

There was also a numbering from the tribe of Levites for service in the tabernacle. We read in *Numbers 3:14-16, And the Lord spake unto Moses in the wilderness of Sinai, saying, Number the children of Levi after the house of their fathers, by their families: every male from a month old and upward shalt thou number them. And Moses numbered them according to the word of the Lord, as he was commanded.* They were servants just like Moses and they had to do all the works related to the tabernacle. It was a service and a burden they had to carry to obey the law. Solomon later also took a census to assign laborers and workers. We see this in *Numbers 4:49, According to the commandment of the Lord they were numbered by the hand of Moses, every one according to his service, and according to his burden: thus were they numbered of him, as the Lord commanded Moses.*

However, the mother of all censuses was taken by David when provoked by the devil. In his whole life, David was cognizant of God's grace and goodness. Although he lived before the cross, he was given new covenant glimpses of Jesus and His finished work. In *1 Samuel 17:33-40,* we read, *And Saul said to David, Thou art not able to go against this Philistine to fight with him: for thou art but a youth, and he a man of war from his youth. And David said unto Saul, Thy servant kept his father's sheep, and there came a lion, and a bear, and took a lamb out of the flock: And I went out after him, and smote him, and delivered it out of his mouth: and when he arose against me, I caught him by his beard, and smote him, and slew him. Thy servant slew both the lion and the bear: and this uncircumcised Philistine shall be as one of them, seeing he hath defied the armies of the living God. David said moreover, The Lord that delivered me out of the paw of the lion, and out of the paw of the bear, he will deliver me out of the hand of this Philistine. And Saul said unto David, Go, and the Lord be with thee.*

And Saul armed David with his armour, and he put an helmet of brass upon his head; also he armed him with a coat of mail. And David girded his sword upon his armour, and he assayed to go; for he had not proved it. And David said unto Saul, I cannot go with these; for I have not proved them. And David put them off him. And he took his staff in his hand, and chose him five smooth stones out of the brook, and put them in a shepherd's bag which he had, even in a scrip; and his sling was in his hand: and he drew near to the Philistine.

When he was but a youth, God delivered up the lion and the bear into his hands. Then God toppled Goliath with one smooth stone. Five stands for grace in the bible. One stone was needed for Goliath while the other four stones were for his four remaining brothers. By Grace, Goliath and his brothers were defeated by David. David needed no armor of self-works when he faced the giant, as Goliath was a defeated foe. David knew he was from Abraham's seed and he was heir to all of the promises, albeit superseded by the law. When he ate the showbread from the temple, he fed on 'Jesus'. We read this in *Matthew 12:3-4, But he said unto them, Have ye not read what David did, when he was an hungred, and they that were with him; How he entered into the house of God, and did eat the shewbread, which was not lawful for him to eat, neither for them which were with him, but only for the priests?* Also, Jesus was often called the Son of David, as David had the genetic right to bear The King who would live forever.

We read of this census in *1 Chronicles 21:1-7, And Satan stood up against Israel, and provoked David to number Israel. And David said to Joab and to the rulers of the people, Go, number Israel from Beer-sheba even to Dan; and bring the number of them to me, that I may know it. And Joab answered, The Lord make his people an hundred times so many more as they be: but, my lord the king, are they not all my lord's servants? why then doth my lord require this thing? why will he be a cause of trespass to Israel? Nevertheless the king's word prevailed against Joab. Wherefore Joab departed, and went throughout all Israel, and came to*

*Jerusalem. And Joab gave the sum of the number of the people
unto David. And all they of Israel were a thousand thousand and
an hundred thousand men that drew sword: and Judah was four
hundred threescore and ten thousand men that drew sword. But
Levi and Benjamin counted he not among them: for the king's word
was abominable to Joab. And God was displeased with this thing;
therefore he smote Israel.*

David, after relying solely on God and feeding on Jesus,
was provoked by Satan to look at his own strength by taking a
census of the might of his army. Joab, David's general, was
displeased with the task of taking the census. It was so unpleasant
to him that he did not even finish the counting process for he left
out the tribes of Levi and Benjamin in the process. However, the
census displeased God even more and He punished Israel for it.
**God's armies would always be innumerable and not to be
counted. For the size of God's army is always adequate and
sufficient in Jesus. The army is always enough as Jesus is
always enough. Christ is always more than sufficient for
anything.**

This account is repeated in 2 Samuel chapter 24. All
discrepancies in the numbers relate to whether the men were
experienced men of war or just men of war. In addition, some men
were serving in frontier lines and were not counted.

The punishment for what David had done in trusting in the
might of his army, instead of God, can be read in *1 Chronicles
21:8-18, And David said unto God, I have sinned greatly, because
I have done this thing: but now, I beseech thee, do away the
iniquity of thy servant; for I have done very foolishly. And the Lord
spake unto Gad, David's seer, saying, Go and tell David, saying,
Thus saith the Lord, I offer thee three things: choose thee one of
them, that I may do it unto thee. So Gad came to David, and said
unto him, Thus saith the Lord, Choose thee, Either three years'
famine; or three months to be destroyed before thy foes, while that
the sword of thine enemies overtaketh thee; or else three days the
sword of the Lord, even the pestilence, in the land, and the angel of
the Lord destroying throughout all the coasts of Israel. Now
therefore advise thyself what word I shall bring again to him that*

*sent me. And David said unto Gad, I am in a great strait: let me
fall now into the hand of the Lord; for very great are his mercies:
but let me not fall into the hand of man. So the Lord sent pestilence
upon Israel: and there fell of Israel seventy thousand men.*

*And God sent an angel unto Jerusalem to destroy it: and as
he was destroying, the Lord beheld, and he repented him of the
evil, and said to the angel that destroyed, It is enough, stay now
thine hand. And the angel of the Lord stood by the threshingfloor
of Ornan the Jebusite. And David lifted up his eyes, and saw the
angel of the Lord stand between the earth and the heaven, having a
drawn sword in his hand stretched out over Jerusalem. Then David
and the elders of Israel, who were clothed in sackcloth, fell upon
their faces. And David said unto God, Is it not I that commanded
the people to be numbered? even I it is that have sinned and done
evil indeed; but as for these sheep, what have they done? let thine
hand, I pray thee, O Lord my God, be on me, and on my father's
house; but not on thy people, that they should be plagued. Then the
angel of the Lord commanded Gad to say to David, that David
should go up, and set up an altar unto the Lord in the
threshingfloor of Ornan the Jebusite.*

When David realized that he was trusting in his own works
and had sinned, he chose the punishment that God had for him.
The three choices were all punishments for sin but only one was
from God. The three years famine was a punishment for man's
works by man's hand; the three months annihilation by his enemies
and the destroyer was a chastisement by the devil; and the three
days pestilence was a correction by God for sin. David chose the
pestilence resulting in the death of seventy thousand men. The
purpose of the census was to show David how much he had but the
end result of his work was that the census showed how much less
he had. The angel of death that bought about this pestilence, not
unlike the angel of death in Exodus, stopped when David built an
altar and offered burnt offerings on it. In Exodus, the angel of
death passed over all the houses with blood on its lentils and side
posts. The blood of The Lamb, in the shape of the cross, always
saves. Here the angel of death sheathed his sword when, once
again, the blood of The Lamb was sacrificed. All punishments that

we deserved came to an end with Jesus. He became The Ransom for the census.

We do not have to suffer the penalty of sin because He took upon Himself all the punishments and castigations that we deserved. In *Isaiah 53:4-5, Surely he hath borne our griefs, and carried our sorrows: yet we did esteem him stricken, smitten of God, and afflicted. But he was wounded for our transgressions, he was bruised for our iniquities: the chastisement of our peace was upon him; and with his stripes we are healed.* Again in *1 Peter 2:24, Who his own self bare our sins in his own body on the tree, that we, being dead to sins, should live unto righteousness: by whose stripes ye were healed.* And in *Matthew 20:28, Even as the Son of man came not to be ministered unto, but to minister, and to give his life a ransom for many.* Grief, sorrow, and sin that were ours to bear were borne by Jesus in our stead. He bore the load that we could not carry. We deserved the striking, the smiting, the afflicting but we obtained an undeserved pardon instead. Our due reward for sin was to be pierced for our transgressions and to be bruised for our iniquities but He made us worthy to receive healing instead. **We merited death but we got unmerited life.**

❧ 14 ❧

JESUS AND THE SPOTTED, SPECKLED AND RINGSTRAKED

Some of the writings in the bible are so strange that if we do not read them properly they border on superstition to downright paganism. We may even consider them fables and fairy tales until the Holy Spirit reveals to us their true meanings. As the Holy Spirit always point to Jesus, we can only comprehend scripture if Jesus is in it.

One of these writings tells of Jacob and of his father-in-law, Laban. We read of this account in *Genesis 30:25-43, And it came to pass, when Rachel had born Joseph, that Jacob said unto Laban, Send me away, that I may go unto mine own place, and to my country. Give me my wives and my children, for whom I have served thee, and let me go: for thou knowest my service which I have done thee. And Laban said unto him, I pray thee, if I have found favour in thine eyes, tarry: for I have learned by experience that the Lord hath blessed me for thy sake. And he said, Appoint me thy wages, and I will give it. And he said unto him, Thou knowest how I have served thee, and how thy cattle was with me. For it was little which thou hadst before I came, and it is now increased unto a multitude; and the Lord hath blessed thee since my coming: and now when shall I provide for mine own house also? And he said, What shall I give thee? And Jacob said, Thou*

*shalt not give me any thing: if thou wilt do this thing for me, I will
again feed and keep thy flock: I will pass through all thy flock to
day, removing from thence all the speckled and spotted cattle, and
all the brown cattle among the sheep, and the spotted and speckled
among the goats: and of such shall be my hire. So shall my
righteousness answer for me in time to come, when it shall come
for my hire before thy face: every one that is not speckled and
spotted among the goats, and brown among the sheep, that shall be
counted stolen with me. And Laban said, Behold, I would it might
be according to thy word. And he removed that day the he goats
that were ringstraked and spotted, and all the she goats that were
speckled and spotted, and every one that had some white in it, and
all the brown among the sheep, and gave them into the hand of his
sons. And he set three days' journey betwixt himself and Jacob:
and Jacob fed the rest of Laban's flocks.*

*And Jacob took him rods of green poplar, and of the hazel
and chesnut tree; and pilled white strakes in them, and made the
white appear which was in the rods. And he set the rods which he
had pilled before the flocks in the gutters in the watering troughs
when the flocks came to drink, that they should conceive when they
came to drink. And the flocks conceived before the rods, and
brought forth cattle ringstraked, speckled, and spotted.*

*And Jacob did separate the lambs, and set the faces of the
flocks toward the ringstraked, and all the brown in the flock of
Laban; and he put his own flocks by themselves, and put them not
unto Laban's cattle. And it came to pass, whensoever the stronger
cattle did conceive, that Jacob laid the rods before the eyes of the
cattle in the gutters, that they might conceive among the rods. But
when the cattle were feeble, he put them not in: so the feebler were
Laban's, and the stronger Jacob's. And the man increased
exceedingly, and had much cattle, and maidservants, and
menservants, and camels, and asses.*

After many years of service to Laban, Jacob requested
payment in terms of sheep, goats, and cattle. Laban's flocks and
herds have increased and multiplied under Jacob's hand. Jacob,
like his grandfather Abraham, was blessed by God unconditionally.
Laban acquiesced to Jacob's request. However, when Jacob chose

his share of the sheep, goats, and cattle, he chose rather unwisely. For he selected only the spotted, speckled, and ringstraked animals! All the spotted animals would be his and all the unspotted and unblemished would belong to Laban.

Then he performed an even stranger process. He cut green boughs from the poplar, hazel, and chestnut trees and stripped them from their barks. The stripped off barks, now resembling white rods, were arranged and put into the watering troughs. When his motley colored animals came to drink of the water, they would see the white rods, mate immediately and conceive soon after. All the offspring of such animals would be spotted. Jacob, true to his nature, would bring stronger pregnant animals before the rods ensuring that their offspring of lambs, kids, and calves would be spotted, speckled, and ringstraked. With the rods, Jacob's flocks and herds multiplied and increased exceedingly.

So are we talking about secret aphrodisiacs, sorcery, love potions, animal hypnotism, or genetic engineering here? Well, none of the above.

Because of the unconditional Abrahamic Covenant, God chose to show His goodness first to Abraham, then to Isaac and now to Jacob as well. No matter how many times Jacob tricked and lied to all those around him, God would still bless him. God honored His covenant despite Jacob's sins. The wooden branches that Jacob cut off from the trees represented Jesus. Jesus had his garments and clothes repeatedly stripped off revealing his nakedness just like the branches had their barks removed. The white rods stand symbolically as Jesus naked skin. Jesus was beaten and flayed with whips until his skin peeled off, revealing his bones. Just as the sap of the branches flowed into the watering troughs, the blood of Jesus poured out as He was flogged and then pierced through.

We read this in *Matthew 27:28-31, And they stripped him, and put on him a scarlet robe. And when they had platted a crown of thorns, they put it upon his head, and a reed in his right hand: and they bowed the knee before him, and mocked him, saying, Hail, King of the Jews! And they spit upon him, and took the reed, and smote him on the head. And after that they had mocked him,*

they took the robe off from him, and put his own raiment on him,
and led him away to crucify him. And then in *Psalm 22:13-18 ,*
They gaped upon me with their mouths, as a ravening and a
roaring lion. I am poured out like water, and all my bones are out
of joint: my heart is like wax; it is melted in the midst of my
bowels. My strength is dried up like a potsherd; and my tongue
cleaveth to my jaws; and thou hast brought me into the dust of
death. For dogs have compassed me: the assembly of the wicked
have inclosed me: they pierced my hands and my feet. I may tell all
my bones: they look and stare upon me. They part my garments
among them, and cast lots upon my vesture.

Grace was given to an undeserving trickster like Jacob. All
the spotted animals that drank from the water were given new life.
New life sprang from their wombs as they looked upon the symbol
of Jesus. Because of God's unconditional promises to Abraham
and God's goodness, Jacob became very blessed and very rich.

And just like the spotted, speckled, and ringstraked
animals, Jesus still chose to approach those categorized as
blemished. The sick, the blind, the dumb, the possessed, the
hungry, the thirsty, the rejected, the oppressed, and even the dead
were given new life. **Look at Jesus and live. Look at Jesus and
be healed. Look at Jesus and see your Provision. Look at Jesus
and be whole again.**

❧ 15 ☙

JESUS AND THE TABERNACLE

We get a first glimpse of the throne room of God in the book of Genesis. We read in *Genesis 2:8-10, 15-17, And the Lord God planted a garden eastward in Eden; and there he put the man whom he had formed. And out of the ground made the Lord God to grow every tree that is pleasant to the sight, and good for food; the tree of life also in the midst of the garden, and the tree of knowledge of good and evil. And a river went out of Eden to water the garden; and from thence it was parted, and became into four heads. And the Lord God took the man, and put him into the garden of Eden to dress it and to keep it. And the Lord God commanded the man, saying, Of every tree of the garden thou mayest freely eat: But of the tree of the knowledge of good and evil, thou shalt not eat of it: for in the day that thou eatest thereof thou shalt surely die.*

After creating man, he put him in the garden of Eden. At the cool of each day, God would commune with Adam and Eve. The garden was situated eastward in the land called Eden. Note that the garden is not Eden; it is just located in Eden. In the middle of the garden were two trees, the tree of life and the tree of knowledge of good and evil. Adam was told not to eat from the tree of knowledge of good and evil.

The garden of Eden prefigured the forthcoming tabernacle. The outer court parallels the land called Eden. The inner court is the garden. And the two trees stand in the innermost sanctum of the garden. We all know the scripture as to what happened next. Reading from *Genesis 3:2-3, 8-9, And the woman said unto the serpent, We may eat of the fruit of the trees of the garden: But of the fruit of the tree which is in the midst of the garden, God hath said, Ye shall not eat of it, neither shall ye touch it, lest ye die. And they heard the voice of the Lord God walking in the garden in the cool of the day: and Adam and his wife hid themselves from the presence of the Lord God amongst the trees of the garden. And the Lord God called unto Adam, and said unto him, Where art thou?*

Adam and Eve sinned and God drove them out of the garden. They were still allowed to live in Eden, or the outer court, but not in the garden. The only entrance to the garden, facing east, was now guarded by cherubims and a flaming sword. Their intimate meetings with God were no more. The free access to the tree of life had ended.

Genesis 3:16-24, Unto the woman he said, I will greatly multiply thy sorrow and thy conception; in sorrow thou shalt bring forth children; and thy desire shall be to thy husband, and he shall rule over thee. And unto Adam he said, Because thou hast hearkened unto the voice of thy wife, and hast eaten of the tree, of which I commanded thee, saying, Thou shalt not eat of it: cursed is the ground for thy sake; in sorrow shalt thou eat of it all the days of thy life; Thorns also and thistles shall it bring forth to thee; and thou shalt eat the herb of the field; In the sweat of thy face shalt thou eat bread, till thou return unto the ground; for out of it wast thou taken: for dust thou art, and unto dust shalt thou return. And Adam called his wife's name Eve; because she was the mother of all living. Unto Adam also and to his wife did the Lord God make coats of skins, and clothed them. And the Lord God said, Behold, the man is become as one of us, to know good and evil: and now, lest he put forth his hand, and take also of the tree of life, and eat, and live forever: Therefore the Lord God sent him forth from the garden of Eden, to till the ground from whence he was taken. So he drove out the man; and he placed at the east of the garden of Eden Cherubims, and a flaming sword which turned every way, to keep the way of the tree of life.

Life in Eden, outside the garden, was difficult for both Adam and Eve. Adam sweated to produce crops as the land was now cursed. His work was not cursed but the land was. With sorrow, Eve bore two children namely Cain and Abel. We read in *Genesis 4:1-7, And Adam knew Eve his wife; and she conceived, and bare Cain, and said, I have gotten a man from the Lord. And she again bare his brother Abel. And Abel was a keeper of sheep, but Cain was a tiller of the ground. And in process of time it came to pass, that Cain brought of the fruit of the ground an offering unto the Lord. And Abel, he also brought of the firstlings of his flock and of the fat thereof. And the Lord had respect unto Abel and to his offering: But unto Cain and to his offering he had not respect. And Cain was very wroth, and his countenance fell. And the Lord said unto Cain, Why art thou wroth? and why is thy countenance fallen? If thou doest well, shalt thou not be accepted? and if thou doest not well, sin lieth at the door. And unto thee shall be his desire, and thou shalt rule over him.*

There was an altar in Eden where Cain and Abel could bring their offerings to God. Abel brought a blood offering but Cain did not. The offerings were to be a sweet savor to God. Cain's offerings of the fruit of the ground were considered unacceptable. It was also untimely. Yet God provided an offering suitable for Cain. There was an offering for sin waiting at The Door. This Sin Offering had a desire to be an offering for Cain, and if Cain had accepted this Sin Offering, he would have dominance over sin. However, Cain rejected the offering provided by God. He rejected the Sin Offering, which was Jesus Christ, choosing to sacrifice his brother's blood instead. Because of his own actions, Cain was driven out from Eden into the land of Nod. The presence of the Lord was not in the land of Nod.

We read of this in *Genesis 4:8-16, And Cain talked with Abel his brother: and it came to pass, when they were in the field, that Cain rose up against Abel his brother, and slew him. And the Lord said unto Cain, Where is Abel thy brother? And he said, I know not: Am I my brother's keeper? And he said, What hast thou done? the voice of thy brother's blood crieth unto me from the ground. And now art thou cursed from the earth, which hath*

*opened her mouth to receive thy brother's blood from thy hand;
When thou tillest the ground, it shall not henceforth yield unto thee
her strength; a fugitive and a vagabond shalt thou be in the earth.
And Cain said unto the Lord, My punishment is greater than I can
bear. Behold, thou hast driven me out this day from the face of the
earth; and from thy face shall I be hid; and I shall be a fugitive
and a vagabond in the earth; and it shall come to pass, that every
one that findeth me shall slay me. And the Lord said unto him,
Therefore whosoever slayeth Cain, vengeance shall be taken on
him sevenfold. And the Lord set a mark upon Cain, lest any finding
him should kill him. And Cain went out from the presence of the
Lord, and dwelt in the land of Nod, on the east of Eden.*

The tabernacle or 'tent of meeting' was a physical place
here on earth with a spiritual counterpart in heaven. It was a place
where God would meet with man, just like the garden in Eden, and
was a shadow of the throne room of God in heaven. In *Hebrews
8:5*, we read, *Who serve unto the example and shadow of heavenly
things, as Moses was admonished of God when he was about to
make the tabernacle: for, See, saith he, that thou make all things
according to the pattern shewed to thee in the mount.* And in
*Hebrews 9:23-24, It was therefore necessary that the patterns of
things in the heavens should be purified with these; but the
heavenly things themselves with better sacrifices than these. For
Christ is not entered into the holy places made with hands, which
are the figures of the true; but into heaven itself, now to appear in
the presence of God for us:*

The tabernacle was portable and could be moved from
place to place. The whole structure was enclosed and surrounded
by a courtyard fence of fine white twined linen. There was only
one door, facing east, whereby people could enter and exit the
linen fence. The white linen fence stands in stark contrast to the
colors of the desert and stands for holiness and purity. The one
door signified Jesus as the only way to the Father. In *John 10:9*,
we read, *I am the door: by me if any man enter in, he shall be
saved.* There is no other way or entrance. *John 14:6* states, *Jesus
saith unto him, I am the way, the truth, and the life: no man cometh
unto the Father, but by me.* And very clearly in *Exodus 20:26*,

Neither shalt thou go up by steps unto mine altar, that thy nakedness be not discovered thereon. There were no steps, representing human works, leading to the door.

The tabernacle is divided into three parts; the outer court, the inner court or the Holy Place, and the Holy of Holies. Like in the garden, God wants to put us in the Holy of Holies. However, due to Adam's sin, He cannot. Therefore, Jesus has to take us in. All the furnishings in the tabernacle represent Jesus and what He did for us. Without Jesus, we cannot enter into the presence of God.

In the outer court, the first furnishing we encounter in the earthly tabernacle is the brass or bronze altar. In *Exodus 27:1-4, And thou shalt make an altar of shittim wood, five cubits long, and five cubits broad; the altar shall be foursquare: and the height thereof shall be three cubits. And thou shalt make the horns of it upon the four corners thereof: his horns shall be of the same: and thou shalt overlay it with brass. And thou shalt make his pans to receive his ashes, and his shovels, and his basons, and his fleshhooks, and his firepans: all the vessels thereof thou shalt make of brass. And thou shalt make for it a grate of network of brass; and upon the net shalt thou make four brasen rings in the four corners thereof.* The burnt offerings were sacrificed and the blood collected here. Innocent animals had their blood shed to bring about reconciliation for sin and consecration. It was made of wood and it had four corners just like the cross. Brass stands for judgment. Jesus was judged in our place on the cross. He is our perfect burnt offering. By His blood, we are reconciled to God and can enjoy everlasting life.

The next furnishing is the brass laver of water. We see in *Exodus 30:17-20, And the Lord spake unto Moses, saying, Thou shalt also make a laver of brass, and his foot also of brass, to wash withal: and thou shalt put it between the tabernacle of the congregation and the altar, and thou shalt put water therein. For Aaron and his sons shall wash their hands and their feet thereat: When they go into the tabernacle of the congregation, they shall wash with water, that they die not; or when they come near to the altar to minister, to burn offering made by fire unto the Lord.* The priests would wash themselves with this water before entering into the Holy Place. They would wash their hands and their feet each time they entered the inner court. This is a water basin, not a blood basin. Similarly, Jesus washes our feet as they get soiled from the pollution and dirt of the world around us. Resting and feeding on Jesus everyday washes our minds clean from self-righteousness and self-works. We are sanctified in our body, mind, and spirit by the words of Jesus. In *John 15:3, Now ye are clean through the word which I have spoken unto you and again in Ephesians 5:26, That he might sanctify and cleanse it with the washing of water by the word,*

The Holy Place and the Holy of Holies are covered by four layers of coverings each representing Jesus. We read this in *Exodus 26:1, 3, 7-9, 14, Moreover thou shalt make the tabernacle with ten curtains of fine twined linen, and blue, and purple, and scarlet: with cherubims of cunning work shalt thou make them. The five curtains shall be coupled together one to another; and other five curtains shall be coupled one to another. And thou shalt make curtains of goats' hair to be a covering upon the tabernacle: eleven curtains shalt thou make. The length of one curtain shall be thirty cubits, and the breadth of one curtain four cubits: and the eleven curtains shall be all of one measure. And thou shalt couple five curtains by themselves, and six curtains by themselves, and shalt double the sixth curtain in the forefront of the tabernacle. And thou shalt make a covering for the tent of rams' skins dyed red, and a covering above of badgers' skins.*

The first covering of linen of blue, purple, and gold represents respectively the divinity, royalty, and deity of Jesus. The next covering of goats' hair symbolizes Jesus as the all-sufficient sacrifice for our sins. Here, unlike any other covering, the five curtains are joined to six curtains but the sixth is doubled and hidden behind the fifth. As the number five stands for grace and six stands for man, man's works are hidden behind grace. It is not about our good works as Jesus did it all for us. The next two coverings of rams' skins dyed red and badgers' skins represent, respectively, the blood sacrifice of Jesus and His humble position as the Son of man, who would eventually save the sons of men.

Under these coverings is the inner court or the Holy Place. There are three items of furnishing here. The first is a seven-branched golden candlestick. In *Exodus 25:31-32,37, And thou shalt make a candlestick of pure gold: of beaten work shall the candlestick be made: his shaft, and his branches, his bowls, his knops, and his flowers, shall be of the same. And six branches shall come out of the sides of it; three branches of the candlestick out of the one side, and three branches of the candlestick out of the other side. And thou shalt make the seven lamps thereof: and they shall light the lamps thereof, that they may give light over against it.* Because of the cross, all punishment had been meted out on Jesus. Judgment was passed and the price was paid. There is now no more punishment for us, which explains why all the furnishings are now made of gold, symbolizing divinity. In Isaiah chapter 11 verse 2, we read of the six aspects of the Holy Spirit with the seventh as the Spirit of the Lord, as symbolized by the golden candlestick. We are now holy and righteous because of Jesus. The Holy Spirit shines His everlasting light on us to remind us that our justification is based upon His knowledge of His finished work, not our knowledge. We got here because Jesus saw the travail of His soul and was satisfied. In *Isaiah 53:11,* it states, *He shall see of the travail of his soul, and shall be satisfied: by his knowledge shall my righteous servant justify many; for he shall bear their iniquities.* Jesus, with full cognizance of His sufficiency, bore our iniquities. The Holy Spirit shines this truth for us to see.

The second piece of furniture in the inner court is the golden table of showbread. On this table were the twelve loaves of bread, signifying the twelve tribes of Israel. These bread would be eaten by the priests every Sabbath. Once the bread was eaten, it had to be replaced. This shadow has now been supplanted once and for all time by the true Bread of Life, Jesus Christ. Those who eat of Him would never die. Just as the showbread was always on the table, those who eat from Jesus will always have health and life. We demonstrate this every time we partake of the bread and juice from the Lord's Supper or Holy Communion. The bread, signifying the body of Christ, reminds us that we are healed by His stripes. The juice, signifying the blood of Christ, reminds us that we have eternal life.

We see this in *Exodus 25:23-30, Thou shalt also make a table of shittim wood: two cubits shall be the length thereof, and a cubit the breadth thereof, and a cubit and a half the height thereof. And thou shalt overlay it with pure gold, and make thereto a crown of gold round about. And thou shalt make unto it a border of an hand breadth round about, and thou shalt make a golden crown to the border thereof round about. And thou shalt make for it four rings of gold, and put the rings in the four corners that are on the four feet thereof. Over against the border shall the rings be for places of the staves to bear the table. And thou shalt make the staves of shittim wood, and overlay them with gold, that the table may be borne with them. And thou shalt make the dishes thereof, and spoons thereof, and covers thereof, and bowls thereof, to cover withal: of pure gold shalt thou make them. And thou shalt set upon the table shewbread before me alway.* And *John 6:33-35* states, *For the bread of God is he which cometh down from heaven, and giveth life unto the world. Then said they unto him, Lord, evermore give us this bread. And Jesus said unto them, I am the bread of life: he that cometh to me shall never hunger; and he that believeth on me shall never thirst.* Then again in *1 Corinthians 10:16-17, The cup of blessing which we bless, is it not the communion of the blood of Christ? The bread which we break, is it not the communion of the body of Christ? For we being many are one bread, and one body: for we are all partakers of that one bread.*

The last item in the Holy Place was the golden altar of incense. In *Exodus 30:1-8, And thou shalt make an altar to burn incense upon: of shittim wood shalt thou make it. A cubit shall be the length thereof, and a cubit the breadth thereof; foursquare shall it be: and two cubits shall be the height thereof: the horns thereof shall be of the same. And thou shalt overlay it with pure gold, the top thereof, and the sides thereof round about, and the horns thereof; and thou shalt make unto it a crown of gold round about. And two golden rings shalt thou make to it under the crown of it, by the two corners thereof, upon the two sides of it shalt thou make it; and they shall be for places for the staves to bear it withal. And thou shalt make the staves of shittim wood, and overlay them with gold.*

And thou shalt put it before the vail that is by the ark of the testimony, before the mercy seat that is over the testimony, where I will meet with thee. And Aaron shall burn thereon sweet incense every morning: when he dresseth the lamps, he shall burn incense upon it. And when Aaron lighteth the lamps at even, he shall burn incense upon it, a perpetual incense before the Lord throughout your generations. And then in *Revelations 8:3-4,* we read, *And another angel came and stood at the altar, having a golden censer; and there was given unto him much incense, that he should offer it with the prayers of all saints upon the golden altar which was before the throne. And the smoke of the incense, which came with the prayers of the saints, ascended up before God out of the angel's hand.*

Aaron, the High Priest, would burn incense upon it twice per day so that there would be perpetual incense before God. We know from Revelations that the smoke from the incense are the prayers of the saints; our prayers in Jesus' mighty name. However, part of the incense is also Jesus praying for us as seen in *John 17:1-4, 9, 12, These words spake Jesus, and lifted up his eyes to heaven, and said, Father, the hour is come; glorify thy Son, that thy Son also may glorify thee: As thou hast given him power over all flesh, that he should give eternal life to as many as thou hast given him. And this is life eternal, that they might know thee the only true God, and Jesus Christ, whom thou hast sent. I have glorified thee on the earth: I have finished the work which thou gavest me to do. I pray for them: I pray not for the world, but for them which thou hast given me; for they are thine. While I was with them in the world, I kept them in thy name: those that thou gavest me I have kept, and none of them is lost, but the son of perdition; that the scripture might be fulfilled.* It is a sweet fragrance before God when Jesus prayed that He gave us eternal life, that He had kept us, and that He had not lost any of us. What a fragrant, aromatic smell for our prayers to rise together with Jesus' before God. In the throne room in heaven, Jesus continuously makes intercession for us.

To enter the third part of the tabernacle, which is also under the coverings, we have to go through the veil. As Jesus' back was torn with whips, He parted the entrance to the Holy of Holies for us. In *Matthew 27:51, And, behold, the veil of the temple was rent in twain from the top to the bottom; and the earth did quake, and the rocks rent* and again in *Hebrews 10:20-22, By a new and living way, which he hath consecrated for us, through the veil, that is to say, his flesh; And having an high priest over the house of God; Let us draw near with a true heart in full assurance of faith, having our hearts sprinkled from an evil conscience, and our bodies washed with pure water.*

It was a new and living way. The old way meant death. When he died for us, the veil that separated us from God was torn in two. We can enter and live. Not only can we enter the Holy of Holies but we can also draw near with a true heart full of Jesus. **We are assured of our salvation because of what Jesus did for us. Because of His righteousness, we are also righteous. Moreover, as righteous people, we can approach God's holy presence without fear. For the price of sin had been paid in full. The punishment had been borne. Death had been defeated.**

In the last part of the tabernacle, called the Holy of Holies, rest a single item, namely the ark of the covenant. Reading from *Exodus 25:10-22, And they shall make an ark of shittim wood: two cubits and a half shall be the length thereof, and a cubit and a half the breadth thereof, and a cubit and a half the height thereof. And thou shalt overlay it with pure gold, within and without shalt thou overlay it, and shalt make upon it a crown of gold round about. And thou shalt cast four rings of gold for it, and put them in the four corners thereof; and two rings shall be in the one side of it, and two rings in the other side of it. And thou shalt make staves of shittim wood, and overlay them with gold. And thou shalt put the staves into the rings by the sides of the ark, that the ark may be borne with them. The staves shall be in the rings of the ark: they shall not be taken from it. And thou shalt put into the ark the testimony which I shall give thee. And thou shalt make a mercy seat of pure gold: two cubits and a half shall be the length thereof, and a cubit and a half the breadth thereof. And thou shalt make two cherubims of gold, of beaten work shalt thou make them, in the two ends of the mercy seat. And make one cherub on the one end, and the other cherub on the other end: even of the mercy seat shall ye make the cherubims on the two ends thereof. And the cherubims shall stretch forth their wings on high, covering the mercy seat with their wings, and their faces shall look one to another; toward the mercy seat shall the faces of the cherubims be. And thou shalt put the mercy seat above upon the ark; and in the ark thou shalt put the testimony that I shall give thee. And there I will meet with thee, and I will commune with thee from above the mercy seat, from between the two cherubims which are upon the ark of the testimony, of all things which I will give thee in commandment unto the children of Israel.*

God's presence rested on the ark. It was made of shittim or acacia wood, covered outside and inside with pure gold. Golden poles, made to carry the ark, were commanded not to be removed from it. On top of the ark was the mercy seat, made from one slab of solid gold. At the ends of the mercy seat were two golden cherubims, with wings outstretched, facing each other. There was also a golden crown on the top of the mercy seat.

Inside the ark itself, there were originally three items. There were the two tablets of blue stone on which the ten commandments were written, an omer of manna, and Aaron's rod. About five hundred years later, in 1Kings chapter 8, only the tablets were left in the ark. The other two items were presumably lost.

As we approach the ark, let us look at it a little closer, with a little bit more detail. Wood stands as a symbol for man in the Old Testament. Shittim or acacia wood was known as incorruptible wood. Together, the wooden ark symbolizes the incorruptible humanity of Jesus. The bark and gum of the acacia branch could be used to treat infectious skin ailments, diarrhea, intestinal problems, and inflammation. The tannins from the branch also have antibacterial properties. In *Zechariah 3:8, Hear now, O Joshua the high priest, thou, and thy fellows that sit before thee: for they are men wondered at: for, behold, I will bring forth my servant the*

BRANCH. Jesus Christ is the Branch. Then again in *Isaiah 11:1, And there shall come forth a rod out of the stem of Jesse, and a Branch shall grow out of his roots.* Here, He is the Rod of the stem. Jesus is the incorruptible Branch and Rod with healing powers.

The ark is overlaid inside and outside completely with pure gold. Gold stood for divinity. Jesus, the incorruptible man, is also fully divine. The golden poles, which were not to be removed from the ark's side, represented the ever-present Jesus who promised to never leave us nor forsake us. The ark never had a permanent resting place. The ark traveled with the Israelites wherever they went. In *Numbers 10:33, And they departed from the mount of the Lord three days' journey: and the ark of the covenant of the Lord went before them in the three days' journey, to search out a resting place for them.* The ark literally sought out a resting place for the Israelites. Similarly, Jesus never rested fully until He did the will of His Father. When He did it, we all found rest in Him. In *Numbers 2:2*, we see that *Every man of the children of Israel shall pitch by his own standard, with the ensign of their father's house: far off about the tabernacle of the congregation shall they pitch.* Whenever the Israelites made camp, the ark would be placed in the center of the camp. The twelve tribes, with their individual banners, would then camp around the ark. Jesus is still and always will be the center and the banner of our lives. He is our Jehovah-Nissi, meaning 'Lord our Banner'.

However, the most important element of the ark was the mercy seat. The golden crown on top of the mercy seat showed royalty. Jesus is the King of Kings and the Lord of Lords. The mercy seat is one solid slab of gold beaten into shape just as Jesus was beaten for us. The two cherubims corresponded to the two angels that Mary saw, one at the head and the other at the foot of Jesus' tomb. In *John 20:11-12*, we read, *But Mary stood without at the sepulchre weeping: and as she wept, she stooped down, and looked into the sepulchre, And seeth two angels in white sitting, the one at the head, and the other at the feet, where the body of Jesus had lain.* God only communed with His people from above the mercy seat, between the two cherubims, and never from inside the ark. When God's manifest presence showed up, the glory cloud would center upon the mercy seat. In *1 Chronicles 13:6, And David went up, and all Israel, to Baalah, that is, to Kirjath-jearim, which belonged to Judah, to bring up thence the ark of God the Lord, that dwelleth between the cherubims, whose name is called on it.* We call this the 'shekinah' glory as it literally means 'that which dwells'.

Every year, the High Priest would enter the Holy of Holies and sprinkle blood on the mercy seat. This was called the Day of Atonement as this gesture atoned for the sins of the people. The mercy seat represented Jesus Christ, with His blood on it poured out for us. As the mercy seat sat on top of the ark that held the tablets of the law, it effectively covered the law. The manna and the rod, both representing man's rebellion against God, was initially in the ark but was lost as the years went by. The ark kept the law. Jesus, the perfect law-keeper kept the law perfectly in its place - under Him. Without Jesus keeping the law at bay, death would result. Many years later, in *1 Samuel 6:19, And he smote the men of Beth-shemesh, because they had looked into the ark of the Lord, even he smote of the people fifty thousand and threescore and ten men: and the people lamented, because the Lord had smitten many of the people with a great slaughter.* When the people of Bethshemesh removed the mercy seat and looked into the ark, 50070 of them died. Bethshemesh meant 'house of the sun'. Without the Son, the people of the house of the sun perished.

Grace is always higher than the law. With Jesus' blood on the mercy seat, God had to look at Jesus first before He could look at the law. And when God looked at what Jesus had done on the cross, mercy ended. For the price had been paid in blood. Punishment had been carried out. Justice had been done. Jesus was punished for our crime of sin so we cannot be punished for the same crime. There had already been a death. We can now ask for justice, as a just God must set us free. We are acquitted as the punishment was fit.

Every part of the ark represented Jesus. We entered the Holy of Holies by Jesus and we are led to see Jesus. As such, the physical ark of the covenant became superfluous and was done away with. In *Jeremiah 3:16, And it shall come to pass, when ye be multiplied and increased in the land, in those days, saith the Lord, they shall say no more, The ark of the covenant of the Lord: neither shall it come to mind: neither shall they remember it; neither shall they visit it; neither shall that be done any more.* It will not be remembered, it will not come to mind, and it will not be visited. Instead, it will be removed.

Many people still look for the physical ark but there is no need to look for it as it is no longer needed nor is it essential. But Jesus, our true ark, would be brought to remembrance. He would be brought to mind, as He is essential. He would be written in our hearts. He would become our new covenant. We see this in *Jeremiah 31:31-34, Behold, the days come, saith the Lord, that I will make a new covenant with the house of Israel, and with the house of Judah: Not according to the covenant that I made with their fathers in the day that I took them by the hand to bring them out of the land of Egypt; which my covenant they brake, although I was an husband unto them, saith the Lord: But this shall be the covenant that I will make with the house of Israel; After those days, saith the Lord, I will put my law in their inward parts, and write it in their hearts; and will be their God, and they shall be my people. And they shall teach no more every man his neighbour, and every man his brother, saying, Know the Lord: for they shall all know me, from the least of them unto the greatest of them, saith the Lord; for I will forgive their iniquity, and I will remember their sin no more.*

We now come to the true tabernacle - the throne room of God. In *Revelation 4:1-3*, we read, *After this I looked, and, behold, a door was opened in heaven: and the first voice which I heard was as it were of a trumpet talking with me; which said, Come up hither, and I will shew thee things which must be hereafter. And immediately I was in the spirit: and, behold, a throne was set in heaven, and one sat on the throne. And he that sat was to look upon like a jasper and a sardine stone: and there was a rainbow round about the throne, in sight like unto an emerald.* John was taken up in the spirit and was shown things which were to come. The first thing he saw was Jesus.

Since no man can see God's face and live, John did not see God sitting on the throne. He saw Jesus, whom he knew intimately on earth. However, Jesus is now in His glorified form and is sitting on the throne, on the right hand side of His Father. *Luke 22:69* states that *Hereafter shall the Son of man sit on the right hand of the power of God.* According to John, Jesus looked like a jasper and a sardius stone. We know that the High Priest in the Old Testament wore a breastplate of judgment that had sixteen stones set in it. In *Exodus 28:15-20, And thou shalt make the breastplate of judgment with cunning work; after the work of the ephod thou shalt make it; of gold, of blue, and of purple, and of scarlet, and of fine twined linen, shalt thou make it. Foursquare it shall be being doubled; a span shall be the length thereof, and a span shall be the breadth thereof. And thou shalt set in it settings of stones, even four rows of stones: the first row shall be a sardius, a topaz, and a carbuncle: this shall be the first row. And the second row shall be an emerald, a sapphire, and a diamond. And the third row a ligure, an agate, and an amethyst. And the fourth row a beryl, and an onyx, and a jasper: they shall be set in gold in their inclosings.* The first stone was sardius and the last was jasper. This breastplate of stones was only worn by the High Priest of the earthly tabernacle.

In this heavenly tabernacle, Jesus is our High Priest, seated on the throne on the Father's right hand side. *Hebrews 8:1-2* states, *Now of the things which we have spoken this is the sum: We have such an high priest, who is set on the right hand of the throne of the Majesty in the heavens; A minister of the sanctuary, and of the true tabernacle, which the Lord pitched, and not man.* He sits on His Father's right hand signifying He is equal to God in glory, position, honor, authority, respect, and power. All things are under His feet and He is the head over all things. We see this in *Ephesians 1:20-22, Which he wrought in Christ, when he raised him from the dead, and set him at his own right hand in the heavenly places, Far above all principality, and power, and might, and dominion, and every name that is named, not only in this world, but also in that which is to come: And hath put all things under his feet, and gave him to be the head over all things to the church.*

John saw the stones in reverse order from that in the Old Testament. In the Old Testament, the Israelites looked forward to the coming of Jesus. The first stone was sardius, a blood red stone, which portended the sacrifice of Jesus on the cross. It was His blood that paid the price for all our sins. The last stone was jasper, a clear white stone auguring complete victory.

But John saw Jesus after the cross. The jasper is now the first stone. Victory over sin and death had already been achieved. The victory was won by Jesus. Moreover, He would come again in victory to set up His kingdom. All because of His blood sacrifice on the cross as symbolized by the sardius stone.

There was also a rainbow around the throne. On earth, we usually see only half a rainbow. In order to see a full rainbow, which is very rare, one has to be higher than the rain droplets suspended in the air.

The first mention of the rainbow was as a token of the covenant that God made with Noah. After the flood had ended, Noah offered burnt offerings to God. We read this in *Genesis 8:20-21, And Noah builded an altar unto the Lord; and took of every clean beast, and of every clean fowl, and offered burnt offerings on the altar. And the Lord smelled a sweet savour; and the Lord said in his heart, I will not again curse the ground any more for man's sake; for the imagination of man's heart is evil from his youth; neither will I again smite any more every thing living, as I have done.*

The sweet savor of the burnt offerings ascended to heaven, and then God bound Himself with a covenant to never destroy the earth again with a flood. The water, which destroyed the earth, now caused the rainbow. We read this in *Genesis 9:11-17, And I will establish my covenant with you; neither shall all flesh be cut off any more by the waters of a flood; neither shall there any more be a flood to destroy the earth. And God said, This is the token of the covenant which I make between me and you and every living creature that is with you, for perpetual generations: I do set my bow in the cloud, and it shall be for a token of a covenant between me and the earth. And it shall come to pass, when I bring a cloud over the earth, that the bow shall be seen in the cloud: And I will remember my covenant, which is between me and you and every living creature of all flesh; and the waters shall no more become a flood to destroy all flesh. And the bow shall be in the cloud; and I will look upon it, that I may remember the everlasting covenant between God and every living creature of all flesh that is upon the earth. And God said unto Noah, This is the token of the covenant, which I have established between me and all flesh that is upon the earth.*

A rainbow consists of seven colors; the number seven signifying perfection. Jesus is perfection. Every time light refracts off Perfection, we see a rainbow. Every time God sees the rainbow, or Jesus, He would remember His unconditional covenant. Because of the rainbow, or Jesus, God's wrath is appeased. God promised that He would never be angry with us because of Jesus! In *Isaiah 54:9-10, For this is as the waters of Noah unto me: for as I have sworn that the waters of Noah should no more go over the earth; so have I sworn that I would not be wroth with thee, nor rebuke thee. For the mountains shall depart, and the hills be removed; but my kindness shall not depart from thee, neither shall the covenant of my peace be removed, saith the Lord that hath mercy on thee.*

Ezekiel 1:28 describes it *As the appearance of the bow that is in the cloud in the day of rain, so was the appearance of the brightness round about. This was the appearance of the likeness of the glory of the Lord.* We now see the full, not partial, rainbow in heaven. A perfect rainbow circle symbolizing eternity. It has no beginning and no end. Furthermore, this rainbow looked like an emerald. Emeralds are green denoting life and freshness. The circular rainbow looking like an emerald is the new covenant with Jesus. Mountains may depart and hills be removed but Jesus' kindness to us would never depart from us. This new covenant is also called the covenant of Peace, as he is the Prince of Peace. Jesus is now seen in His complete, perfected state of fullness.

He came down to lift us up to where He is. He took us through the tabernacle, from the outer court to the inner court to the Holy of Holies. He took us home to be with Him

forevermore. He made us sit with Him on His throne. No priest ministering in the earthly tabernacle could ever sit, as his work was never finished. There were no golden chairs in the earthly tabernacle. But Jesus accomplished it all. That is why there are chairs in the throne room. *Hebrews 10:12-14* states, *But this man, after he had offered one sacrifice for sins forever, sat down on the right hand of God; From henceforth expecting till his enemies be made his footstool. For by one offering he hath perfected for ever them that are sanctified.* By one sacrifice for sins forever, He sat down on the right hand of God.

    Psalms 103:10-12 further declare that *He hath not dealt with us after our sins; nor rewarded us according to our iniquities. For as the heaven is high above the earth, so great is his mercy toward them that fear him. As far as the east is from the west, so far hath he removed our transgressions from us.* As far as the east is from the west, which is infinite as they never meet, He removed our transgressions from us.

    Furthermore, we read in *Ephesians 2:4-6, But God, who is rich in mercy, for his great love wherewith he loved us, Even when we were dead in sins, hath quickened us together with Christ, (by grace ye are saved;) And hath raised us up together, and made us sit together in heavenly places in Christ Jesus.* Also in *Revelation 3:21, To him that overcometh will I grant to sit with me in my throne, even as I also overcame, and am set down with my Father in his throne.* God now gives us seats in heaven next to Jesus. When we sit with Jesus on His right hand side, He puts out His right arm and places His arm over our shoulders. And if we were to look at God, we would see His right arm on Jesus' shoulder as well. For whatever the Father does, Jesus also does. We will finally understand why Jesus said that He and His Father are one. When we were dead in our sins, God showed His infinite love towards us by giving His all, Jesus, to us. And Jesus showed His infinite love towards us by perfecting and sanctifying us to everlasting life with Him on the throne. **We have eternal life with Jesus because of Jesus!**

❧ 16 ❧

JESUS AND A YOUNG RED COW

Under the law, the Israelites had to perform numerous offerings to God. The purpose of these offerings was to temporarily cover up sins committed by the people. All the offerings are shadows or types fore-signifying Jesus Christ. A shadow represents or suggests the form of something or someone that is real. It is not the real thing or person but alludes to that thing or person.

The most common offerings to God are found in the book of Leviticus. There are five offerings mentioned here. They are (1) the burnt offering, (2) the sin offering, (3) the trespass offering, (4) the meal offering, and (5) the peace offering. As mentioned before, these five offerings prefigure Christ.

Let us read from *Leviticus 1:1-9* about the burnt offering, *And the Lord called unto Moses, and spake unto him out of the tabernacle of the congregation, saying, Speak unto the children of Israel, and say unto them, If any man of you bring an offering unto the Lord, ye shall bring your offering of the cattle, even of the herd, and of the flock. If his offering be a burnt sacrifice of the herd, let him offer a male without blemish: he shall offer it of his own voluntary will at the door of the tabernacle of the congregation before the Lord. And he shall put his hand upon the head of the burnt offering; and it shall be accepted for him to make atonement for him. And he shall kill the bullock before the Lord:*

and the priests, Aaron's sons, shall bring the blood, and sprinkle the blood round about upon the altar that is by the door of the tabernacle of the congregation. And he shall flay the burnt offering, and cut it into his pieces. And the sons of Aaron the priest shall put fire upon the altar, and lay the wood in order upon the fire: And the priests, Aaron's sons, shall lay the parts, the head, and the fat, in order upon the wood that is on the fire which is upon the altar: But his inwards and his legs shall he wash in water: and the priest shall burn all on the altar, to be a burnt sacrifice, an offering made by fire, of a sweet savour unto the Lord.

Leviticus 4:1-6 writes about the sin offering, And the Lord spake unto Moses, saying, Speak unto the children of Israel, saying, If a soul shall sin through ignorance against any of the commandments of the Lord concerning things which ought not to be done, and shall do against any of them: If the priest that is anointed do sin according to the sin of the people; then let him bring for his sin, which he hath sinned, a young bullock without blemish unto the Lord for a sin offering. And he shall bring the bullock unto the door of the tabernacle of the congregation before the Lord; and shall lay his hand upon the bullock's head, and kill the bullock before the Lord. And the priest that is anointed shall take of the bullock's blood, and bring it to the tabernacle of the congregation: And the priest shall dip his finger in the blood, and sprinkle of the blood seven times before the Lord, before the vail of the sanctuary.

And the trespass offering is found in Leviticus 5:15-16, If a soul commit a trespass, and sin through ignorance, in the holy things of the Lord; then he shall bring for his trespass unto the Lord a ram without blemish out of the flocks, with thy estimation by shekels of silver, after the shekel of the sanctuary, for a trespass offering: And he shall make amends for the harm that he hath done in the holy thing, and shall add the fifth part thereto, and give it unto the priest: and the priest shall make an atonement for him with the ram of the trespass offering, and it shall be forgiven him.

Notice that there are similarities in the three offerings above. The offerings involve a male bullock, or some other animal, with no blemish. The sinner brings the spotless offering. He has to make sure that it is spotless; otherwise, it will be rejected as an acceptable sacrifice. After checking that the bullock is indeed spotless, the sinner brings it before the priest. The priest now examines the same bullock that the man has already examined earlier. The priest checks over the animal thoroughly but the sinner is not examined by the priest. When the bullock is pronounced acceptable, the animal is killed. The whole bullock, minus its skin, is burnt on the altar.

However, before the bullock is killed, the sinner lays his hand upon the bullock's head. This act signifies that the unblemished perfection of the animal is transferred to the sinner. At the same time, the sins of the sinner are transferred to the bullock. The bullock dies in the place of the sinner who walks away free and sinless. In each case, the offering is examined. The sinner who brings the offering is never examined.

Jesus Christ is the only sweet smelling savor to God. We do not smell sweet to God at all. Jesus is sinless. He is the Spotless Lamb of God. In this great exchange, He took our sins upon Himself and transferred His perfection to us. We become perfect because of Jesus. If not for what Jesus did on the cross, we would never be acceptable to God. It would be pointless for us to consider whether we are acceptable to God based on our actions. We can examine ourselves minutely for past, present, and future sins; fast and pray fervently; confess and re-confess our sins to no avail. We are sinners and can never be accepted by God based on our own works. **But Jesus is the Perfect Sacrifice and because He is perfectly acceptable to God, we become perfectly acceptable to God as well. Because God looks at Jesus, not us, we smell just as sweet as Jesus. Because of Jesus offering of Himself as the perfect sacrifice, we walk away sinless. Not only sinless but adopted and accepted as His children as well.**

The burnt offering is a sweet savor to God. The sin and trespass offerings are not. Another difference between the burnt offering and the sin and trespass offerings are that the last two offerings were burned outside the tabernacle. As they represented sin, they were not sweet savors.

The trespass offering also involved the blood of an animal. After the animal was sacrificed, the trespasser would be similarly forgiven after the atonement by the blood of the offering. Sometimes restitution had to be made for the trespass and a fifth part added to the original. This was the first sign that Jesus not only took away our sins and paid our debt but He added a fifth part more to it. **The Sacrifice overpaid the debt bringing more glory to God and more blessings to man**. However, all the three offerings here had the same significance. And that is of Jesus taking our place and then, more than paying for our debt.

We read of this in the scriptures below.

Leviticus 22:20, But whatsoever hath a blemish, that shall ye not offer: for it shall not be acceptable for you.

2 Corinthians 5:21, For he hath made him to be sin for us, who knew no sin; that we might be made the righteousness of God in him.

John 1:29, The next day John seeth Jesus coming unto him, and saith, Behold the Lamb of God, which taketh away the sin of the world.

1 Peter 1:18-19, Forasmuch as ye know that ye were not redeemed with corruptible things, as silver and gold, from your vain conversation received by tradition from your fathers; But with the precious blood of Christ, as of a lamb without blemish and without spot:

1 Corinthians 5:7, Purge out therefore the old leaven, that ye may be a new lump, as ye are unleavened. For even Christ our passover is sacrificed for us:

Ephesians 5:2, And walk in love, as Christ also hath loved us, and hath given himself for us an offering and a sacrifice to God for a sweet smelling savour.

The next two offerings, the meal and peace offerings were sweet savors to God. We find the meal offering in *Leviticus 2:1-2, And when any will offer a meal offering unto the Lord, his offering shall be of fine flour; and he shall pour oil upon it, and put frankincense thereon: And he shall bring it to Aaron's sons the priests: and he shall take thereout his handful of the flour thereof, and of the oil thereof, with all the frankincense thereof; and the priest shall burn the memorial of it upon the altar, to be an offering made by fire, of a sweet savour unto the Lord:*

Leviticus 3:1-5 describes the peace offering, *And if his oblation be a sacrifice of peace offering, if he offer it of the herd; whether it be a male or female, he shall offer it without blemish before the Lord. And he shall lay his hand upon the head of his offering, and kill it at the door of the tabernacle of the congregation: and Aaron's sons the priests shall sprinkle the blood upon the altar round about. And he shall offer of the sacrifice of the peace offering an offering made by fire unto the Lord; the fat that covereth the inwards, and all the fat that is upon the inwards, And the two kidneys, and the fat that is on them, which is by the flanks, and the caul above the liver, with the kidneys, it shall he take away. And Aaron's sons shall burn it on the altar upon the burnt sacrifice, which is upon the wood that is on the fire: it is an offering made by fire, of a sweet savour unto the Lord.*

The fine flour in the meal offering represented Jesus; the oil the Holy Spirit working throughout His life; and the frankincense the fragrance of His Person. The peace offering was shared between God, the priests, and the offerer. It represented our fellowship with God, Jesus, and one another. This fellowship and communion was made possible by Jesus.

There were also two other common offerings mentioned numerous times in the bible. These two offerings were given to the priests, as representatives of God. The two offerings were (1) the wave offering and (2) the heave offering.

Some of the scripture explaining these offerings are as follows: *Numbers 5:9-10, And every offering of all the holy things of the children of Israel, which they bring unto the priest, shall be his. And every man's hallowed things shall be his: whatsoever any man giveth the priest, it shall be his.*
Ezekiel 44:29-30, They shall eat the meat offering, and the sin offering, and the trespass offering; and every dedicated thing in Israel shall be theirs. And the first of all the firstfruits of all things, and every oblation of all, of every sort of your oblations, shall be the priest's: ye shall also give unto the priest the first of your dough, that he may cause the blessing to rest in thine house.

Exodus 29:22-24, Also thou shalt take of the ram the fat and the rump, and the fat that covereth the inwards, and the caul above the liver, and the two kidneys, and the fat that is upon them, and the right shoulder; for it is a ram of consecration: And one loaf of bread, and one cake of oiled bread, and one wafer out of the basket of the unleavened bread that is before the Lord: And thou shalt put all in the hands of Aaron, and in the hands of his sons; and shalt wave them for a wave offering before the Lord.
Numbers 15:19-21, Then it shall be, that, when ye eat of the bread of the land, ye shall offer up an heave offering unto the Lord. Ye shall offer up a cake of the first of your dough for an heave offering: as ye do the heave offering of the threshing floor, so shall ye heave it. Of the first of your dough ye shall give unto the Lord an heave offering in your generations.
Numbers 31:28-29, And levy a tribute unto the Lord of the men of war which went out to battle: one soul of five hundred, both of the persons, and of the beeves, and of the asses, and of the sheep: Take it of their half, and give it unto Eleazar the priest, for an heave offering of the Lord.
Exodus 29:25-27, And thou shalt receive them of their hands, and burn them upon the altar for a burnt offering, for a sweet savour before the Lord: it is an offering made by fire unto the Lord. And thou shalt take the breast of the ram of Aaron's consecration, and wave it for a wave offering before the Lord: and it shall be thy part. And thou shalt sanctify the breast of the wave offering, and the shoulder of the heave offering, which is waved, and which is heaved up, of the ram of the consecration, even of that which is for Aaron, and of that which is for his sons.

Whether it was parts of the burnt offering, firstfruits of bread, grain and oil, parts of spoil taken in war, tenth of all tithes, or other gifts, the ceremony was the same. The wave offering was carried by the offerer to the priest. They would stand facing each other. The priest would then place his hands under the offerer's hands. Together both of them would move the offering to and fro in a wave like horizontal motion. On the other hand, the heave offering was heaved up and down vertically by the priest before God, just like wheat being threshed. These two motions, one horizontal and the other vertical, signify the cross of Christ. He is the perfect offering before God.

There is another very important offering that seemed to be cloaked in mystery. It is the Red Heifer (in Hebrew, Parah Adumah) offering. It is found in *Numbers 19:1-10, And the Lord spake unto Moses and unto Aaron, saying, This is the ordinance of the law which the Lord hath commanded, saying, Speak unto the children of Israel, that they bring thee a red heifer without spot, wherein is no blemish, and upon which never came yoke: And ye shall give her unto Eleazar the priest, that he may bring her forth without the camp, and one shall slay her before his face: And Eleazar the priest shall take of her blood with his finger, and sprinkle of her blood directly before the tabernacle of the congregation seven times: And one shall burn the heifer in his sight; her skin, and her flesh, and her blood, with her dung, shall he burn: And the priest shall take cedar wood, and hyssop, and scarlet, and cast it into the midst of the burning of the heifer.*

Then the priest shall wash his clothes, and he shall bathe his flesh in water, and afterward he shall come into the camp, and the priest shall be unclean until the even. And he that burneth her shall wash his clothes in water, and bathe his flesh in water, and shall be unclean until the even. And a man that is clean shall gather up the ashes of the heifer, and lay them up without the camp in a clean place, and it shall be kept for the congregation of the children of Israel for a water of separation: it is a purification for sin. And he that gathereth the ashes of the heifer shall wash his clothes, and be unclean until the even: and it shall be unto the children of Israel, and unto the stranger that sojourneth among them, for a statute forever.

The cow had to be completely red. Even a few strands of white or black hair on the cow would disqualify it as being without spot or blemish. After the sacrifice, the whole cow would be burnt. Not a single part of the cow was kept. Even the blood was burnt in the fire. This whole ritual was performed outside the tabernacle. The blood, before burning, was not put on the altar. The priest who performed this ritual would become unclean but the ashes of the burnt heifer, mixed with water, would become the water of separation for the Israelites. This water with the ashes of the burnt heifer in it would serve as water for purification of sin. Anyone sprinkled by this water would become clean.

It is actually quite easy for a New Covenant believer to see Jesus in this red cow offering. As the cow was unique, Jesus was unique. He was spotless as He fulfilled the whole law. He was sacrificed and crucified outside the city walls and His blood more than paid our debt for sin. He is the water of separation that separates us from sin and death. He is the living water that gives life to us. All of the offerings established by the law were fulfilled fully and completely by Jesus Christ. As such, when the 'real' appeared the 'shadows' disappeared.

We read in *Hebrews 10:1-14, For the law having a shadow of good things to come, and not the very image of the things, can never with those sacrifices which they offered year by year continually make the comers thereunto perfect. For then would they not have ceased to be offered? because that the worshippers once purged should have had no more conscience of sins. But in those sacrifices there is a remembrance again made of sins every year. For it is not possible that the blood of bulls and of goats should take away sins.*

Wherefore when he cometh into the world, he saith, Sacrifice and offering thou wouldest not, but a body hast thou prepared me: In burnt offerings and sacrifices for sin thou hast had no pleasure. Then said I, Lo, I come (in the volume of the book it is written of me,) to do thy will, O God. Above when he said, Sacrifice and offering and burnt offerings and offering for sin thou wouldest not, neither hadst pleasure therein; which are offered by the law; Then said he, Lo, I come to do thy will, O God. He taketh away the first, that he may establish the second. By the which will we are sanctified through the offering of the body of Jesus Christ once for all.

And every priest standeth daily ministering and offering oftentimes the same sacrifices, which can never take away sins: But this man, after he had offered one sacrifice for sins for ever, sat down on the right hand of God; From henceforth expecting till

his enemies be made his footstool. For by one offering he hath
perfected for ever them that are sanctified.

When Jesus became our High Priest, the Levitical high
priest was removed. Today, we are under a new priesthood after
the order of Melchisedec. It replaces the old Levitical priesthood of
Aaron. When Jesus became the greater and perfect tabernacle, the
old tabernacle was displaced. When Jesus became our perfect
Offering, all the offerings of meats and drinks became obsolete. By
His one sacrifice for all time, the yearly animal sacrifices became
extinct. By His complete sacrifice, every priest can now sit down
at the throne of His Grace by His side. There was no longer any
need to stand and continue the daily ministries of offerings and the
annual reminder of sins. **When Jesus made us perfect by His**
sacrifice, we can lay down our sacrifices of animals and gifts
forevermore. We can enter into the presence of God and not
have to stand at a distance outside.

The sacrifice of animals could never make us perfect as
pertaining to the conscience. The conscience is the knowledge of
good and evil. With our conscience and the resulting ability to
discern right from wrong, we fall into the tendency to do right to
appease God by our own strength. We try to save ourselves by our
own knowledge on how to 'do right'. This false confidence in our
ability to save ourselves because we know right from wrong is
extremely dangerous, as we cannot do right all the time. Therefore,
when we do wrong, we feel condemned and we hide from God,
just like Adam and Eve. We feel we have lost our salvation and
consequently, we work even harder to do more 'rights' to right our
'wrongs'. All these works are known as dead works.

Hebrews 9:6-15 states, *Now when these things were thus*
ordained, the priests went always into the first tabernacle,
accomplishing the service of God. But into the second went the
high priest alone once every year, not without blood, which he
offered for himself, and for the errors of the people: The Holy
Ghost this signifying, that the way into the holiest of all was not yet
made manifest, while as the first tabernacle was yet standing:
Which was a figure for the time then present, in which were offered
both gifts and sacrifices, that could not make him that did the

service perfect, as pertaining to the conscience; Which stood only in meats and drinks, and divers washings, and carnal ordinances, imposed on them until the time of reformation.

But Christ being come an high priest of good things to come, by a greater and more perfect tabernacle, not made with hands, that is to say, not of this building; Neither by the blood of goats and calves, but by his own blood he entered in once into the holy place, having obtained eternal redemption for us. For if the blood of bulls and of goats, and the ashes of an heifer sprinkling the unclean, sanctifieth to the purifying of the flesh: How much more shall the blood of Christ, who through the eternal Spirit offered himself without spot to God, purge your conscience from dead works to serve the living God? And for this cause he is the mediator of the new testament, that by means of death, for the redemption of the transgressions that were under the first testament, they which are called might receive the promise of eternal inheritance.

However, the blood of Christ purges our conscience clean. There is now no need to do right to cover up wrongs. By His blood all our sins were blotted out, not just covered. All our works came to nought. It is by His sacrifice alone that we have eternal redemption and eternal inheritance. We are sanctified through the offering of Jesus Christ once for all time. When the new covenant of Jesus came, the old covenant of works and law was done away with. He took away the first to establish the second. The second is the new covenant of Grace. The new covenant rested on Jesus' completed work and only on His completed work. We are set free from depending on our works. For by one offering He has perfected us that are sanctified. *Hebrews 5:9-10* states, *And being made perfect, he became the author of eternal salvation unto all them that obey him; Called of God an high priest after the order of Melchisedec.* Our salvation is not after the old Levitical priesthood but after the new priesthood of Melchisedec. Also, in *1 John 5:11, And this is the record, that God hath given to us eternal life, and this life is in his Son.* Jesus, our new High Priest, gives us eternal salvation and life. Jesus is our life and He is more than sufficient for us.

❧ 17 ❧

JESUS AND ADAM

In *Romans 5:12-14,* we read, *Wherefore, as by one man sin entered into the world, and death by sin; and so death passed upon all men, for that all have sinned: (For until the law sin was in the world: but sin is not imputed when there is no law. Nevertheless death reigned from Adam to Moses, even over them that had not sinned after the similitude of Adam's transgression, who is the figure of him that was to come.* Due to Adam's disobedience in the garden of Eden, sin entered into the world and spiritual death followed. This spiritual death was passed onto all men after Adam. As Adam was the first man created, all of us who came after were similarly condemned. Through the disobedient act of one man, spiritual death came to all men.

As we saw in the preceding chapter, the sacrifices in the Old Testament were never sufficient to cleanse the people from their sins and trespasses. Every sacrifice offered was consumed and then more was demanded. Their sins could be covered for a short period of time but because of their sinful or 'old man' nature, the animal sacrifices had to be performed over and over again. It never sufficed.

Then Grace came by Jesus Christ. *Romans 3:22-28* states that *Even the righteousness of God which is by faith of Jesus Christ unto all and upon all them that believe: for there is no difference: For all have sinned, and come short of the glory of God; Being justified freely by his grace through the redemption that is in Christ Jesus: Whom God hath set forth to be a*

*propitiation through faith in his blood, to declare his righteousness
for the remission of sins that are past, through the forbearance of
God; To declare, I say, at this time his righteousness: that he
might be just, and the justifier of him which believeth in Jesus.
Where is boasting then? It is excluded. By what law? of works?
Nay: but by the law of faith. Therefore we conclude that a man is
justified by faith without the deeds of the law.*

Because of His obedience, sin was conquered fully and
spiritual life ensued. By His sacrifice on the cross, this spiritual life
became freely available to all men. However, not all men wanted
this spiritual life freely given by Jesus. Many people chose to not
have faith in Jesus, choosing instead to have faith in other gods and
in self-works. Therefore, while life and righteousness in Jesus is
freely available to all, not all men wanted this free gift. But for
those who chose by faith to believe in Jesus, they are justified
freely by His Grace. All men who believe in Jesus by faith are
justified as fully righteous without any deeds of the law or self-
works.

However, just as the trespass offering mentioned in the last
chapter, the restitution amounted to more than the initial trespass.
**Jesus' finished work on the cross is much greater than Adam's
sin.**

We see this in *Romans 5:15-21, But not as the offence, so
also is the free gift. For if through the offence of one many be
dead, much more the grace of God, and the gift by grace, which is
by one man, Jesus Christ, hath abounded unto many. And not as it
was by one that sinned, so is the gift: for the judgment was by one
to condemnation, but the free gift is of many offences unto
justification. For if by one man's offence death reigned by one;
much more they which receive abundance of grace and of the gift
of righteousness shall reign in life by one, Jesus Christ. Therefore
as by the offence of one judgment came upon all men to
condemnation; even so by the righteousness of one the free gift
came upon all men unto justification of life. For as by one man's
disobedience many were made sinners, so by the obedience of one
shall many be made righteous. Moreover the law entered, that the
offence might abound. But where sin abounded, grace did much*

more abound: That as sin hath reigned unto death, even so might
grace reign through righteousness unto eternal life by Jesus Christ
our Lord.

In Adam, because of one sin, all men became spiritually
dead. In Jesus, even for a multitude of sins, all men who have faith
in Him became spiritually alive. In Adam, we become condemned
and death began to reign. In Jesus, we become justified and life
began to reign. From being slaves to sin, we become overcomers
of sin. From being punished due to the single offense, we now
receive an abundance of gifts even if we had offended greatly.
Although the law multiplied our sins, the Grace of Jesus more than
multiplied to take away our sins. Because of Jesus' completed
work, the new man in Jesus is not only greater but complete as
well. Adam fell but Jesus lifted us up much higher than the fall.

By God sending His own Son in the likeness of sinful flesh,
sin was condemned in the flesh. Sin now has no dominion over the
new man. In his spirit, man cannot sin and is completely free from
the law of sin and death. We are justified, sanctified, and made
fully and completely righteous by Jesus Christ. Adam's sin no
longer affects us because Jesus defeated that sin. No one can be
condemned because of what Adam did in the garden because there
is no condemnation for those who are in Jesus. In *Romans 8:1-4*,
we read that *There is therefore now no condemnation to them*
which are in Christ Jesus, who walk not after the flesh, but after
the Spirit. For the law of the Spirit of life in Christ Jesus hath
made me free from the law of sin and death. For what the law
could not do, in that it was weak through the flesh, God sending
his own Son in the likeness of sinful flesh, and for sin, condemned
sin in the flesh: That the righteousness of the law might be fulfilled
in us, who walk not after the flesh, but after the Spirit.

We are no longer 'in Adam' but in Christ. No one can die
spiritually because spiritual life in Jesus has come. We die
spiritually only when we reject the free gift that we have in Jesus.

When the law was given to Moses, sin multiplied. But the
law was faulty and was replaced by Grace when Jesus came. We
read in *Hebrews 8:6-13, But now hath he obtained a more*
excellent ministry, by how much also he is the mediator of a better

covenant, which was established upon better promises. For if that first covenant had been faultless, then should no place have been sought for the second. For finding fault with them, he saith, Behold, the days come, saith the Lord, when I will make a new covenant with the house of Israel and with the house of Judah: Not according to the covenant that I made with their fathers in the day when I took them by the hand to lead them out of the land of Egypt; because they continued not in my covenant, and I regarded them not, saith the Lord. For this is the covenant that I will make with the house of Israel after those days, saith the Lord; I will put my laws into their mind, and write them in their hearts: and I will be to them a God, and they shall be to me a people: And they shall not teach every man his neighbour, and every man his brother, saying, Know the Lord: for all shall know me, from the least to the greatest. For I will be merciful to their unrighteousness, and their sins and their iniquities will I remember no more. In that he saith, A new covenant, he hath made the first old. Now that which decayeth and waxeth old is ready to vanish away.

The law was never meant as the final revelation or provision for mankind. It always pointed to our need for a savior, Jesus. Jesus' ministry was more excellent than the law because it is eternal and not temporal. The new covenant was better than the old covenant for under the new covenant of grace, we have assurance of salvation by Jesus. Under the law, there were no assurances but only provisions and conditions. The promises under the new covenant were better and surer than the old covenant promises. Blessings under the law required obedience but punishments and death followed disobedience. Because of what Jesus did, all the promises are now 'yes' and not dependent upon our works and performance. We say 'amen' to His yes. The promises are now absolute and not conditional. The law required righteousness but did not provide for it. Under the new covenant, Jesus' righteousness was imputed to us.

The power of Jesus living in us enables and empowers us to have dominion over sin, live righteously and to abound in good works. In *1 Corinthians 3:11-15*, we read, *For other foundation can no man lay than that is laid, which is Jesus Christ. Now if any man build upon this foundation gold, silver, precious stones, wood, hay, stubble; Every man's work shall be made manifest: for the day shall declare it, because it shall be revealed by fire; and the fire shall try every man's work of what sort it is. If any man's work abide which he hath built thereupon, he shall receive a reward. If any man's work shall be burned, he shall suffer loss: but he himself shall be saved; yet so as by fire.* And when we overcome sin and live righteously without effort and bear good fruits of gold, silver, and precious stones, we are further rewarded at the judgment seat of Christ. *2 Corinthians 5:9-10* states that *Wherefore we labour, that, whether present or absent, we may be accepted of him. For we must all appear before the judgment seat of Christ; that every one may receive the things done in his body, according to that he hath done, whether it be good or bad.* He not only rewards us abundantly in this life but He rewards us in the afterlife as well. This can also be seen in *Revelation 22:12, And, behold, I come quickly; and my reward is with me, to give every man according as his work shall be.*

John 10:10 states that *The thief cometh not, but for to steal, and to kill, and to destroy: I am come that they might have life, and that they might have it more abundantly.* **Not only does Jesus give us life but He gives us life more abundantly. This abundant life in Jesus is distinctly different from our old life in Adam. When we are 'in Adam', curses, lack, poverty, sickness, diseases, and death affected our lives. But being 'in Jesus' frees us from the cursed blood line of Adam. We become separated from the fallen Adam's family. We become free from the maleficent life and can now enjoy an abundant life instead.**

The new covenant promises are internalized in our new spirit. The new bottles store the new wine internally. We see this in *Luke 5:37-38, And no man putteth new wine into old bottles; else the new wine will burst the bottles, and be spilled, and the bottles shall perish. But new wine must be put into new bottles; and both are preserved.* The new man stores the knowledge and wisdom of Jesus in him. *Colossians 3:9-10* states, *Lie not one to another, seeing that ye have put off the old man with his deeds; And have put on the new man, which is renewed in knowledge after the image of him that created him.* The old man is dead. In *Ephesians 4:24, And that ye put on the new man, which after God is created in righteousness and true holiness.* The new man is created by God in righteousness and true holiness. His spirit is unable to sin and his mind and flesh cannot be dominated by sin. The new man is far superior to the dead old man as the new man is spiritual and not carnal. Everything under the new covenant is better because of Jesus. Best yet, this new covenant, while it is promised to everyone who believes, is also personalized and individualized for you and me. You and I have a Personal Savior who knows us by name.

ᕤ 18 ᕦ

JESUS AND THE FLAMING SWORD

We know that the sword in the bible represents the word of God. However, there is also a physical sword that seems to be woven throughout the bible, from Genesis to Revelation.

We read in *Genesis 2:15-17, And the Lord God took the man, and put him into the garden of Eden to dress it and to keep it. And the Lord God commanded the man, saying, Of every tree of the garden thou mayest freely eat:But of the tree of the knowledge of good and evil, thou shalt not eat of it: for in the day that thou eatest thereof thou shalt surely die.* While God commanded Adam to not eat from the tree of the knowledge of good and evil, Eve was deceived by the devil, resulting in Adam disobeying a direct command from God. The consequence was spiritual and physical death.

However, physical death could be avoided if either or both of them ate from the tree of life. They would then have lived physically forever but at the same time be spiritually dead forever because of sin. To prevent this from happening, God drove them out of the garden. There was no law, so the sin of breaking the direct commandment from God was not imputed on them. They were accountable for their actions but as there was no law, there was no punishment for their sin. The sole reason for driving them out of the garden was to preclude them eating from the tree of life and to live forever physically. *Genesis 3:22-24* states that *And the*

Lord God said, Behold, the man is become as one of us, to know
good and evil: and now, lest he put forth his hand, and take also of
the tree of life, and eat, and live for ever: Therefore the Lord God
sent him forth from the garden of Eden, to till the ground from
whence he was taken. So he drove out the man; and he placed at
the east of the garden of Eden Cherubims, and a flaming sword
which turned every way, to keep the way of the tree of life.

To restraint them from going back into the garden, God
stationed cherubims and a physical flaming sword that turned
every way at the entrance gate to the garden, which faced east. The
flaming sword (the sword, in Hebrew, hahereb, can also mean any
sharp weapon or tool) effectively prevented anyone from ever
eating from the tree of life.

After the law was given, the sword became a sword of
judgment. It would come down against all nations. It would
destroy and slaughter nations because of the curse of the law. The
sword would run with blood from the sacrifices of nations. There
would be no hiding from its judgment. The sword would also come
against Israel. The sword would be drawn out of its sheath and it
would not be re-sheathed. It would go out against all flesh and sin
and cut asunder. It would be sharpened and it would be polished. It
would glitter like lightning as it turns every way bringing a great
slaughter. Because of the curse, no one who followed the law
would be spared. The flaming sword, while making sure that none
would eat from the tree of life, continued to kill all those under the
law.

We see this destruction in the following scriptures. *Isaiah*
34:1-8, Come near, ye nations, to hear; and hearken, ye people: let
the earth hear, and all that is therein; the world, and all things that
come forth of it. For the indignation of the Lord is upon all
nations, and his fury upon all their armies: he hath utterly
destroyed them, he hath delivered them to the slaughter. Their
slain also shall be cast out, and their stink shall come up out of
their carcases, and the mountains shall be melted with their blood.
And all the host of heaven shall be dissolved, and the heavens shall
be rolled together as a scroll: and all their host shall fall down, as
the leaf falleth off from the vine, and as a falling fig from the fig

*tree. For my sword shall be bathed in heaven: behold, it shall
come down upon Idumea, and upon the people of my curse, to
judgment. The sword of the Lord is filled with blood, it is made fat
with fatness, and with the blood of lambs and goats, with the fat of
the kidneys of rams: for the Lord hath a sacrifice in Bozrah, and a
great slaughter in the land of Idumea. And the unicorns shall
come down with them, and the bullocks with the bulls; and their
land shall be soaked with blood, and their dust made fat with
fatness. For it is the day of the Lord's vengeance, and the year of
recompences for the controversy of Zion.
Ezekiel 21:1-5, 8-15, And the word of the Lord came unto me,
saying, Son of man, set thy face toward Jerusalem, and drop thy
word toward the holy places, and prophesy against the land of
Israel, And say to the land of Israel, Thus saith the Lord; Behold, I
am against thee, and will draw forth my sword out of his sheath,
and will cut off from thee the righteous and the wicked. Seeing then
that I will cut off from thee the righteous and the wicked, therefore
shall my sword go forth out of his sheath against all flesh from the
south to the north: That all flesh may know that I the Lord have
drawn forth my sword out of his sheath: it shall not return any
more.*

*Again the word of the Lord came unto me, saying, Son of
man, prophesy, and say, Thus saith the Lord; Say, A sword, a
sword is sharpened, and also furbished: It is sharpened to make a
sore slaughter; it is furbished that it may glitter: should we then
make mirth? it contemneth the rod of my son, as every tree.*

*And he hath give it to be furbished, that it may be handled:
this sword is sharpened, and it is furbished, to give it into the hand
of the slayer. Cry and howl, son of man: for it shall be upon my
people, it shall be upon all the princes of Israel: terrors by reason
of the sword shall be upon my people: smite therefore upon thy
thigh. Because it is a trial, and what if the sword contemn even the
rod? it shall be no more, saith the Lord God. Thou therefore, son
of man, prophesy, and smite thine hands together, and let the
sword be doubled the third time, the sword of the slain: it is the
sword of the great men that are slain, which entereth into their
privy chambers. I have set the point of the sword against all their*

gates, *that their heart may faint, and their ruins be multiplied: ah!*
it is made bright, it is wrapped up for the slaughter.

Then one day, the flaming sword 'contemneth the rod of
my son'. The flaming sword in its despicable role of keeping
people away from the tree of life would strike the rod of My Son!
The King's Son would be struck by the flaming, turning sword.
Jesus would be struck by that sword. *Isaiah 53:4-5*, states, *Surely*
he hath borne our griefs, and carried our sorrows: yet we did
esteem him stricken, smitten of God, and afflicted. But he was
wounded for our transgressions, he was bruised for our iniquities:
the chastisement of our peace was upon him; and with his stripes
we are healed.

He would be stricken, smitten, and afflicted. We read
further in *John 19:34-37, But one of the soldiers with a spear*
pierced his side, and forthwith came there out blood and water.
And he that saw it bare record, and his record is true: and he
knoweth that he saith true, that ye might believe. For these things
were done, that the scripture should be fulfilled, A bone of him
shall not be broken. And again another scripture saith, They shall
look on him whom they pierced. And again in *Psalm 22:16, For*
dogs have compassed me: the assembly of the wicked have
inclosed me: they pierced my hands and my feet. His hands, his
feet, and his side would be pierced and cut. He would be pierced
for our transgressions. In piercing Jesus, the use of the sword was
overturned. In *Ezekiel 21:27*, we read, *I will overturn, overturn,*
overturn, it: and it shall be no more, until he come whose right it
is; and I will give it him. The sword's purpose of keeping people
away would be no more. It was given over to Jesus and it would be
transformed. Jesus had the right to change the sword that struck
Him.

The sword is now no longer the sword of judgment. Jesus,
by taking the sword's punishment beat it, changed it, and
transformed it into plowshares, pruning hooks, and sickles. We see
this in *Revelation 14:14-16, And I looked, and behold a white*
cloud, and upon the cloud one sat like unto the Son of man, having
on his head a golden crown, and in his hand a sharp sickle. And
another angel came out of the temple, crying with a loud voice to

him that sat on the cloud, Thrust in thy sickle, and reap: for the time is come for thee to reap; for the harvest of the earth is ripe. And he that sat on the cloud thrust in his sickle on the earth; and the earth was reaped. And again in *Isaiah 2:4, And he shall judge among the nations, and shall rebuke many people: and they shall beat their swords into plowshares, and their spears into pruninghooks: nation shall not lift up sword against nation, neither shall they learn war any more.*

What kept people away had been transformed into something that plants, grows, and reaps. **In Jesus' hands, the sword is now an implement of harvest as He gathers and draws all men to Him. The sword that kept all away from the old tree of life has been transformed by Jesus into a sickle, which gathers all into the new Tree of Life, Jesus Himself!**

The same eastern gate where the flaming sword kept all at bay is now the entrance where Jesus would come in. We read this in *Ezekiel 43:1-2, Afterward he brought me to the gate, even the gate that looketh toward the east: And, behold, the glory of the God of Israel came from the way of the east: and his voice was like a noise of many waters: and the earth shined with his glory* and in *Matthew 24:27, For as the lightning cometh out of the east, and shineth even unto the west; so shall also the coming of the Son of man be.*

And where Jesus is, there is life and healing. And He is going to bring us in, through the gate and then through the door, as well. There would not only be eternal healing but eternal life. There is no sickness and death in Jesus. A beautiful picture of this is described in *Ezekiel 47:1-10, Afterward he brought me again unto the door of the house; and, behold, waters issued out from under the threshold of the house eastward: for the forefront of the house stood toward the east, and the waters came down from under from the right side of the house, at the south side of the altar. Then brought he me out of the way of the gate northward, and led me about the way without unto the utter gate by the way that looketh eastward; and, behold, there ran out waters on the right side.*

And when the man that had the line in his hand went forth eastward, he measured a thousand cubits, and he brought me through the waters; the waters were to the ankles. Again he measured a thousand, and brought me through the waters; the waters were to the knees. Again he measured a thousand, and brought me through; the waters were to the loins. Afterward he measured a thousand; and it was a river that I could not pass over: for the waters were risen, waters to swim in, a river that could not be passed over.

And he said unto me, Son of man, hast thou seen this? Then he brought me, and caused me to return to the brink of the river. Now when I had returned, behold, at the bank of the river were very many trees on the one side and on the other. Then said he unto me, These waters issue out toward the east country, and go down into the desert, and go into the sea: which being brought forth into the sea, the waters shall be healed. And it shall come to pass, that every thing that liveth, which moveth, whithersoever the rivers shall come, shall live: and there shall be a very great multitude of fish, because these waters shall come thither: for they shall be healed; and every thing shall live whither the river cometh. And it shall come to pass, that the fishers shall stand upon it from En-gedi even unto En-eglaim; they shall be a place to spread forth nets; their fish shall be according to their kinds, as the fish of the great sea, exceeding many.

This healing, cleansing, life giving water of Jesus would spread out, starting from the east. This water would first cover our ankles, and then reach our knees, and then our loins, to ultimately become a river that could not be passed over. It had become a sea. Nets would be spread out in this great sea. Multitudes of people as numerous as fishes would be brought in. We, who are in Christ, would be brought in. A great harvest would be reaped. Eternal death has been replaced by eternal life because of Jesus. **In Jesus Christ, we can live forever!**

❧ 19 ❧

JESUS AND GENERATIONAL CURSES

The good thing about being a missionary is that you get to experience events that you would normally never encounter. The bad thing about being a missionary is that you also get to experience events that you would normally never encounter. For example, while in the missions' field, I have been cursed countless times by countless people while preaching the goodness of God. These innumerable curses upon my life would have produced incalculable damage had they any power over me. Of course, the curses were powerless but why do people believe and practice this in the first place?

In *Exodus 34:6-7*, we read, *And the Lord passed by before him, and proclaimed, The Lord, The Lord God, merciful and gracious, longsuffering, and abundant in goodness and truth, Keeping mercy for thousands, forgiving iniquity and transgression and sin, and that will by no means clear the guilty; visiting the iniquity of the fathers upon the children, and upon the children's children, unto the third and to the fourth generation.* God said this of Himself, 'The Lord God is merciful and gracious, longsuffering, and abundant in goodness and truth, keeping mercy for thousands, forgiving iniquity and transgression and sin'. God is always good. He wanted to show His goodness to His people so He made an unconditional covenant through Abraham to bless His people. However, His people rejected Him and opted for a conditional covenant through Moses. Because of this conditional covenant, the people came under the curse of the law. God will now not clear the guilty and will visit the iniquity of the fathers upon the children, upon the children's children, unto the third and fourth generation. Generational curses came because of the law of Moses.

The Israelites suffered greatly because of this curse. But they accepted the curse and even made a proverb out of it. We read this in *Ezekiel 18:1-2, The word of the Lord came unto me again, saying, What mean ye, that ye use this proverb concerning the land of Israel, saying, The fathers have eaten sour grapes, and the children's teeth are set on edge?* 'The fathers have eaten sour grapes and the children's teeth are set on edge' simply means that because the fathers' ate acidic grapes the children had cavities or rotten teeth. Jews blamed their parents for committing sins. Because of their parents sins they were cursed, and their children and their children's children would be similarly cursed.

On the missions' field, you can be cursed for setting people free from legalism. You can be cursed if someone you prayed for does not become instantaneously healed. You can be cursed for not giving money to complete strangers. You can be cursed for the color of your skin. You can be cursed for the adverse weather. You can be cursed for the bad harvest. You can be cursed if the cow does not produce milk or if the hen that had been mauled by the dog dies. You can be cursed for the heavy traffic in the city. But hands down you will receive the most curses for preaching Jesus Christ.

Of course, in exchange for money, you can have all the curses removed from your life and even, on demand, order new curses to be heaped upon the people who cursed you in the first place, what I call COD or curses on demand. These people who allegedly can put and take away curses from your life end up being very rich as curses are slung back and forth between people caught up in the curse-race; which originated from the law of Moses.

Then came the prophets from God prophesying a new covenant. We read this in *Ezekiel 18:3, 18-20, As I live, saith the Lord God, ye shall not have occasion any more to use this proverb in Israel. As for his father, because he cruelly oppressed, spoiled his brother by violence, and did that which is not good among his people, lo, even he shall die in his iniquity. Yet say ye, Why? doth not the son bear the iniquity of the father? When the son hath done that which is lawful and right, and hath kept all my statutes, and hath done them, he shall surely live. The soul that sinneth, it shall die. The son shall not bear the iniquity of the father, neither shall the father bear the iniquity of the son: the righteousness of the righteous shall be upon him, and the wickedness of the wicked shall be upon him.* This old proverb would be taken away. The son will no longer bear the iniquities and sins of the father; neither shall the father bear the iniquities and sins of the son. A man shall die in his/her own iniquity and it will not be passed down from generation to generation. Every man who eats sour grapes would have his own teeth spoilt.

In *Jeremiah 31:29-34,* we read, *In those days they shall say no more, The fathers have eaten a sour grape, and the children's teeth are set on edge. But every one shall die for his own iniquity: every man that eateth the sour grape, his teeth shall be set on edge. Behold, the days come, saith the Lord, that I will make a new covenant with the house of Israel, and with the house of Judah:*

Not according to the covenant that I made with their fathers in the day that I took them by the hand to bring them out of the land of Egypt; which my covenant they brake, although I was an husband unto them, saith the Lord: But this shall be the covenant that I will make with the house of Israel; After those days, saith the Lord, I will put my law in their inward parts, and write it in their hearts; and will be their God, and they shall be my people. And they shall teach no more every man his neighbour, and every man his brother, saying, Know the Lord: for they shall all know me, from the least of them unto the greatest of them, saith the Lord; for I will forgive their iniquity, and I will remember their sin no more. In the new covenant, everyone is responsible for either accepting or rejecting Jesus Christ. Those who accept Him by faith would have their iniquities forgiven and their sins would be remembered no more.

As believers, how did Jesus remove the curse from us? Under Mosaic law, a man would be hung on a tree if he committed a sin worthy of death. *Deuteronomy 21:22-23* clearly states, *And if a man have committed a sin worthy of death, and he be to be put to death, and thou hang him on a tree: His body shall not remain all night upon the tree, but thou shalt in any wise bury him that day; (for he that is hanged is accursed of God;) that thy land be not defiled, which the Lord thy God giveth thee for an inheritance.* The man so hung would be a curse. Jesus hung on the cross for us taking with Him the curse that was meant for us.

We see many instances in the bible where the people wanted to catch hold of Jesus and kill Him. However, it was never accomplished. Below are some of these instances.

John 10:31-33, 39, Then the Jews took up stones again to stone him. Jesus answered them, Many good works have I shewed you from my Father; for which of those works do ye stone me? The Jews answered him, saying, For a good work we stone thee not; but for blasphemy; and because that thou, being a man, makest thyself God. Therefore they sought again to take him: but he escaped out of their hand,

Matthew 27:33-34, And when they were come unto a place called Golgotha, that is to say, a place of a skull, They gave him vinegar to drink mingled with gall: and when he had tasted thereof, he would not drink.

Psalm 69:21, They gave me also gall for my meat; and in my thirst they gave me vinegar to drink.

John 19:28-30, After this, Jesus knowing that all things were now accomplished, that the scripture might be fulfilled, saith, I thirst. Now there was set a vessel full of vinegar: and they filled a spunge with vinegar, and put it upon hyssop, and put it to his mouth. When Jesus therefore had received the vinegar, he said, It is finished: and he bowed his head, and gave up the ghost.

During His ministry, the Jews wanted to stone Him to death but He always escaped. When He arrived at Golgotha, and before He was crucified, He was given vinegar mingled with gall to drink. The word gall in Greek 'chole' literally means poison that is bitter in taste. He tasted the mixture, realized what it was, and would not drink it. Later as He hung on the cross, He accepted the vinegar drink that had no gall. Jesus could not be stoned or poisoned, as He

had to become a curse for us. We read this in *Galatians 3:13-14,
Christ hath redeemed us from the curse of the law, being made a
curse for us: for it is written, Cursed is every one that hangeth on a
tree: That the blessing of Abraham might come on the Gentiles
through Jesus Christ; that we might receive the promise of the
Spirit through faith.*

He had to fulfill scripture so He died hanging on the cross.
With His sacrifice for us, the curse of the law was lifted and the
unconditional Abrahamic covenant would now come on the
gentiles. **We cannot be cursed because Jesus took the curse
upon Himself for us. It is too late if someone wants to curse us.
It is too late because Jesus already took away the curse. Too
late! Too late! Too late! Jesus did it already!**

Because of Jesus, we only get to enjoy all His blessings.
**The new covenant of Jesus can be viewed as an extension as
well as an amplification of the Abrahamic Covenant.** He did it
for me and He did it for you. That is why I am blessed and can
never be cursed. That is why you are blessed and can never be
cursed.

Jesus is greater than any Old Testament curse. We see
another example of this in the city of Jericho. Jericho was a cursed
city in the days of Joshua. We see in *Joshua 6:26, And Joshua
adjured them at that time, saying, Cursed be the man before the
Lord, that riseth up and buildeth this city Jericho: he shall lay the
foundation thereof in his firstborn, and in his youngest son shall he
set up the gates of it.* It was not to be rebuilt but it was. Therefore,
it stayed cursed until the cure came.

The cure was provided by Elisha. In *2 Kings 2:18-22, And
when they came again to him, (for he tarried at Jericho,) he said
unto them, Did I not say unto you, Go not? And the men of the city
said unto Elisha, Behold, I pray thee, the situation of this city is
pleasant, as my lord seeth: but the water is naught, and the ground
barren. And he said, Bring me a new cruse, and put salt therein.
And they brought it to him. And he went forth unto the spring of
the waters, and cast the salt in there, and said, Thus saith the Lord,
I have healed these waters; there shall not be from thence any*

more death or barren land. So the waters were healed unto this day, according to the saying of Elisha which he spake.

Elisha the prophet had been staying in Jericho when the inhabitants of the city approached him. Although the rebuilt city itself had a pleasant look, it was dying as the water was still cursed making the ground barren. No amount of self-works by the inhabitants could heal the water. They could plan, construct, repair, plant, and seed but to no avail. The curse remained.

The cure was simple. Elisha asked specifically for a new cruse with salt within. An old cruse would not do. It had to be new. The new vessel was filled with salt, then taken to the spring and cast in. Immediately the water was healed and the curse lifted. Grace is always greater than the curse of the law. The new covenant of Grace is the new cruse. We are the salt inside Grace. *Matthew 5:13* states that *Ye are the salt of the earth.* Jesus or Grace envelops us completely. Whoever is wrapped up in the righteousness of Christ is immune to curses. Not only that but whatever cursed object that person covered by Grace touched, that object would also be healed. The name of Jesus is mightier than any curse. At His name every curse, every disease, every hurt, every problem, and every demon must bow down and confess that He is Lord. In Jesus' name, there would be no more barrenness nor death caused by curses. We are completely healed by Jesus.

ॐ 20 ॐ

JESUS AND THE SABBATH

Before the Mosaic Law was given, the Israelites did have knowledge of the Sabbath. We see this in the following scriptures. *Exodus 16:23-28, And he said unto them, This is that which the Lord hath said, Tomorrow is the rest of the holy sabbath unto the Lord: bake that which ye will bake to day, and seethe that ye will seethe; and that which remaineth over lay up for you to be kept until the morning. And they laid it up till the morning, as Moses bade: and it did not stink, neither was there any worm therein. And Moses said, Eat that to day; for to day is a sabbath unto the Lord: to day ye shall not find it in the field. Six days ye shall gather it; but on the seventh day, which is the sabbath, in it there shall be none. And it came to pass, that there went out some of the people on the seventh day for to gather, and they found none. And the Lord said unto Moses, How long refuse ye to keep my commandments and my laws?*
Exodus 20:8-11, Remember the sabbath day, to keep it holy. Six days shalt thou labour, and do all thy work: But the seventh day is the sabbath of the Lord thy God: in it thou shalt not do any work, thou, nor thy son, nor thy daughter, thy manservant, nor thy maidservant, nor thy cattle, nor thy stranger that is within thy gates: For in six days the Lord made heaven and earth, the sea, and all that in them is, and rested the seventh day: wherefore the Lord blessed the sabbath day, and hallowed it.

*Exodus 31:15-17, Six days may work be done; but in the seventh is
the sabbath of rest, holy to the Lord: whosoever doeth any work in
the sabbath day, he shall surely be put to death. Wherefore the
children of Israel shall keep the sabbath, to observe the sabbath
throughout their generations, for a perpetual covenant. It is a sign
between me and the children of Israel for ever: for in six days the
Lord made heaven and earth, and on the seventh day he rested,
and was refreshed.*

*Deuteronomy 5:15, And remember that thou wast a servant in the
land of Egypt, and that the Lord thy God brought thee out thence
through a mighty hand and by a stretched out arm: therefore the
Lord thy God commanded thee to keep the sabbath day*

As God rested on the seventh day of creation, the people
were commanded to also not work on the seventh day. This
included their children, their servants, and all strangers within their
charge. To be disobedient to God was sin but because the law was
not yet given, the sin could not be imputed upon the people. They
would not be punished if they broke the Sabbath. For example, if
an Israelite went out on the Sabbath to look for manna, which he
was not supposed to do, he would not be put to death even if he
were clearly breaking a commandment. With the arrival of the law,
the Sabbath became part of the Ten Commandments. Now sin was
imputed. If anyone were to work on the Sabbath day, they would
be put to death. As mentioned in a previous chapter, a man found
gathering sticks to, presumably, light a fire for a meal was stoned
to death.

As time went on, the Pharisees enumerated 39 categories of
labor that were forbidden based on the types of work that were
related to the construction of the tabernacle, which ceased on the
Sabbath. I have listed the categories in Appendix B at the end of
the book. It is interesting to note that mundane activities such as
turning on the lights or any other electrical appliance in the house,
tearing of toilet paper, striking a match or turning on a stove,
picking the bones out of a fish, tearing through the writing on a
package of food, and carrying money and house keys are all
forbidden on the Sabbath.

Because the whole Sabbath law involves the work of the flesh, Jesus, who followed the Sabbath perfectly, did not put much importance on it. For He is Lord even of the Sabbath. His disciples plucked the corn from a cornfield, cooked and ate it on the Sabbath. Immediately after He was rebuked by the Pharisees for His disciples' behavior, He healed the man with a withered hand! We read this in *Matthew 12:1-14, At that time Jesus went on the sabbath day through the corn; and his disciples were an hungred, and began to pluck the ears of corn, and to eat. But when the Pharisees saw it, they said unto him, Behold, thy disciples do that which is not lawful to do upon the sabbath day. But he said unto them, Have ye not read what David did, when he was an hungred, and they that were with him; How he entered into the house of God, and did eat the shewbread, which was not lawful for him to eat, neither for them which were with him, but only for the priests? Or have ye not read in the law, how that on the sabbath days the priests in the temple profane the sabbath, and are blameless? But I say unto you, That in this place is one greater than the temple. But if ye had known what this meaneth, I will have mercy, and not sacrifice, ye would not have condemned the guiltless. For the Son of man is Lord even of the sabbath day.*

And when he was departed thence, he went into their synagogue: And, behold, there was a man which had his hand withered. And they asked him, saying, Is it lawful to heal on the sabbath days? that they might accuse him. And he said unto them, What man shall there be among you, that shall have one sheep, and if it fall into a pit on the sabbath day, will he not lay hold on it, and lift it out? How much then is a man better than a sheep? Wherefore it is lawful to do well on the sabbath days. Then saith he to the man, Stretch forth thine hand. And he stretched it forth; and it was restored whole, like as the other. Then the Pharisees went out, and held a council against him, how they might destroy him.

In *Luke 13:10-19,* we read, *And he was teaching in one of the synagogues on the sabbath. And, behold, there was a woman which had a spirit of infirmity eighteen years, and was bowed together, and could in no wise lift up herself. And when Jesus saw her, he called her to him, and said unto her, Woman, thou art loosed from thine infirmity. And he laid his hands on her: and immediately she was made straight, and glorified God. And the ruler of the synagogue answered with indignation, because that Jesus had healed on the sabbath day, and said unto the people, There are six days in which men ought to work: in them therefore come and be healed, and not on the sabbath day. The Lord then answered him, and said, Thou hypocrite, doth not each one of you on the sabbath loose his ox or his ass from the stall, and lead him away to watering? And ought not this woman, being a daughter of Abraham, whom Satan hath bound, lo, these eighteen years, be loosed from this bond on the sabbath day? And when he had said these things, all his adversaries were ashamed: and all the people rejoiced for all the glorious things that were done by him. Then said he, Unto what is the kingdom of God like? and whereunto shall I resemble it? It is like a grain of mustard seed, which a man took, and cast into his garden; and it grew, and waxed a great tree; and the fowls of the air lodged in the branches of it.* Jesus taught the Jews on the Sabbath and then He healed and loosed a woman who had a spirit of infirmity for eighteen years on the same day. The Pharisees observed the Sabbath but not the woman. They only saw their self-righteous ways threatened and disrupted, while completely ignoring the sick and infirm around them.

To address the hypocritical self-righteous Pharisees, Jesus told a parable that seemed at first glance out of context. Many people have misinterpreted it to mean that the gospel, starting out small, has grown into maturity and now provided shelter for all. If this were correct, the Pharisees would be beside themselves with joy for they would be the great tree giving shelter and hope to many. But this parable of the mustard seed could only be understood in Jesus' context as He was addressing the Pharisees.

The kernel of mustard seed is our faith in Jesus. The field is the earth. The mustard seed will grow as we become more and more aware of what Jesus has done for us. The more we feed on Jesus, the more aware we are of our inheritance in Him. The mustard seed will grow into a big bush naturally without any striving. However, the mustard seed here has grown into a tree. A mustard seed cannot grow into a tree so something must have happened to it. What started out as faith in Jesus was corrupted by the law and changed to faith in works. What was to be simple faith in Jesus became a very big tree of religion with many branches and divisions, all trusting in self-righteousness and dead works. This big religious tree gives shelter to many fowls of the air and other birds of prey. The birds are satan and his demons. It also illustrates the religious Pharisees sitting as birds all lined up on the branches under the shadow of the law.

We first saw this tree in *Daniel 4:10-14, Thus were the visions of mine head in my bed; I saw, and behold a tree in the midst of the earth, and the height thereof was great. The tree grew, and was strong, and the height thereof reached unto heaven, and the sight thereof to the end of all the earth: The leaves thereof were fair, and the fruit thereof much, and in it was meat for all: the beasts of the field had shadow under it, and the fowls of the heaven dwelt in the boughs thereof, and all flesh was fed of it. I saw in the visions of my head upon my bed, and, behold, a watcher and an holy one came down from heaven;He cried aloud, and said thus, Hew down the tree, and cut off his branches, shake off his leaves, and scatter his fruit: let the beasts get away from under it, and the fowls from his branches.* Nebuchadnezzar's vast empire of spiritual darkness provided shelter and meat for all manners of bird, beasts, and men. However, it was an evil tree soon to be hewn down and its branches, leaves, and fruit destroyed.

As Christians, we do not need a tree to shelter and protect us. Our protection comes from Jesus. We do not live in the shadow or the darkness of the law but in the light of Jesus. His light does not reveal the law to us. His light reveals truth, righteousness, holiness, beauty, and perfection that is our blood bought right in Him.

In the Old Testament, in the earthly Jerusalem, the law dictated that no burdens be borne on the Sabbath. We read in *Jeremiah 17:19-27, Thus said the Lord unto me; Go and stand in the gate of the children of the people, whereby the kings of Judah come in, and by the which they go out, and in all the gates of Jerusalem; And say unto them, Hear ye the word of the Lord, ye kings of Judah, and all Judah, and all the inhabitants of Jerusalem,*

that enter in by these gates: Thus saith the Lord; Take heed to
yourselves, and bear no burden on the sabbath day, nor bring it in
by the gates of Jerusalem; Neither carry forth a burden out of your
houses on the sabbath day, neither do ye any work, but hallow ye
the sabbath day, as I commanded your fathers. But they obeyed
not, neither inclined their ear, but made their neck stiff, that they
might not hear, nor receive instruction. And it shall come to pass,
if ye diligently hearken unto me, saith the Lord, to bring in no
burden through the gates of this city on the sabbath day, but
hallow the sabbath day, to do no work therein;
    Then shall there enter into the gates of this city kings and
princes sitting upon the throne of David, riding in chariots and on
horses, they, and their princes, the men of Judah, and the
inhabitants of Jerusalem: and this city shall remain for ever. And
they shall come from the cities of Judah, and from the places about
Jerusalem, and from the land of Benjamin, and from the plain, and
from the mountains, and from the south, bringing burnt offerings,
and sacrifices, and meat offerings, and incense, and bringing
sacrifices of praise, unto the house of the Lord. But if ye will not
hearken unto me to hallow the sabbath day, and not to bear a
burden, even entering in at the gates of Jerusalem on the sabbath
day; then will I kindle a fire in the gates thereof, and it shall
devour the palaces of Jerusalem, and it shall not be quenched.

    If the Israelites obeyed the law, then they would enter
Jerusalem like fleshly kings and princes riding on chariots pulled
by horses. Their city would be blessed. But if they broke the law,
then a fire would be kindled under them and their buildings would
be burnt down with an unquenchable fire.

    However, one day in the New Jerusalem, the city of our
king Jesus, we would finally carry no burdens at all. The Sabbath
was fulfilled wholly in Jesus. We will enter the New Jerusalem like
real kings and princes. It will be our new home and we shall
remain there forever.

    There is another good example that provides a very clear
contrast between the Sabbath in the Old Testament and the Lord of
the Sabbath in the New Testament, Jesus Christ. In *John 5:1-16*,
we read, *After this there was a feast of the Jews; and Jesus went up*

to Jerusalem. Now there is at Jerusalem by the sheep market a pool, which is called in the Hebrew tongue Bethesda, having five porches. In these lay a great multitude of impotent folk, of blind, halt, withered, waiting for the moving of the water. For an angel went down at a certain season into the pool, and troubled the water: whosoever then first after the troubling of the water stepped in was made whole of whatsoever disease he had. And a certain man was there, which had an infirmity thirty and eight years. When Jesus saw him lie, and knew that he had been now a long time in that case, he saith unto him, Wilt thou be made whole?

The impotent man answered him, Sir, I have no man, when the water is troubled, to put me into the pool: but while I am coming, another steppeth down before me. Jesus saith unto him, Rise, take up thy bed, and walk. And immediately the man was made whole, and took up his bed, and walked: and on the same day was the sabbath.

The Jews therefore said unto him that was cured, It is the sabbath day: it is not lawful for thee to carry thy bed. He answered them, He that made me whole, the same said unto me, Take up thy bed, and walk. Then asked they him, What man is that which said unto thee, Take up thy bed, and walk? And he that was healed wist not who it was: for Jesus had conveyed himself away, a multitude being in that place. Afterward Jesus findeth him in the temple, and said unto him, Behold, thou art made whole: sin no more, lest a worse thing come unto thee. The man departed, and told the Jews that it was Jesus, which had made him whole. 16 And therefore did the Jews persecute Jesus, and sought to slay him, because he had done these things on the sabbath day.

The Lord of the Sabbath came on the Sabbath to the pool. Due to the veil of the law, not even a single sick person by the pool recognized that the Healer was there. They were stuck in their self-works mentality on who could get into the water first after the angel had troubled the pool water. Jesus saw a man there who had an infirmity for thirty-eight years. This man faced his Healer and all he could say was 'I have no man...' The man wanted to work for his healing, to deserve his healing, to merit by being the first man into the pool after the angel. Though the man did not know

Jesus, Jesus healed him completely. Unmerited healing was given
freely. Then the man took up his bed and walked. He had in his
arms what had him before. The Pharisees saw him carrying the bed
on the Sabbath, which was not lawful, and challenged him.
Although the bed was no longer a burden to the man, he did not
know it yet.

The man answered that he did not know who it was that
had healed him and that had asked him to carry the bed. He was
healed by Grace but not freed by Grace yet. Although healed, he
was still caught up by works. Jesus found him in the temple later
and told him to sin no more. The only sin he was guilty of was the
sin of not knowing Jesus. By not knowing Jesus, worse things
could come upon him than his previous infirmity. Therefore, he got
to know Jesus and was made whole! He went back to the Pharisees
who had previously questioned him and told them that it was Jesus
who not only had healed him but also now has made him whole.
He was now freed from the law to follow Grace.

Paul who knew Jesus apart from the law, constantly
preached on the Sabbath. In *Acts 13:14-16, But when they departed
from Perga, they came to Antioch in Pisidia, and went into the
synagogue on the sabbath day, and sat down. And after the
reading of the law and the prophets the rulers of the synagogue
sent unto them, saying, Ye men and brethren, if ye have any word
of exhortation for the people, say on. Then Paul stood up, and
beckoning with his hand said, Men of Israel, and ye that fear God,
give audience.* And again in *Acts 17:1-3, Now when they had
passed through Amphipolis and Apollonia, they came to
Thessalonica, where was a synagogue of the Jews: And Paul, as
his manner was, went in unto them, and three sabbath days
reasoned with them out of the scriptures, Opening and alleging,
that Christ must needs have suffered, and risen again from the
dead; and that this Jesus, whom I preach unto you, is Christ.*

As the Jews met on the Sabbath day in their synagogues,
Paul would work on the Sabbath to bring the gospel of Grace to
them. In some cities, almost the whole city, Jews and gentiles
alike, came out on the Sabbath to hear Paul share about Jesus. In
Acts 13:27-28, 42-44, we read, For they that dwell at Jerusalem,

*and their rulers, because they knew him not, nor yet the voices of
the prophets which are read every sabbath day, they have fulfilled
them in condemning him. And though they found no cause of death
in him, yet desired they Pilate that he should be slain. And when
the Jews were gone out of the synagogue, the Gentiles besought
that these words might be preached to them the next sabbath. Now
when the congregation was broken up, many of the Jews and
religious proselytes followed Paul and Barnabas: who, speaking to
them, persuaded them to continue in the grace of God. And the
next sabbath day came almost the whole city together to hear the
word of God.*

We, like the man who was healed, as well as Paul, should
desire to be whole and share what Jesus had done for us.
Wholeness can only be found apart from our own works. It comes
only by resting in the finished work of Jesus. We should never turn
to weak and beggarly elements like observing days. In *Galatians
4:9-11, But now, after that ye have known God, or rather are
known of God, how turn ye again to the weak and beggarly
elements, whereunto ye desire again to be in bondage? Ye observe
days, and months, and times, and years. I am afraid of you, lest I
have bestowed upon you labour in vain.* Paul mentioned that his
labor would be in vain if the Galatians did not understand this
simple point. Every day is alike as they were all made and given by
God. *Romans 14:5-6* clearly states that *One man esteemeth one
day above another: another esteemeth every day alike. Let every
man be fully persuaded in his own mind. He that regardeth the
day, regardeth it unto the Lord; and he that regardeth not the day,
to the Lord he doth not regard it.* And in *Colossians 2:16-17*, we
read, *Let no man therefore judge you in meat, or in drink, or in
respect of an holyday, or of the new moon, or of the sabbath days:
Which are a shadow of things to come; but the body is of Christ.*
The Sabbath was only a shadow of our real rest, which is in Jesus.

The hypocritical Pharisees twisted and watered down the
law to make it 'keepable'. It gave people a false sense of security
when they found that, with enough self-discipline, they could
actually keep all 39 categories of the Sabbath. In fact, if they could
keep the law, why would they need a savior? Of course, they

forgot that the law is a whole. If they offended in one point, they would be guilty of all. In *Galatians 5:3*, we read, *For I testify again to every man that is circumcised, that he is a debtor to do the whole law.* And again in *James 2:10, For whosoever shall keep the whole law, and yet offend in one point, he is guilty of all.* **The only person who could keep the whole law was the same person who came to take it away**.

Matthew 11:27-30 states, *All things are delivered unto me of my Father: and no man knoweth the Son, but the Father; neither knoweth any man the Father, save the Son, and he to whomsoever the Son will reveal him. Come unto me, all ye that labour and are heavy laden, and I will give you rest. Take my yoke upon you, and learn of me; for I am meek and lowly in heart: and ye shall find rest unto your souls. For my yoke is easy, and my burden is light.* Jesus came to set free all those who are caught up in the heavy yoke of the law and those who labor to follow the law. **He did not die for us so that we could keep the law. But He fulfilled the law for us so we would not have to struggle, strive, and squirm under its oppressive burden. His yoke is easy and His burden is light because He did it for us already.**

In *Hebrews 4:1-11*, we read, *Let us therefore fear, lest, a promise being left us of entering into his rest, any of you should seem to come short of it. For unto us was the gospel preached, as well as unto them: but the word preached did not profit them, not being mixed with faith in them that heard it. For we which have believed do enter into rest, as he said, As I have sworn in my wrath, if they shall enter into my rest: although the works were finished from the foundation of the world.*

For he spake in a certain place of the seventh day on this wise, And God did rest the seventh day from all his works. And in this place again, If they shall enter into my rest. Seeing therefore it remaineth that some must enter therein, and they to whom it was first preached entered not in because of unbelief: Again, he limiteth a certain day, saying in David, To day, after so long a time; as it is said, To day if ye will hear his voice, harden not your hearts.

For if Jesus had given them rest, then would he not afterward have spoken of another day. There remaineth therefore a rest to the people of God. For he that is entered into his rest, he also hath ceased from his own works, as God did from his. Let us labour therefore to enter into that rest, lest any man fall after the same example of unbelief.

We can find rest in our souls and spirits when we rest in His finished work for us. He was prepared as our sacrifice before the foundations of the world were laid. It was finished even before it began. He was provided before there was the need for Him. Sin was defeated by Grace before Adam was created.

There is no need to speak of the Sabbath any more. For we can enter into our rest in Jesus. We can cease from our own works. Let us try hard to stop doing and performing to satisfy and earn favor with God. Let us labor to cease from our own self-righteous ways and works. Instead, let us rest in the rest that Jesus gave to us. As stated before, rest does not mean inactivity. It means that everything we do starts from this rest and point of completeness in Jesus. It becomes all about Jesus working His works in and through us.

✤ 21 ✤

JESUS AND THE THREE PRODIGALS

God is very unfair. He is very unfairly good to us. When we do not deserve any goodness at all, he showers goodness on us. When we deserve the worst, He gave us His best. Let us see this in the most beautiful parable in the bible - the parable of the two prodigal sons and their prodigal father. Prodigal means extravagant. The parable was told to the Pharisees but the sinners got to hear it as well. It is much more than a beautiful parable. It is about Jesus and it is about His relationship to us.

We read from *Luke 15:1-3, 11-13, Then drew near unto him all the publicans and sinners for to hear him. And the Pharisees and scribes murmured, saying, This man receiveth sinners, and eateth with them. And he spake this parable unto them, saying,*

And he said, A certain man had two sons: And the younger of them said to his father, Father, give me the portion of goods that falleth to me. And he divided unto them his living. And not many days after the younger son gathered all together, and took his journey into a far country, and there wasted his substance with riotous living.

The parable was simple. A certain father had two sons whom he loved. One day the younger of the two sons came to ask his father for his inheritance. Under the law, this is sacrilegious as the inheritance is only divided and given when the father is dying.

It is a spit in the father's face to ask for the inheritance when the father is still alive. Such rebellious, unheard of behavior deserves death by stoning according to the law. In *Deuteronomy 21:17-22*, we read, *But he shall acknowledge the son of the hated for the firstborn, by giving him a double portion of all that he hath: for he is the beginning of his strength; the right of the firstborn is his. If a man have a stubborn and rebellious son, which will not obey the voice of his father, or the voice of his mother, and that, when they have chastened him, will not hearken unto them: Then shall his father and his mother lay hold on him, and bring him out unto the elders of his city, and unto the gate of his place; And they shall say unto the elders of his city, This our son is stubborn and rebellious, he will not obey our voice; he is a glutton, and a drunkard. And all the men of his city shall stone him with stones, that he die: so shalt thou put evil away from among you; and all Israel shall hear, and fear. And if a man have committed a sin worthy of death, and he be to be put to death, and thou hang him on a tree:*

However, the father took the insult and apportioned to his younger son his one-third share of the inheritance. As the whole village heard about this law-breaking gesture of the father, they were incensed and wanted to punish the son. How dared he ask for his inheritance earlier than the appropriate time? Did he manage to influence the other boys in the village? Would they also ask for their inheritance earlier? They had to punish this boy to purify the whole village.

To escape the wrath and condemnation of the whole village, the younger son had to leave the village hurriedly. He left not because of his father's condemnation but because of the other villagers' condemnation. To escape the guilt heaped upon him, he left for a far country. As expected, the younger son wasted his whole inheritance on riotous living. He was prodigal in that he was extravagant in his spending and lost all that he had.

We read in *Luke 15:14-24, And when he had spent all, there arose a mighty famine in that land; and he began to be in want. And he went and joined himself to a citizen of that country; and he sent him into his fields to feed swine. And he would fain have filled his belly with the husks that the swine did eat: and no*

*man gave unto him. And when he came to himself, he said, How
many hired servants of my father's have bread enough and to
spare, and I perish with hunger! I will arise and go to my father,
and will say unto him, Father, I have sinned* against *heaven, and
before thee, And am no more worthy to be called thy son: make me
as one of thy hired servants.*
*And he arose, and came to his father. But when he was yet a great
way off, his father saw him, and had compassion, and ran, and fell
on his neck, and kissed him. And the son said unto him, Father, I
have sinned against heaven, and in thy sight, and am no more
worthy to be called thy son. But the father said to his servants,
Bring forth the best robe, and put it on him; and put a ring on his
hand, and shoes on his feet: And bring hither the fatted calf, and
kill it; and let us eat, and be merry: For this my son was dead, and
is alive again; he was lost, and is found. And they began to be
merry.*

Even guiltier now and in order to stay alive, the younger
son took the most detestable and lowest job in that far off country.
His job was to feed the pigs but he was prohibited from eating the
husks that was fed to the pigs. No man gave him any husks to eat,
as the famine was so severe. Under Jewish law, pigs were unclean
and their carcasses should not be touched. *Leviticus 11:7-8* states,
*And the swine, though he divide the hoof, and be clovenfooted, yet
he cheweth not the cud; he is unclean to you.8 Of their flesh shall
ye not eat, and their carcase shall ye not touch; they are unclean to
you.*

Taking care of the pigs made the younger son, if possible,
even more unclean. Not allowed to eat the husks given to the pigs
meant he was treated lower than the unclean pigs. Living under the
strict law brought him guilt, condemnation, fear, hunger, and
'unclean-ness'. When he finally came to his senses, he
remembered his father back home. Although he could go back
home, he thought it would not be as before. He would no longer be
a son but he could go back as a hired servant. He would pay back
with interest what he had taken from his father. He would work for
his father. His righteous works would earn him the right to food

and lodgings. He focused on the money lost, with never a thought that he was the lost one.

Meanwhile, the father who had missed his younger son sorely was waiting for his son's return. As he did not know when, if ever, his son would return he would climb a hill each day. From this vantage point, he could look a great way off. Each day would be as the preceding day. His son did not return. He would climb down the hill. Then the next day, without fail, he would climb up the same hill and peer off into the distance yet again. Maybe today would be the day! Maybe his son would return today!

Then one day it happened. He saw his son from a great way off. Compassion and love sprang up from his guts. He gathered up his robes, exposing his knees and legs, and ran out of the village to meet his son. The villagers saw the father streaking out with his legs ridiculously exposed and thought about condemning him. Then they too saw the return of the younger son. What drama would there be? What punishment would the father mete out to the son who had humiliated him so much? There were many big sticks lying around the village. A good beating might suffice but a good stoning would be even better!

The younger son started to confess his sins and to say that he was no longer worthy to be called 'son' when his father stopped him. His father could have his son stoned but he would not. Instead, he embraced, kissed, and supported him; and continued to kiss his son as they walked back home together. The shame of the son, the smell of his 'unclean-ness', and the dirt of his deeds were borne by his father. He took the guilt of his son by unconditionally accepting him. That day, grace was shown to the whole village. Nobody could judge the son because of the father. Upon reaching home, he honored his son with the best robe, his ring of authority, and sandals fit for a son. The son was honored based on the father's goodness, riches, and grace. It had nothing to do with the son's mistakes, poverty, needs, or repentance. In his father's eyes, the son would always remain a son, as he was a son by birth, not by works. He had the position of a son so he could never lose it. A son would always be accepted simply by birth but a servant had to earn acceptance. By the law, the son would be disqualified and stoned. However, by Grace, he was accepted and loved. There was great rejoicing in the house as the father celebrated the return of his son. The father was prodigal in that he was extravagant in his love for his son.

God's Grace, Jesus Christ, is still extended to all of us today. **We cannot ever be rejected because acceptance is not based upon our works but by His goodness**. After Adam and Eve sinned, God still made garments for them to wear. When the Israelites grumbled, God not only parted the Red Sea but also dried the seabed so that their sandals would not become encrusted with mud. When Adam lost the ring of spiritual authority through sin, Jesus bought it back for us. When we deserved nothing, He gave us everything. *Isaiah 55:8-12* states, *For my thoughts are not your thoughts, neither are your ways my ways, saith the Lord. For as the heavens are higher than the earth, so are my ways higher than your ways, and my thoughts than your thoughts. For as the rain cometh down, and the snow from heaven, and returneth not thither, but watereth the earth, and maketh it bring forth and bud, that it may give seed to the sower, and bread to the eater: So shall my word be that goeth forth out of my mouth: it shall not return unto me void, but it shall accomplish that which I please, and it shall prosper in the thing whereto I sent it. For ye shall go out with joy, and be led forth with peace: the mountains and the hills shall break forth before you into singing, and all the trees of the field shall clap their hands.*

His thoughts are not our thoughts and His ways are not our ways. His thoughts and ways are always infinitely higher. When His Word, Jesus, goes out, He will not return void but will bring back with Him a plentiful and prosperous harvest. You and I are part of that harvest. There will be joy, peace, singing, and clapping of hands as you and I go back home one day to be with our Father.

Meanwhile, the elder son was prodigal as he was extravagant in good works. By law, as the elder son, he was entitled to two-thirds of the inheritance. He was addicted to good works and was still working when he stumbled upon the party thrown by his father for his brother. We read in *Luke 15:25-32, Now his elder son was in the field: and as he came and drew nigh to the house, he heard musick and dancing. And he called one of the servants, and asked what these things meant. And he said unto him, Thy brother is come; and thy father hath killed the fatted calf, because he hath received him safe and sound. And he was angry, and would not go in: therefore came his father out, and intreated him. And he answering said to his father, Lo, these many years do I serve thee, neither transgressed I at any time thy commandment: and yet thou never gavest me a kid, that I might make merry with my friends: But as soon as this thy son was come, which hath devoured thy living with harlots, thou hast killed for him the fatted calf. And he said unto him, Son, thou art ever with me, and all that I have is thine. It was meet that we should make merry, and be glad: for this thy brother was dead, and is alive again; and was lost, and is found.*

Hearing the music, the dancing and the return of his good-for-nothing brother, he became furious. He could walk into the party as a son but he would not. He stood outside like a servant. He insulted his father by not entering in. As such, his father came out to him and entreated him. Immediately, he justified himself by his list of works and accomplishments. He had served, he had sacrificed, he had obeyed, he had not transgressed, he had stayed home, he had raised the fatted calf, he had not been lazy, and he had not sinned. His brother was so odious to him that he referred to him as 'your son' and not as 'my brother'. Then he accused his brother of living with harlots, a false accusation, as he had no idea what his brother had been doing until then. Spewing hatred and pride, he lambasted the grace of his father. His father answered him and replied that it was meet that they should have a celebration for the dead had been made alive and the lost had been found. While the parable does not have an ending, it could easily have one. It could go something like this.

The eldest son, representing the Pharisees who were listening closely to this parable, did not like the father's answer and seethed with anger. Seeing the many big sticks lying on the ground, he picked one up, thrust it at his father with all his might, pierced him through and killed him. Likewise, the Pharisees hated Jesus, pierced Him, hung Him on a wooden cross, and killed Him.

∂₂ 22 ₂∂

JESUS AND THE FIG TREE

We find a very strange account of Jesus in *Mark 11:12-14, 20-22, And on the morrow, when they were come from Bethany, he was hungry: And seeing a fig tree afar off having leaves, he came, if haply he might find any thing thereon: and when he came to it, he found nothing but leaves; for the time of figs was not yet. And Jesus answered and said unto it, No man eat fruit of thee hereafter for ever. And his disciples heard it. And in the morning, as they passed by, they saw the fig tree dried up from the roots. And Peter calling to remembrance saith unto him, Master, behold, the fig tree which thou cursedst is withered away. And Jesus answering saith unto them, Have faith in God.*

Jesus was walking from Bethany to Jerusalem, about a two-mile walk, when He saw a fig tree from afar off. As He was hungry, he walked towards the tree and started looking for some ripe figs to eat. All the while, He knew it was not the time for figs yet. Was Jesus shortsighted? Did He see figs when there was none? Finding no figs, He cursed the tree. The next day, when Jesus and His disciples walked past the same tree, the tree had withered away. What had the tree done to Him to deserve such vengeance? Was He a tree hater? Was Jesus not green and eco friendly?

Jesus is truly a marvel in revealing secrets to us. He utilizes everyday examples to show us His grace and His love for us. This example is one of the best. Let us discover what it really says.

Jesus was traveling in and out of Jerusalem with His disciples when He saw a fig tree from afar off. It is well known that the fig tree represents the Jews. In Jeremiah, the Jews are likened to two baskets of figs, one good and one naughty. *Jeremiah 24:1-2, The Lord shewed me, and, behold, two baskets of figs were set before the temple of the Lord, after that Nebuchadrezzar king of Babylon had carried away captive Jeconiah the son of Jehoiakim king of Judah, and the princes of Judah, with the carpenters and smiths, from Jerusalem, and had brought them to Babylon. One basket had very good figs, even like the figs that are first ripe: and the other basket had very naughty figs, which could not be eaten, they were so bad.* And again in *Nahum 3:12, All thy strong holds shall be like fig trees with the first ripe figs: if they be shaken, they shall even fall into the mouth of the eater.* Here the Jews were likened to fig trees with the first ripened figs.

Jesus wanted to teach His disciples an unforgettable truth with the fig tree. Therefore, He walked to the fig tree that He knew had no figs at all, as it was not the season for figs yet. There was something that was not there as well which the disciples were not aware of.

Fig trees bear leaves about the end of March. The leaves are usually accompanied by a crop of small knobs called taqsh that can be readily eaten. This taqsh will drop off before the formation of the real figs about two months on. If there are no taqsh on the fig tree, there will be no figs later on. Jesus not only knew that there were no figs on the tree but that there were no taqsh there as well. He chose a completely barren fig tree to use as His object lesson.

In Genesis, after Adam and Eve sinned, they sewed fig leaves together to cover up their nakedness. *Genesis 3:7* reads, *And the eyes of them both were opened, and they knew that they were naked; and they sewed fig leaves together, and made themselves aprons.* By their own works, they tried to cover up their sin. Self-righteousness cannot cover sin. It is impossible for us to redeem ourselves. God killed an animal later on to cover up their nakedness. *Genesis 3:21, Unto Adam also and to his wife did the*

Lord God make coats of skins, and clothed them. However, that was temporary, for we can only be fully covered up by God. When we are clothed we Jesus, His righteousness makes us righteous as well.

However, the Jews were self-righteous. They were the chosen people yet many of them denied Jesus, choosing to come under the curse of the law. They are spiritually dead and barren. Trusting in their own works, they would end up withered and wasted. The decay was so bad that even the roots shriveled up and died. The withered fig tree represented the spiritual leaders of Israel at that time. For a show, they made long prayers and dressed in long robes. We read in *Luke 20:45-47, Then in the audience of all the people he said unto his disciples, Beware of the scribes, which desire to walk in long robes, and love greetings in the markets, and the highest seats in the synagogues, and the chief rooms at feasts; Which devour widows' houses, and for a shew make long prayers: the same shall receive greater damnation.* They loved to be greeted in the marketplace and occupied the highest seats in the synagogues and the chief rooms at feasts. At the same time they enforced the heavy yoke of the law upon the people.

This can be clearly seen in *Luke 21:1-4, And he looked up, and saw the rich men casting their gifts into the treasury. And he saw also a certain poor widow casting in thither two mites. And he said, Of a truth I say unto you, that this poor widow hath cast in more than they all: For all these have of their abundance cast in unto the offerings of God: but she of her penury hath cast in all the living that she had.* Notice that immediately after Jesus had talked about the scribes devouring widows' houses, Jesus looked up and saw the poor widow casting into the treasury her two mites. He did not comment on her generous giving as many people had taught on. But rather, she had to give to the temple because it was the law. We do not know whether she bought a prayer or paid for a sacrificial offering but we know that she was being devoured! It was all that she had and the spiritual leaders took it from her.

Such leaders were represented by this barren tree that was devoid of even the smallest fruit. *Luke 3:9* states, *And now also the axe is laid unto the root of the trees: every tree therefore which bringeth not forth good fruit is hewn down, and cast into the fire.* These trees withered from the roots up and they must be hewn down and cast into the fire. While this is what they deserved, they did not end up getting what they deserved. While God is not slack in His promises, He is patient towards us. We read in *2 Peter 3:8-9, But, beloved, be not ignorant of this one thing, that one day is with the Lord as a thousand years, and a thousand years as one day. The Lord is not slack concerning his promise, as some men count slackness; but is longsuffering to us-ward, not willing that any should perish, but that all should come to repentance.* God wants none of us to perish but for all of us to know Jesus. Hell was created for the devil. It was not created for us even though we may deserve it.

Jesus then told another parable on the fig tree to illustrate what was in store for us. In *Luke 13:6-9, He spake also this parable; A certain man had a fig tree planted in his vineyard; and he came and sought fruit thereon, and found none. Then said he unto the dresser of his vineyard, Behold, these three years I come seeking fruit on this fig tree, and find none: cut it down; why cumbereth it the ground? And he answering said unto him, Lord, let it alone this year also, till I shall dig about it, and dung it: And if it bear fruit, well: and if not, then after that thou shalt cut it down.* The owner of a vineyard had a fig tree planted in his vineyard. He came looking for fruit for three years and found none. Frustrated, he asked the dresser of the vineyard to cut down the tree. The dresser asked for another year to see whether the tree would produce fruit before cutting it down.

The owner of the vineyard was God. In the vineyard, He planted a fig tree. The dresser of the vineyard was Jesus as He gives the Living Water to all the plants. Now, fig trees bear fruit only after three years. The owner came after these three years had passed and started looking for fruit upon this tree. He did this for the next three years. 3+3=6. Six years have now passed. The number six in the bible stands for 'man'. After six years, man's efforts to produce fruit have failed. Men cannot produce the desired fruit. If men were to be judged by his own works, he would be cut down. The axe would be put to his root and he would be hewn down. But Jesus said, 'One more year!' As one day is with the Lord as a thousand years and a thousand years as one day, Jesus asked for a period of grace so that no men would perish but that all would be given time to repent. Jesus would dig and He would put fertilizer around this tree during this period of grace. The price for this period of grace is His life. He would pay this price to redeem us, an unfruitful non-producing tree, from being hewn down and thrown into the fire. God's perfect patience allowed this to happen. The price for one more year was Jesus Christ. He is perfection Himself as $3+3+1=7$; seven being the perfect number in the bible. When the first six years of man's work is over, the seventh year of Jesus' work starts. **When we give up on our strength and on our works, then Jesus takes over**. When Jesus takes over, the tree is transformed. It becomes a new creation!

Before Jesus told the parable of the fig tree, He told the crowd gathered at the synagogue something significant. The Jews had been taught that bad things happen to people because they were bad sinners. This can be found in *Luke 13:1-5, There were present at that season some that told him of the Galilaeans, whose blood Pilate had mingled with their sacrifices. And Jesus answering said unto them, Suppose ye that these Galilaeans were sinners above all the Galilaeans, because they suffered such things? I tell you, Nay: but, except ye repent, ye shall all likewise perish. Or those eighteen, upon whom the tower in Siloam fell, and slew them, think ye that they were sinners above all men that dwelt in Jerusalem? I tell you, Nay: but, except ye repent, ye shall all likewise perish.*

In the first account, Pilate had taxed the Jews for a water system that was built for Jerusalem. When the temple had to pay those taxes as well, the Jews revolted and were subsequently massacred. The blood of these massacred Galileans was mixed with the blood of their animal sacrifices on the floor of the temple. It was always supposed that these massacred Galileans were the worst sinners among all the other Galileans resulting in their suffering. The second account was about an accident at the tower in Siloam in which eighteen people died. The Jews were similarly taught that the eighteen died in the accident because they were bad sinners. However, Jesus refuted these teachings. He said that they perished because they did not believe in Him, not because they were bad sinners! And then Jesus added that all men would perish if they did not believe in Him. Men who trusted in their works would perish, for all of us are sinners. Whether we are Jews or not, none of us can earn our righteousness; no, not one.

We strive for the first six years by our deeds. However, it does not bring justification. **No matter how hard we try, we still come short of the glory of God.** *Romans 3:10-12, 20-28* states, *As it is written, There is none righteous, no, not one: There is none that understandeth, there is none that seeketh after God. They are all gone out of the way, they are together become unprofitable; there is none that doeth good, no, not one. Therefore by the deeds of the law there shall no flesh be justified in his sight: for by the law is the knowledge of sin. But now the righteousness of God without the law is manifested, being witnessed by the law and the prophets; Even the righteousness of God which is by faith of Jesus Christ unto all and upon all them that believe: for there is no difference: For all have sinned, and come short of the glory of God; Being justified freely by his grace through the redemption that is in Christ Jesus: Whom God hath set forth to be a propitiation through faith in his blood, to declare his righteousness for the remission of sins that are past, through the forbearance of God; To declare, I say, at this time his righteousness: that he might be just, and the justifier of him which believeth in Jesus. Where is boasting then? It is excluded. By what law? of works? Nay: but by the law of faith. Therefore we conclude that a man is justified by faith without the deeds of the law.*

Our obedience and performance is never enough. The standard is too high, the chasm too wide. However, in the seventh year, the righteousness of God without the law, Jesus, was made manifest, being witnessed by the law and the prophets. Jesus met the standard and closed the chasm. Only His obedience and performance is enough. He did what we could not do. He lived the live we could not live. He justified us freely by His grace. He redeemed us by Himself. He became a propitiation for our sins. He appeased God's anger towards sin and reconciled us back to God. He became our righteousness for the remission of sins. Because of Jesus, we can bear new fruit. In the seventh year, as we have faith in what Jesus had done, we all become new creations.

In *John 15:1-6*, we read, *I am the true vine, and my Father is the husbandman. Every branch in me that beareth not fruit he taketh away: and every branch that beareth fruit, he purgeth it, that it may bring forth more fruit. Now ye are clean through the word which I have spoken unto you. Abide in me, and I in you. As the branch cannot bear fruit of itself, except it abide in the vine; no more can ye, except ye abide in me. I am the vine, ye are the branches: He that abideth in me, and I in him, the same bringeth forth much fruit: for without me ye can do nothing. If a man abide not in me, he is cast forth as a branch, and is withered; and men gather them, and cast them into the fire, and they are burned.* People who are not attached to The True Vine, Jesus, are not new creations. These branches are not joined to Jesus. As they are not connected to Jesus, they produce the same old fruits. These same old fruits bring death. Ultimately, they wither away, are gathered up, and cast into the fire. We can read this in *Revelations 22:19, And if any man shall take away from the words of the book of this prophecy, God shall take away his part out of the book of life, and out of the holy city, and from the things which are written in this book.* There are people who profess to be Christians but are not joined to Christ. By their many self-works, they assume their names are written in the book of life when it is actually not. But rather than attaching themselves to Christ, they would rather tamper with the words of the bible to fit their self-righteous views.

However, people who are new creations are entirely different. They do not want to tamper with the words in the bible, as they are branches connected to The True Vine, Jesus. **Their very nature changes as Jesus now dwells in them.** They are not copies of Jesus but they abide in Jesus as Jesus abides in them. Jesus becomes an integral part of them and becomes inseparable from them. They in turn cannot be isolated or be severed from Jesus. They are clean and they remain clean because of Jesus. If dirt from sin comes upon them, they are unaffected. Jesus does not discard branches because they are dirty, only to re-attach these same branches when they become clean again. As they are already forgiven and made clean, there is no need for them to be saved and to be cleaned repeatedly. The new is made new by Jesus and maintains its newness by Jesus. They are forever clean because of Jesus.

True believers cannot earn their salvation by their own works nor can they lose their salvation by their own works. They cannot lose their salvation because of their works because they did not earn their salvation by their works. Just as sinners cannot earn salvation by doing good works, believers cannot lose their salvation by their own works. They are made new because they are connected to Jesus.

All that comes to Jesus will never be cast away. In *John 6:37-40*, we read that *All that the Father giveth me shall come to me; and him that cometh to me I will in no wise cast out. For I came down from heaven, not to do mine own will, but the will of him that sent me. And this is the Father's will which hath sent me, that of all which he hath given me I should lose nothing, but should raise it up again at the last day. And this is the will of him that sent me, that every one which seeth the Son, and believeth on him, may have everlasting life: and I will raise him up at the last day.* Furthermore, *John 10:28-30* states, *And I give unto them eternal life; and they shall never perish, neither shall any man pluck them out of my hand. My Father, which gave them me, is greater than all; and no man is able to pluck them out of my Father's hand. I and my Father are one.* **Those who are in Jesus have the assurance that no man, no woman, no demon, and no devil will ever be able to pluck them out of Jesus' hand. The will of the Father is that Jesus loses none and as Jesus always and only does the will of the Father, therefore Jesus loses nothing and no one. When we are connected to Jesus, we have everlasting life and will never perish.**

This is reinforced in *Ephesians 4:30, And grieve not the holy Spirit of God, whereby ye are sealed unto the day of redemption.* We are sealed with Christ and nobody is going to break this seal. Finally, we have Jesus' promise of eternal salvation in *Revelations 3:5, He that overcometh, the same shall be clothed in white raiment; and I will not blot out his name out of the book of life, but I will confess his name before my Father, and before his angels.* All believers are overcomers. **We are clothed with Jesus and guaranteed that our names would never be blotted out of the book of life. That is a promise and the Promiser is Jesus Himself, who will confess our names before God. What a Savior we have in Jesus!**

At the same time, we who are connected to Jesus also automatically start to bear good fruits. Because of Jesus in us, we cannot help but produce fruit. Grapes are produced effortlessly when connected to the vine. There is no striving to produce fruits. All those that rest in The Vine, Jesus, produce fruit. Without The Vine, we can do nothing. We bear nothing. Without Jesus, we have no righteousness, sanctification, blessings, and forgiveness. The source of our righteousness, sanctification, blessings, and forgiveness is from The Vine, Jesus. That is why the leaf of a grape vine has five ribs, the number five representing grace. It has place for six ribs but there is only five. Six represents man and man has to be taken out. Otherwise, it would no longer be Grace or Jesus. We receive all when we rest in our vine, Jesus. They may be times when we are pruned for the purpose of producing more fruit but we are never cast away. **We produce fruit because of Jesus and we continue to produce fruit because of Jesus.**

❧ 23 ❧

JESUS AND THE HOUSE OF FISH

I always believed that Jesus was the answer to everything in my life until I became a full time missionary in Eastern Europe in 1999. In that part of the world, I was told that the answer was not Jesus but righteous self-works! At that time, all the churches, without a single exception, preached legalism. Many times it was extreme and but at other times, a mixture. It was quite amazing to see and hear real-life Pharisees and Sadducees. As a missionary, one of the most frequently asked question was, "How do you preach Grace to a legalist?" Not surprisingly, the answer was given by Jesus more than two thousand years ago.

In *Matthew 13:33, Another parable spake he unto them; The kingdom of heaven is like unto leaven, which a woman took, and hid in three measures of meal, till the whole was leavened.* The common explanation for this parable was that the woman represented the church. She hid the gospel or leaven secretly in man as represented by the meal. After a period of time, because of the gospel in man, the whole world became saved.

There are some problems with this explanation, chiefly because the whole world is not saved. Also, the gospel is not to be secretly hidden in man. The light of the gospel is to be shone from the top of a hill for all to see in order for God to be glorified. We see in *Matthew 5:14-16, Ye are the light of the world. A city that is*

*set on an hill cannot be hid. Neither do men light a candle, and put
it under a bushel, but on a candlestick; and it giveth light unto all
that are in the house. Let your light so shine before men, that they
may see your good works, and glorify your Father which is in
heaven.* And again in *John 8:12, Then spake Jesus again unto
them, saying, I am the light of the world: he that followeth me shall
not walk in darkness, but shall have the light of life.*

In *Luke 12:1,* we read, *In the mean time, when there were
gathered together an innumerable multitude of people, insomuch
that they trode one upon another, he began to say unto his
disciples first of all, Beware ye of the leaven of the Pharisees,
which is hypocrisy.* Jesus reminded His disciples to beware of the
leaven of the Pharisees, which was hypocrisy or false religion.
False religion or the law makes people hypocritical. It gives them a
false sense of security while trying to please and earn favor with
God. It results in self-righteousness. His disciples did not
understand fully and thought Jesus was talking about bread or the
lack of bread. It was not easy for the disciples to understand as the
leaven was hidden inside the meal and had eluded detection for a
very long time. They had ears to hear, eyes to see, and heads to
remember but the leaven was so cunningly and secretly hidden that
it was near impossible to detect.

Leaven ferments the meal or dough, from a sweet to a sour
taste. The meal becomes corrupted by the leaven. The woman
represented a false religion that demanded a self-righteous and a
self-preoccupied way to earn salvation and favor from God. This
self-righteous way is called the law. It is not put into the church
openly but is hidden stealthily into it, disguised as good works and
noble deeds. As such, the unleavened becomes leavened. The
sweet becomes sour. The pure becomes impure. In the natural, the
process is irreversible. Leaven cannot be removed from the dough.
The infected cannot be cured.

But this leaven is a spiritual problem, not a natural
problem. To fight a spiritual problem with worldly weapons is to
ask for defeat. **Spiritual problems can only be solved by
spiritual means. To reverse the corruption, the revelation of
Grace or Jesus must come upon the church. Jesus had to be**

revealed supernaturally to tear away the veil that blinded the people. Only Jesus can make us see Himself clearly.

We have such an example in *Mark 8:22-26, And he cometh to Bethsaida; and they bring a blind man unto him, and besought him to touch him. And he took the blind man by the hand, and led him out of the town; and when he had spit on his eyes, and put his hands upon him, he asked him if he saw ought. And he looked up, and said, I see men as trees, walking. After that he put his hands again upon his eyes, and made him look up: and he was restored, and saw every man clearly. And he sent him away to his house, saying, Neither go into the town, nor tell it to any in the town.* Jesus spitted once but touched the blind man's eyes twice before he could see clearly. The leaven of the Pharisees would quickly point to the law governing spitting into someone's face. In *Numbers 12:14,* we read, *And the Lord said unto Moses, If her father had but spit in her face, should she not be ashamed seven days? let her be shut out from the camp seven days, and after that let her be received in again.* Spitting into someone's face makes the person ashamed and unclean for seven days. Furthermore, the person must be put outside the city walls till the seven days had passed. Breaking the spitting law would bring punishment.

The leaven could also be disguised and hidden as self-righteous or holier-than-thou attitude. It would assign the apparent failure of Jesus to the man's faith, or lack of it, as the reason why he was not healed with the first spit. He was a man of little faith so what he needed was to have more faith. Or maybe Jesus needed to do more too because He may not have spat enough the first time around rendering Him liable for more spit. More faith. More spit. More works. Work harder. Try more. More, more, more!

Bethsaida is of Aramaic origin and means the 'house of fish'. Jesus fed people with fish and loaves and called his disciples to become fishers of men. The 'house of fish' represented the 'house of God'. The fish symbol was widely used among early Christians. When they met, one would draw the arc of a simple fish outline. The other would complete the drawing by another arc. This simple fish symbol helped them tell friends from foes.

However, the 'house of God' had been transformed by the religious leaders into the 'house of fish' and it stank with the law and self-righteousness. Jesus took the blind man by his hand and led him out of the house of fish. Also, if the Pharisees had seen what Jesus was about to do, they would have put the blind man outside anyway and labeled him unclean. Jesus preempted the religious leaders by taking the blind man's hand, holding him gently, and leading him out of the house of fish where law was king. Two kings cannot inhabit the same place. One has to come out. In this account, Jesus took the blind man out of the house of fish where self was glorified. Babylon, representing the world system resided in the house of fish. We see in *Revelation 18:4-7, And I heard another voice from heaven, saying, Come out of her, my people, that ye be not partakers of her sins, and that ye receive not of her plagues. For her sins have reached unto heaven, and God hath remembered her iniquities. Reward her even as she rewarded you, and double unto her double according to her works: in the cup which she hath filled fill to her double. How much she hath glorified herself, and lived deliciously, so much torment and sorrow give her: for she saith in her heart, I sit a queen, and am no widow, and shall see no sorrow.*

Outside the temple, Jesus began to work. He spat into the blind man's eyes and laid hands on him. The blind man then looked up and saw blurred figures of men walking like trees. Wood represents humanity or man in the bible. The blind man was still caught up by fallen man and his works. He only saw through the veil of Moses. It was still not clear to him although Jesus, the Healer, was standing right next to him. Many people coming from a legalistic background cannot see clearly, even if Jesus and His Grace is expounded to them. The leaven was still in them. They need a revelation! A revelation of Grace! A revelation Of Jesus! Only Jesus can reverse the leavened bread. Only Jesus can cure the spiritually sick. Only Jesus can make the corrupted incorruptible.

Jesus then laid hands on the man's eyes a second time. This time he received the revelation of Grace. No more veil. No more law. No more self-righteousness, which brought spiritual blindness. No more works for Jesus accomplished it all. He had eyes and he could see. Clearly. Not blurry as before. The religious leaders had eyes but they could not see or they could only see from behind the veil of Moses. You cannot preach grace to a legalist. It is a spiritual issue. **The only solution for people caught up with legalism is a personal revelation of Jesus.**

And when the blind man could see clearly, Jesus instructed him to not return to the house of fish. To become entangled again with the many lines of the fish-law would only entrap him and make him worse off than before. We see in *2 Peter 2:20-22, For if after they have escaped the pollutions of the world through the knowledge of the Lord and Saviour Jesus Christ, they are again entangled therein, and overcome, the latter end is worse with them than the beginning. For it had been better for them not to have known the way of righteousness, than, after they have known it, to turn from the holy commandment delivered unto them. But it is happened unto them according to the true proverb, The dog is turned to his own vomit again; and the sow that was washed to her wallowing in the mire.* For there is only one holy commandment and that is to believe and have faith in the finished work of Jesus Christ. Jesus did it all so that we can see clearly.

In the book of Acts, every healing and miracle happened outside the temple. Public squares, prisons, private homes, public streets, and even the beach were scenes of miraculous acts. Of all the many supernatural acts, from raising the dead to delivering out of prison, none took place in a synagogue or other religious house. In *Acts 18:4-8*, we read, *And he reasoned in the synagogue every sabbath, and persuaded the Jews and the Greeks. And when Silas and Timotheus were come from Macedonia, Paul was pressed in the spirit, and testified to the Jews that Jesus was Christ. And when they opposed themselves, and blasphemed, he shook his raiment, and said unto them, Your blood be upon your own heads; I am clean: from henceforth I will go unto the Gentiles. And he departed thence, and entered into a certain man's house, named Justus, one that worshipped God, whose house joined hard to the synagogue. And Crispus, the chief ruler of the synagogue, believed on the Lord with all his house; and many of the Corinthians hearing believed, and were baptized.*

Paul had to leave a synagogue before he could testify of Jesus. The religious leaders could not see because of the law. Paul had to physically leave the synagogue to go to an adjoining house before the people could see Jesus revealed. The house owned by Justus was next door to the synagogue and there was no law in his house. The absence of the law opened the way for Jesus to work and it resulted in many salvations. Even the chief ruler of the synagogue, Crispus, had to leave the synagogue to meet Jesus next door. Grace and law do not mix as one precludes the other.

❧ 24 ❧

JESUS AND NAMES

One of the most popular scriptures from the bible is on Daniel and his three friends. It is also popular because it has been used innumerable times to illustrate Daniel's strength of resolve and determination. However, it is actually more an account about Jesus' than Daniel's strength.

We read in *Daniel 1:1-7, In the third year of the reign of Jehoiakim king of Judah came Nebuchadnezzar king of Babylon unto Jerusalem, and besieged it. And the Lord gave Jehoiakim king of Judah into his hand, with part of the vessels of the house of God: which he carried into the land of Shinar to the house of his god; and he brought the vessels into the treasure house of his god. And the king spake unto Ashpenaz the master of his eunuchs, that he should bring certain of the children of Israel, and of the king's seed, and of the princes; Children in whom was no blemish, but well favoured, and skilful in all wisdom, and cunning in knowledge, and understanding science, and such as had ability in them to stand in the king's palace, and whom they might teach the learning and the tongue of the Chaldeans. And the king appointed them a daily provision of the king's meat, and of the wine which he drank: so nourishing them three years, that at the end thereof they might stand before the king. Now among these were of the children of Judah, Daniel, Hananiah, Mishael, and Azariah: Unto whom the prince of the eunuchs gave names: for he gave unto Daniel the name of Belteshazzar; and to Hananiah, of Shadrach; and to Mishael, of Meshach; and to Azariah, of Abed-nego.*

The story begins with the conquering of Jerusalem by the Babylonian king, Nebuchadnezzar. As well as plundering the house of God, Nebuchadnezzar ordered that some of the brilliant children of Israel be brought back to Babylon. The purpose of bringing Daniel and his friends to Babylon was so that their Jewish teaching could be erased, to be replaced by Babylonian teachings. These teachings would be under the Chaldeans who lived in southern Babylon. Not only were the Chaldeans warriors but they were educated and well instructed in the sciences, especially in astrology and astronomy. They are usually credited for the star reading abilities of the three wise men from the East who would discover and then worship the newborn Jesus. The Chaldeans would rise to become Babylonian kings, and in time, the term Chaldean and Babylon became synonymous.

The Chaldeans would spend the next three years re-educating Daniel and his friends. In that time, they would be fed a daily provision of the king's meat and a portion of his wine. This re-education of a conquered nation was not uncommon as serfs and slaves were always in demand. It would have been unremarkable except that among the many children of Israel so chosen were Daniel and his three friends; Hananiah, Mishael, and Azariah.

In Hebrew, Daniel means 'God is my judge', Hananiah means 'Jah who is gracious', Mishael means 'who is what God is', and Azariah means 'Jah has helped'. However, the Babylonians changed their names. Daniel became Belteshazzar meaning 'Bel protects his life or Bel's prince'. Hananiah became Shadrach meaning 'the great scribe', Mishael became Meshach meaning 'guest of the king', and Azariah became Abednego meaning 'servant of Nebo', a false god.

Let us look at their original names a little closer. When 'God is my judge', He sees us righteous and holy. We know that Jesus is our judge but Jesus is also our advocate. He defends and makes us righteous and holy and then judges us as righteous and holy. Because of Grace, we are no longer under fear, guilt, and condemnation. As 'Jah who is gracious' to us, we have life and we have it abundantly. Because of His Grace, we are set free from the law and sin. We become 'who is what God is'. We are what God is. As Jesus is, so are we. *1 John 4:17* states, *Herein is our love made perfect, that we may have boldness in the day of judgment: because as he is, so are we in this world.* As Jesus is in heaven, so are we here on earth. Jesus was great when He was living on earth but He is even greater now seated at the right hand of the Father in heaven. Jesus is perfect, so are we. Jesus is sinless, so are we in our spirit. Jesus is Prince of Peace, so are we. Jesus is Life, so are we. We have health, joy, favor, power, wisdom, and life because of Jesus. We are exactly like Him who is in heaven.

That is why Jesus told His disciples that they would do greater works than Him because He goes to His Father in heaven. In *John 14:12-13*, we read, *Verily, verily, I say unto you, He that believeth on me, the works that I do shall he do also; and greater works than these shall he do; because I go unto my Father. And whatsoever ye shall ask in my name, that will I do, that the Father may be glorified in the Son.* They would be like Him in heaven, not earth. We are greater than Jesus when He was here on earth because Jesus is in heaven and we are exactly like Him. 'Jah has helped' me through every circumstance in my life. Never would we be alone, helpless, and forsaken. Our helper is Jesus Himself. That is what the children of Israel had in their original names.

We remember that when God took Abram out of Chaldee, his name was changed to Abraham meaning 'father of a multitude'. He was 'one' but he would be 'multiplied' by God. When the Babylonians changed the Israelites names, they tried to blot out God's blessings upon their lives. They were the antithesis to what God had done.

However, Daniel and his friends' Babylonian names were servile and ingratiating. 'Bel protects his life' is a lie as the devil does not protect anyone's life. The devil seeks to steal, kill, and destroy our lives, not protect it. 'The great scribe' points us back to the law as the scribes copied the law. It puts us back in bondage and slavery to the law. We become 'guest to the king'. No longer are we sons but guests. Guests are temporary but The Son is forever. We are no longer adopted into the family of God and we have no inheritance as guests. Lastly, we sink to become 'servant of Nebo', a false god. We now have to take orders from a false god. We lose our Sonship and priestly nature. Now we have to serve and perform again. Once again, we have to do and earn our salvation. Jesus was a Son but Moses was a servant. Babylon strips us of Grace bringing us back to the law of death. Babylon degrades us from being a prince to being a servant.

The world of Babylon will feed you with choice meat and drink. It is to make you strong so that you will look at yourself and forget about Jesus. **Anything that takes your eyes off Jesus will end up killing you.** That is why Daniel and his three friends rejected the king's food and drink. They chose to eat pulses and to drink water instead. We read this in *Daniel 1:8-20, But Daniel purposed in his heart that he would not defile himself with the portion of the king's meat, nor with the wine which he drank: therefore he requested of the prince of the eunuchs that he might not defile himself. Now God had brought Daniel into favour and tender love with the prince of the eunuchs. And the prince of the eunuchs said unto Daniel, I fear my lord the king, who hath appointed your meat and your drink: for why should he see your faces worse liking than the children which are of your sort? then shall ye make me endanger my head to the king. Then said Daniel to Melzar, whom the prince of the eunuchs had set over Daniel, Hananiah, Mishael, and Azariah, Prove thy servants, I beseech thee, ten days; and let them give us pulse to eat, and water to drink. Then let our countenances be looked upon before thee, and the countenance of the children that eat of the portion of the king's meat: and as thou seest, deal with thy servants. So he consented to them in this matter, and proved them ten days. And at the end of ten days their countenances appeared fairer and fatter in flesh than all the children which did eat the portion of the king's meat.*

Thus Melzar took away the portion of their meat, and the wine that they should drink; and gave them pulse. As for these four children, God gave them knowledge and skill in all learning and wisdom: and Daniel had understanding in all visions and dreams. Now at the end of the days that the king had said he should bring them in, then the prince of the eunuchs brought them in before

Nebuchadnezzar. And the king communed with them; and among them all was found none like Daniel, Hananiah, Mishael, and Azariah: therefore stood they before the king. And in all matters of wisdom and understanding, that the king inquired of them, he found them ten times better than all the magicians and astrologers that were in all his realm.

Pulses are uncooked seeds and grains. They chose to eat the promised Seed of Life and to drink the Living Water. They rested and ate spiritual food, not worldly food. They fed on Jesus for ten days. The number ten in the bible stands for perfection. They fed on Perfection for a perfect time and so they became spiritually perfect. As Jesus is perfect, so are we spiritually! At the end of the ten days, they were fairer and fatter than all the rest of the children of Israel.

Not only were they fatter and healthier, but their knowledge, skill in learning and wisdom were ten times more than the smartest Chaldean. Jesus is Wisdom, so are we. In Jesus is all knowledge, so we become. Jesus is perfection ten times over, so are we. **Our blessings are multiplied ten times as we rest and feed on Jesus.**

❧ 25 ❧

JESUS AND WINE

In my time as a missionary, I encountered many priests and pastors who told me in no uncertain terms what the punishments would be for sinners. When I asked them to define who sinners were, the answer would always be the same. Sinners were all those who did not do what they, the priests and pastors, said! Their answers indubitably revolved around works and performance but never about Jesus and the finished work on the cross. When I asked them about the punishments, they referred me to the bible.

In the bible, I came across some ghastly punishments. Stoning, hanging, burning, drowning, torturing, chaining, flaying, mocking and other indignities, crucifixion, decapitation, sawing and cutting into pieces, dashing in pieces, pounding in a mortar, plucking off the hair, blinding or putting out of eyes, cutting off of limbs, passing through fire, chastising with scorpions, precipitation or throwing off from some high point or cliff, thrusting through with spear and sword, banishment, confiscation of property, throwing to wild beasts, imprisonment, mutilation, scourging, gallows, retaliation or life for life, slavery, stocks, stripes or whipping, exile, restitution and compensation, and wearing of prison garments were all used and accepted. With that list, small wonder the people lived in absolute fear of God and His representatives here on earth, the church leaders.

And it would seem like they are correct! In Exodus, we note the terrible punishments God inflicted upon the Egyptians for not listening to and obeying God's servant, Moses. The first punishment was severe and it represented the first miracle of Moses. All the waters in Egypt were turned into blood. Starting from the mighty Nile to the tributary rivers, from the streams to the ponds, from wells to the pots of water in their houses, all water turned into blood. As the life giving water was replaced with blood, the result was great destruction and death in all the land. All the fish died and the country stunk with the stench that comes from death.

We read this in *Exodus 7:15-21, Get thee unto Pharaoh in the morning; lo, he goeth out unto the water; and thou shalt stand by the river's brink against he come; and the rod which was turned to a serpent shalt thou take in thine hand. And thou shalt say unto him, The Lord God of the Hebrews hath sent me unto thee, saying, Let my people go, that they may serve me in the wilderness: and, behold, hitherto thou wouldest not hear. Thus saith the Lord, In this thou shalt know that I am the Lord: behold, I will smite with the rod that is in mine hand upon the waters which are in the river, and they shall be turned to blood. And the fish that is in the river shall die, and the river shall stink; and the Egyptians shall lothe to drink of the water of the river. And the Lord spake unto Moses, Say unto Aaron, Take thy rod, and stretch out thine hand upon the waters of Egypt, upon their streams, upon their rivers, and upon their ponds, and upon all their pools of water, that they may become blood; and that there may be blood throughout all the land of Egypt, both in vessels of wood, and in vessels of stone. And Moses and Aaron did so, as the Lord commanded; and he lifted up the rod, and smote the waters that were in the river, in the sight of Pharaoh, and in the sight of his servants; and all the waters that were in the river were turned to blood. And the fish that was in the river died; and the river stank, and the Egyptians could not drink of the water of the river; and there was blood throughout all the land of Egypt.*

Then came the other plagues as further punishments upon the people of Egypt. Fetor frogs came forth from the putrid and

fetid water; lice sprouted from the dust of the earth; flies emerged
from the rotting malodorous flesh and plant life; livestock died
from infectious diseases; boils and pus-filled carbuncles broke out
among men and beasts such that they could not stand; gigantic
hailstorms ravaged men, animals, trees, and plants; locusts
devastated the food supplies; and a supernatural darkness that was
tangible invaded the land. Thirst, hunger, pain, wretchedness,
despair, misery, and suffering came to all who disobeyed Moses,
who stood for the inflexibility of the law that was to come. The
finger of God that wrote in these plagues would later write the law
onto the stone tablets. As the Egyptians struggled in their works
and tried to find a way out from their plagues, the Israelites were
protected from these maladies because they were still under God's
unconditional promise to Abraham.

We read of all these plagues in the following scriptures.
*Exodus 8:3-4, 16-17, 19, 21-22, And the river shall bring forth
frogs abundantly, which shall go up and come into thine house,
and into thy bedchamber, and upon thy bed, and into the house of
thy servants, and upon thy people, and into thine ovens, and into
thy kneadingtroughs: And the frogs shall come up both on thee,
and upon thy people, and upon all thy servants.*
*And the Lord said unto Moses, Say unto Aaron, Stretch out thy rod,
and smite the dust of the land, that it may become lice throughout
all the land of Egypt. And they did so; for Aaron stretched out his
hand with his rod, and smote the dust of the earth, and it became
lice in man, and in beast; all the dust of the land became lice
throughout all the land of Egypt.*
*Then the magicians said unto Pharaoh, This is the finger of God:
Else, if thou wilt not let my people go, behold, I will send swarms
of flies upon thee, and upon thy servants, and upon thy people, and
into thy houses: and the houses of the Egyptians shall be full of
swarms of flies, and also the ground whereon they are. And I will
sever in that day the land of Goshen, in which my people dwell,
that no swarms of flies shall be there; to the end thou mayest know
that I am the Lord in the midst of the earth.*
*Exodus 9:3-4, 8-11, 18-19, 25-26, Behold, the hand of the Lord is
upon thy cattle which is in the field, upon the horses, upon the*

*asses, upon the camels, upon the oxen, and upon the sheep: there
shall be a very grievous murrain. And the Lord shall sever between
the cattle of Israel and the cattle of Egypt: and there shall nothing
die of all that is the children's of Israel.*

*And the Lord said unto Moses and unto Aaron, Take to you
handfuls of ashes of the furnace, and let Moses sprinkle it toward
the heaven in the sight of Pharaoh. And it shall become small dust
in all the land of Egypt, and shall be a boil breaking forth with
blains upon man, and upon beast, throughout all the land of Egypt.
And they took ashes of the furnace, and stood before Pharaoh; and
Moses sprinkled it up toward heaven; and it became a boil
breaking forth with blains upon man, and upon beast. And the
magicians could not stand before Moses because of the boils; for
the boil was upon the magicians, and upon all the Egyptians.
Behold, tomorrow about this time I will cause it to rain a very
grievous hail, such as hath not been in Egypt since the foundation
thereof even until now. Send therefore now, and gather thy cattle,
and all that thou hast in the field; for upon every man and beast
which shall be found in the field, and shall not be brought home,
the hail shall come down upon them, and they shall die.*

*And the hail smote throughout all the land of Egypt all that was in
the field, both man and beast; and the hail smote every herb of the
field, and brake every tree of the field. Only in the land of Goshen,
where the children of Israel were, was there no hail.*

*Exodus 10:4-5, 15, 21-23, Else, if thou refuse to let my people go,
behold, to morrow will I bring the locusts into thy coast: And they
shall cover the face of the earth, that one cannot be able to see the
earth: and they shall eat the residue of that which is escaped,
which remaineth unto you from the hail, and shall eat every tree
which groweth for you out of the field:*

*For they covered the face of the whole earth, so that the land was
darkened; and they did eat every herb of the land, and all the fruit
of the trees which the hail had left: and there remained not any
green thing in the trees, or in the herbs of the field, through all the
land of Egypt.*

*And the Lord said unto Moses, Stretch out thine hand toward
heaven, that there may be darkness over the land of Egypt, even*

darkness which may be felt. And Moses stretched forth his hand toward heaven; and there was a thick darkness in all the land of Egypt three days: They saw not one another, neither rose any from his place for three days: but all the children of Israel had light in their dwellings.

The tragedies culminated in the death of every firstborn, man and beast, in all of Egypt. We read in *Exodus 11:5-7, And all the firstborn in the land of Egypt shall die, from the firstborn of Pharaoh that sitteth upon his throne, even unto the firstborn of the maidservant that is behind the mill; and all the firstborn of beasts. And there shall be a great cry throughout all the land of Egypt, such as there was none like it, nor shall be like it any more. But against any of the children of Israel shall not a dog move his tongue, against man or beast: that ye may know how that the Lord doth put a difference between the Egyptians and Israel.* Without Jesus, the church leaders who informed me about punishments were correct. We deserved the punishments. We are sunk without Jesus. Just like Peter sinking into the different world under Jesus' feet, we have no hope without Jesus.

But everything changed when Jesus appeared. The first miracle of Jesus was to turn water into wine. We read this in *John 2:1-11, And the third day there was a marriage in Cana of Galilee; and the mother of Jesus was there: And both Jesus was called, and his disciples, to the marriage. And when they wanted wine, the mother of Jesus saith unto him, They have no wine. Jesus saith unto her, Woman, what have I to do with thee? mine hour is not yet come. His mother saith unto the servants, Whatsoever he saith unto you, do it. And there were set there six waterpots of stone, after the manner of the purifying of the Jews, containing two or three firkins apiece. Jesus saith unto them, Fill the waterpots with water. And they filled them up to the brim. And he saith unto them, Draw out now, and bear unto the governor of the feast. And they bare it. When the ruler of the feast had tasted the water that was made wine, and knew not whence it was: (but the servants which drew the water knew;) the governor of the feast called the bridegroom, And saith unto him, Every man at the beginning doth set forth good wine; and when men have well drunk, then that which is worse: but thou hast kept the good wine until now. This beginning of miracles did Jesus in Cana of Galilee, and manifested forth his glory; and his disciples believed on him.*

This new wine represented the new covenant of Jesus. It was the best wine and it was kept until the end of the marriage ceremony. Jesus was now revealed. What was once veiled and hidden is now displayed clearly. The new covenant of Grace would replace the old covenant. We could not fulfill all the requirements of the law but the new covenant would take care of what we could not do. Jesus was the guest but He took care of the host. From His infinite riches, He blessed His host with the finest wine. Similarly, He blessed us to the brim with His new wine.

The contrast between old and new is staggering. With Moses, the water turned into blood bringing death and mourning. With Jesus, the water turned into wine bringing life and celebration. With Moses, there was death in the waters. With Jesus, there was life above the waters. With Moses, all the fishes died, fouling the air. With Jesus, we smell the aroma of grilled fish on the fire for breakfast. With Moses, frogs came out of the bloodied, rank water. With Jesus, a huge catch of fresh sweet fish came out from the sea. On one occasion, a fish even came with money in its mouth. With Moses, the dust of the earth turned to lice. With Jesus, the dust of the earth turned to balm for healing. The blind saw. With Moses, swarms of flies infested the people. With Jesus, swarms and legions of demons left the people. With Moses, the livestock died. With Jesus, the livestock multiplied and the people were blessed abundantly. With Moses, the people could not stand because of the boils and carbuncles. With Jesus, the lame, crippled, and paralyzed walked and carried their beds. With Moses, hailstorms and storms from heaven destroyed the food supply. With Jesus, blessings from heaven multiplied the food supply. Small fishes and loaves of bread multiplied, feeding tens of thousands of people. Storms ceased and waters became calm with Jesus. With Moses, locusts destroyed the last food supplies. The enemy, as the locust, came to steal, kill, and destroy us. With Jesus, the harvest was so plentiful that it was still being collected as the next season of planting began. In Jesus, the enemy has no power over us. We have life and super abundant life in Jesus. With Moses, darkness and sin overran the earth. With Jesus, light overcame the darkness and sin has no dominion over us. With Moses, death came to every firstborn. With Jesus as firstborn, life came to everyone who believed in Him. The dead were raised and they walked with the living. **With Moses, we have condemnation, bondage, and punishments. With Jesus, we have no condemnation, liberty, and grace. Jesus took our punishments and suffered our indignities. He took what we deserved and gave us what we did not deserve. That is amazing Grace and His name is Jesus!**

❧ 26 ❧

JESUS AND SHEEP AND GOATS

The breed of sheep in the Middle East, in Jesus' time, closely resembled goats. From a distance, it is impossible to distinguish between the two. Upon closer inspection, one can see that a sheep's tail is pointed downwards while a goat's tail is pointed upwards. Shepherds often separated the two for various reasons. Sheep are low grazers while goats are low to high grazers. Where there is scant vegetation on the ground, it is advisable to let goats graze first as they will pick off the leaves of shrubs and bushes as well. If sheep are let in first, they will eat all the grass and leave nothing for the goats. Of course, sheep and goats are also separated because they may mate with one another. The offspring is often stillborn. If the offspring survives, called a geep, it is usually infertile. Of course, sheep and goats are often separated because their milk, when processed into cheese, tastes different.

From such mundane, bucolic and rustic pastoral scenes, we switch to see Jesus coming in His glory taking up His place on the throne. Then in this majestic and glorious setting, Jesus begins to separate the nations just like the shepherd above separating the sheep from the goats.

We read this in *Matthew 25:31-46, When the Son of man shall come in his glory, and all the holy angels with him, then shall he sit upon the throne of his glory: And before him shall be gathered all nations: and he shall separate them one from another,*

*as a shepherd divideth his sheep from the goats: And he shall set
the sheep on his right hand, but the goats on the left.*

*Then shall the King say unto them on his right hand, Come,
ye blessed of my Father, inherit the kingdom prepared for you from
the foundation of the world: For I was an hungred, and ye gave me
meat: I was thirsty, and ye gave me drink: I was a stranger, and ye
took me in: Naked, and ye clothed me: I was sick, and ye visited
me: I was in prison, and ye came unto me. Then shall the righteous
answer him, saying, Lord, when saw we thee an hungred, and fed
thee? or thirsty, and gave thee drink?   When saw we thee a
stranger, and took thee in? or naked, and clothed thee? Or when
saw we thee sick, or in prison, and came unto thee? And the King
shall answer and say unto them, Verily I say unto you, Inasmuch as
ye have done it unto one of the least of these my brethren, ye have
done it unto me.*

*Then shall he say also unto them on the left hand, Depart
from me, ye cursed, into everlasting fire, prepared for the devil and
his angels: For I was an hungred, and ye gave me no meat: I was
thirsty, and ye gave me no drink: I was a stranger, and ye took me
not in: naked, and ye clothed me not: sick, and in prison, and ye
visited me not. Then shall they also answer him, saying, Lord,
when saw we thee an hungred, or athirst, or a stranger, or naked,
or sick, or in prison, and did not minister unto thee? Then shall he
answer them, saying, Verily I say unto you, Inasmuch as ye did it
not to one of the least of these, ye did it not to me. And these shall
go away into everlasting punishment: but the righteous into life
eternal.*

At first glance, the answer seems obvious enough. The
sheep, on the right hand of Jesus, did many good works. They gave
food to the hungry; they gave water to the thirsty; they gave shelter
to the stranger; they gave clothes to the poor; and they visited the
sick in the hospitals and the incarcerated in the prisons. They
deserved eternal life for all their good works. The goats, on the left
hand side of Jesus, did none of those things mentioned. They may
have been egotistical, narcissistic, and selfish, caring only about
themselves. Since they did nothing, they deserved nothing but
everlasting punishment. The conclusion would be that 'good

works' are rewarded while 'no works' would be punished. With this scripture alone, we can make people feel guilty and condemned unless they donate their time, energy, money, and other resources to start or advance good works in and around the world. It would have been settled had not Jesus taught further.

In *Matthew 7:21-27*, we read, *Not every one that saith unto me, Lord, Lord, shall enter into the kingdom of heaven; but he that doeth the will of my Father which is in heaven. Many will say to me in that day, Lord, Lord, have we not prophesied in thy name? and in thy name have cast out devils? and in thy name done many wonderful works? And then will I profess unto them, I never knew you: depart from me, ye that work iniquity. Therefore whosoever heareth these sayings of mine, and doeth them, I will liken him unto a wise man, which built his house upon a rock: And the rain descended, and the floods came, and the winds blew, and beat upon that house; and it fell not: for it was founded upon a rock. And every one that heareth these sayings of mine, and doeth them not, shall be likened unto a foolish man, which built his house upon the sand: And the rain descended, and the floods came, and the winds blew, and beat upon that house; and it fell: and great was the fall of it.*

There seems to be a direct contradiction here. Those who have done many good and wonderful works are now rejected by Jesus. How unfair is this? First, He asks us to do good works, promising us rewards. Then when we ask for the rewards, after we have sacrificed all, He throws us out. Sound very much like my terrible boss here on earth, some of you will say. We did the work and he did not pay us.

Obviously, we have misinterpreted the true meaning behind the sheep and the goats' scripture! In the first case, the sheep did many good works but the goats did not. In the second case, both the sheep and the goats did many good works but only the goats were rejected. They may even have done the same exact works, nonetheless only the goats were rejected. So the separation cannot be based upon their works, otherwise the goats must be accepted.

The key here is that the sheep did the will of God but the goats did not. The will of the Father is that we, as sheep, built our house upon a rock. There is only one Solid Rock that we are called to build upon and that Solid Rock is Jesus. The goats also built a house but upon their works, not Jesus. This is akin to them building on sand. **The sheep knew Jesus while the goats did not. It did not matter how hard the goats worked because it is only Jesus that saves, not good works. There is only one 'work' of God that we need do and that is to believe in Jesus.**

In other words, it did not matter if the goats worked like the sheep or not. It did not matter if they looked like sheep. It did not matter if they behaved like sheep. It did not matter if they sounded like sheep. It did not matter if their tails pointed down like sheep. If they did not know Jesus, they would be rejected. For the sheep knew their Shepherd, Jesus Christ. In *John 6:28-29*, we read, *Then said they unto him, What shall we do, that we might work the works of God? Jesus answered and said unto them, This is the work of God, that ye believe on him whom he hath sent.*

Jesus also warned us of false prophets coming in sheep's clothing. In *Matthew 7:15-20, Beware of false prophets, which come to you in sheep's clothing, but inwardly they are ravening wolves. Ye shall know them by their fruits. Do men gather grapes of thorns, or figs of thistles? Even so every good tree bringeth forth good fruit; but a corrupt tree bringeth forth evil fruit. A good tree cannot bring forth evil fruit, neither can a corrupt tree bring forth good fruit. Every tree that bringeth not forth good fruit is hewn down, and cast into the fire. Wherefore by their fruits ye shall know them.*

Any prophet or teacher coming to us prophesying or teaching salvation based on works is a ravening wolf. The works may appear pious and charitable. These teachers may share food and sustenance; they may visit hospitals and prisons; and they may practice long prayers and bible study. But are they teaching the truth? If not, their fruits or their teaching is wrong. The fruits they offer are called thorns and thistles. They bear evil fruits and will be hewn down and cast into the fire. *Luke 6:43-45* states, *For a good tree bringeth not forth corrupt fruit; neither doth a corrupt tree bring forth good fruit. For every tree is known by his own fruit. For of thorns men do not gather figs, nor of a bramble bush gather they grapes. A good man out of the good treasure of his heart bringeth forth that which is good; and an evil man out of the evil treasure of his heart bringeth forth that which is evil: for of the abundance of the heart his mouth speaketh.* The only good fruit is Jesus. Our teaching should be like a good treasure coming out from our hearts. From our hearts or spirits, we should speak and teach abundantly about Jesus. Once again, the only good abundant fruit is Jesus Christ.

❧ 27 ❦

JESUS AND MIXTURES

One of the best examples in the bible about goats trying to behave like sheep is found in the account of Ananias and his wife, Sapphira. At that time, the apostles filled with the Holy Spirit, began to preach the Word of God, Jesus Christ, with boldness. We read in *Acts 4:31-37, And when they had prayed, the place was shaken where they were assembled together; and they were all filled with the Holy Ghost, and they spake the word of God with boldness. And the multitude of them that believed were of one heart and of one soul: neither said any of them that ought of the things which he possessed was his own; but they had all things common. And with great power gave the apostles witness of the resurrection of the Lord Jesus: and great grace was upon them all. Neither was there any among them that lacked: for as many as were possessors of lands or houses sold them, and brought the prices of the things that were sold, And laid them down at the apostles' feet: and distribution was made unto every man according as he had need. And Joses, who by the apostles was surnamed Barnabas, (which is, being interpreted, The son of consolation,) a Levite, and of the country of Cyprus, Having land, sold it, and brought the money, and laid it at the apostles' feet.*

Great Grace was upon them and because of this Grace; they sold land and houses and distributed the proceeds to those in need. They were sheep in that they knew Jesus. Sheep do good works

because of Grace. Their focus was not on their works but on Jesus
who was in them. Because of Grace, everyone had more than
enough. For example, Joses had land, sold it, brought the money,
and laid it at the apostles' feet. Everyone was blessed by Joses'
action.

Right after Joses, we have the account of Ananias and
Sapphira. They too sold land but only brought a part of the sale
proceeds to the apostles. When questioned by Peter, they lied and
were punished with death. Many teachers concluded that
Christians, just like Ananias and Sapphira, would drop dead if their
lives are not perfectly right before God. Lie to God or to others and
you would die!

This account is found in *Acts 5:1-16, But a certain man
named Ananias, with Sapphira his wife, sold a possession, And
kept back part of the price, his wife also being privy to it, and
brought a certain part, and laid it at the apostles' feet. But Peter
said, Ananias, why hath Satan filled thine heart to lie to the Holy
Ghost, and to keep back part of the price of the land? Whiles it
remained, was it not thine own? and after it was sold, was it not in
thine own power? why hast thou conceived this thing in thine
heart? thou hast not lied unto men, but unto God. And Ananias
hearing these words fell down, and gave up the ghost: and great
fear came on all them that heard these things. And the young men
arose, wound him up, and carried him out, and buried him.*

*And it was about the space of three hours after, when his
wife, not knowing what was done, came in. And Peter answered
unto her, Tell me whether ye sold the land for so much? And she
said, Yea, for so much. Then Peter said unto her, How is it that ye
have agreed together to tempt the Spirit of the Lord? behold, the
feet of them which have buried thy husband are at the door, and
shall carry thee out. Then fell she down straightway at his feet, and
yielded up the ghost: and the young men came in, and found her
dead, and, carrying her forth, buried her by her husband. And
great fear came upon all the church, and upon as many as heard
these things.*

*And by the hands of the apostles were many signs and
wonders wrought among the people; (and they were all with one*

accord in Solomon's porch. And of the rest durst no man join himself to them: but the people magnified them. And believers were the more added to the Lord, multitudes both of men and women.) Insomuch that they brought forth the sick into the streets, and laid them on beds and couches, that at the least the shadow of Peter passing by might overshadow some of them. There came also a multitude out of the cities round about unto Jerusalem, bringing sick folks, and them which were vexed with unclean spirits: and they were healed every one.

The above explanation cannot be correct as we see liars everywhere who do not drop dead when they lie. Therefore, there must be some other explanation for this scripture.

Seeing the great blessing brought on by this unprecedented outpouring of the Holy Spirit and Grace, the goats got excited too and tried to emulate the sheep. However, they did not know Jesus, thus their motives were entirely different. For their identity was not in Jesus but in their works. They did not operate from pure Grace but a mixture.

Ananias, in Hebrew, is Hannaniyah meaning the 'grace of Yah' or the grace of God. Sapphira means sapphire, reminding us of the sapphire tablets that the Ten Commandments or law was written on. Together, Ananias and Sapphira represent a mixture of grace and law. They were goats trying to behave and to look like sheep. They wanted to be blessed based upon their own works. They hung out with the early Christians but were not Christians.

Ananias and Sapphira, living under the law mixture, were judged by the law. Under the law, their sin was imputed to them and they were punished with death. If they had been under Grace, there would have been no punishment as Jesus had already taken their punishment upon Himself. Seeing the death of both Ananias and Sapphira, great fear fell upon the people. However, it was not the fear of death by lying but the fear of mixing Jesus or Grace with the law. Mixing grace and law does result in death. While pure law shows us our need for Jesus, a mixture disguises goats as sheep and deceives goats into thinking that they are saved when they are not.

Fearing this mixture, the people quickly rolled up the bodies, like the scrolls of the law, carried them out and buried them. **The mixture had to be buried as it brought death**. After the removal of the mixture of grace and law, many signs and wonders happened. Pure Grace was re-established and reigned in the cities. The sick were brought out into the streets and every one of them was healed. Pure Grace brought complete healing. Jesus, without mixture, resulted in healing everywhere for He is Healer! At the same time, multitudes of believers were added because of Jesus.

The mixture of law and grace is deadly as it gives a false sense of security to the people. The people think that they are saved when they are actually not. In *2 Kings 4:38-41*, we read, *And Elisha came again to Gilgal: and there was a dearth in the land; and the sons of the prophets were sitting before him: and he said unto his servant, Set on the great pot, and seethe pottage for the sons of the prophets. And one went out into the field to gather herbs, and found a wild vine, and gathered thereof wild gourds his lap full, and came and shred them into the pot of pottage: for they knew them not. So they poured out for the men to eat. And it came to pass, as they were eating of the pottage, that they cried out, and said, O thou man of God, there is death in the pot. And they could not eat thereof. But he said, Then bring meal. And he cast it into the pot; and he said, Pour out for the people, that they may eat. And there was no harm in the pot.*

This mixture nearly brought death to Elisha and his students. They were in Gilgal when one of the student prophets went to gather herbs for a stew. He found some good herbs but he also found a wild vine with gourds on it. The good herbs symbolized grace while the wild gourds are from the vine of the law. When the stew was finished, the men ate hungrily. To their dismay, the wild gourds turned out poisonous. The resulting mixture was called death in the pot. A mixture of law and grace leads to death. The only cure for death is Jesus. Elisha called for some meal, which was cast into the deathly mixture. We know that Jesus is our meal offering. When they ate the meal, they were instantaneously healed. Jesus is and always will be our Healer.

Another parable of Jesus illustrates this false sense of security lucidly. In *Luke 18:9-14*, we read, *And he spake this parable unto certain which trusted in themselves that they were righteous, and despised others: Two men went up into the temple to pray; the one a Pharisee, and the other a publican. The Pharisee stood and prayed thus with himself, God, I thank thee, that I am not as other men are, extortioners, unjust, adulterers, or even as this publican. I fast twice in the week, I give tithes of all that I possess. And the publican, standing afar off, would not lift up so much as his eyes unto heaven, but smote upon his breast, saying, God be merciful to me a sinner. I tell you, this man went down to his house justified rather than the other: for every one that exalteth himself shall be abased; and he that humbleth himself shall be exalted.*

The Pharisee was convinced that because of his good and pious acts, he was saved. There was no question in his mind that he was not. The Pharisee fasted, tithed, and abstained from extortions, unjust acts, adultery, and collecting taxes for the Romans. He made the law keepable and was smug in his self-righteousness. While he was far from perfect, he thought he was. He qualified himself before God. Meanwhile, as the Pharisee was congratulating himself for his qualifications, the publican or tax collector was convinced that his acts were evil and sought God's mercy. There was no smugness in his face as he smote his chest and pleaded for mercy. He was not looking for any mixture. He needed Grace and nothing else. He had no qualifications. Therefore, he was qualified by Grace or Jesus.

As I mentioned before in a previous chapter, the problem with people quagmired in mixtures is that it is often difficult to tell them apart from those operating in Grace. On the surface, they tend to look exactly alike. In another parable found in *Matthew 13:24-30, Another parable put he forth unto them, saying, The kingdom of heaven is likened unto a man which sowed good seed in his field: But while men slept, his enemy came and sowed tares among the wheat, and went his way. But when the blade was sprung up, and brought forth fruit, then appeared the tares also. So the servants of the householder came and said unto him, Sir, didst*

not thou sow good seed in thy field? from whence then hath it
tares? He said unto them, An enemy hath done this. The servants
said unto him, Wilt thou then that we go and gather them up? But
he said, Nay; lest while ye gather up the tares, ye root up also the
wheat with them. Let both grow together until the harvest: and in
the time of harvest I will say to the reapers, Gather ye together
first the tares, and bind them in bundles to burn them: but gather
the wheat into my barn.

In this parable of the tares in the field, the sower is Jesus
and the good seed are His sons and daughters. The enemy is satan
and he sowed the tares. Tares are weeds that look very much like
wheat as it is growing up. It is impossible to dig up the tares
without destroying the wheat too as they look alike. However,
when the harvest season comes, the seed heads would look
completely different. Only then can the tares be separated from the
wheat. The wheat are those who know the Living Word while the
tares are those who know only the written word. But even the devil
knows the written word and it is not going to help him either.

Similarly in *Matthew 13:47-48*, we read, *Again, the*
kingdom of heaven is like unto a net, that was cast into the sea, and
gathered of every kind: Which, when it was full, they drew to
shore, and sat down, and gathered the good into vessels, but cast
the bad away.

The seawaters represent the world and the fishes in it
represent the multitudes of people from every nation and tongue.
The net is the gospel and it caught a huge catch of fish. However,
not all the fishes in the sea are caught in the net. Many people
reject the gospel and are not in the net. Those caught in the net
look very much alike until they are brought to the shore. Then the
good fish are separated from the bad fish. The good fishes are
those whose faith is in Jesus and His finished work. These are
gathered into vessels representing the rooms in heaven. The bad
fishes, which look exactly the same, are those whose faith is in
their works and achievements. These are gathered and cast away
from Jesus.

However, the separation of good from bad is not for us to
do. It is unwise for anyone to judge their brothers and sisters based

on good works and performance for we do not know the hearts of our brothers and sisters. While good works may indicate a transformed man, it is never a perfect indicator. A person doing many good works may be very self-righteous or he may not be. Just remember that there are many unbelievers who perform many, many good works also.

A person who judges others has forgotten that he was also cleansed from his own sins. *2 Peter 1:9* states, *But he that lacketh these things is blind, and cannot see afar off, and hath forgotten that he was purged from his old sins.* The truth is that he has forgotten Jesus! He has also forgotten that the devil is the sower of tares, confusion, and mixtures. As the devil turned Eve away from God to self-works in the garden, he is still trying to turn us away from Jesus to our own works. We see in *Revelation 12:10, And I heard a loud voice saying in heaven, Now is come salvation, and strength, and the kingdom of our God, and the power of his Christ: for the accuser of our brethren is cast down, which accused them before our God day and night.* Then in *1 John 2:1,* we read, *And if any man sin, we have an advocate with the Father, Jesus Christ the righteous* and in *John 5:22, For the Father judgeth no man, but hath committed all judgment unto the Son.* The devil is the accuser of all of us while Jesus is both our advocate and judge. **Only a Perfect Judge can tell what is truly in a person's heart. And that judge is Jesus, not us!**

When the time of separation comes, the lukewarm or mixture of hot and cold would be spewed out by the Judge. In *Revelation 3:15-16,* we read, *I know thy works, that thou art neither cold nor hot: I would thou wert cold or hot. So then because thou art lukewarm, and neither cold nor hot, I will spue thee out of my mouth.* Jesus prefers us to be cold or hot, not lukewarm. If we were as cold as the law, we would see our absolute need for Him. If we were hot, we would see that all of our works are a result of being loved by Him first. However, if we were lukewarm, we would think that we are saved when we are actually not.

❧ 28 ❦

JESUS AND BRICKS

There was a commercial in the eighties about donuts. The commercial showed a baker mouthing incessantly that it was time to make the donuts! Morning till night, in all seasons, and in all temperatures, he would make donuts.

There is a similar story in the bible but instead of donuts, it was about bricks. How many bricks can you make in your lifetime? Every day, 24/7, for the rest of your life regardless of circumstances you are to make bricks! Or thinking of ways to make bricks. Bricks in the morning, bricks in the afternoon, and bricks in the night. Then one day everything changed. Somebody stood up and declared that you do not have to make bricks anymore but that you are to have a well-deserved rest! Let us read this account in *Exodus 5:1-9, And afterward Moses and Aaron went in, and told Pharaoh, Thus saith the Lord God of Israel, Let my people go, that they may hold a feast unto me in the wilderness. And Pharaoh said, Who is the Lord, that I should obey his voice to let Israel go? I know not the Lord, neither will I let Israel go. And they said, The God of the Hebrews hath met with us: let us go, we pray thee, three days' journey into the desert, and sacrifice unto the Lord our God; lest he fall upon us with pestilence, or with the sword.*

And the king of Egypt said unto them, Wherefore do ye, Moses and Aaron, let the people from their works? get you unto your burdens. And Pharaoh said, Behold, the people of the land now are many, and ye make them rest from their burdens. And Pharaoh commanded the same day the taskmasters of the people, and their officers, saying, Ye shall no more give the people straw to make brick, as heretofore: let them go and gather straw for themselves. And the tale of the bricks, which they did make heretofore, ye shall lay upon them; ye shall not diminish ought thereof: for they be idle; therefore they cry, saying, Let us go and sacrifice to our God. Let there more work be laid upon the men, that they may labour therein; and let them not regard vain words.

The Israelites had been making bricks for Pharaoh's fortified cities. It was all toil and grind. The process of making bricks was onerous. The Israelites would be given straw, which would be mixed with the clay they had collected from the river. The straw was needed to reinforce the loose clay particles, which would give stability to the brick. Then came the mixing, the trampling, the forming, the drying, the firing and the transportation of the bricks to the cities. It was endless drudgery. One day, Moses came and announced a rest for the people. The purpose of the rest was to allow the people to go and worship God at Mount Sinai. *Exodus 3:11-12* states, *And Moses said unto God, Who am I, that I should go unto Pharaoh, and that I should bring forth the children of Israel out of Egypt? And he said, Certainly I will be with thee; and this shall be a token unto thee, that I have sent thee: When thou hast brought forth the people out of Egypt, ye shall serve God upon this mountain.* The journey there would only take three days. Hearing that, the people gladly laid down their brick-making burdens and prepared themselves for a rest.

However, Pharaoh refused Moses' request outright. He was incensed that the people had rested from their works. Therefore, he decreed that, while still meeting the daily quota of bricks, no more straw would be provided for the people. Instead, they would have to collect stubble and make do with that. Stubble is inferior to straw, making the bricks more prone to crumbling. If their daily quota of bricks were not met, they would be berated and beaten. The end result of asking for rest from Pharaoh was more work.

We see in *Exodus 5:10-21, And the taskmasters of the people went out, and their officers, and they spake to the people, saying, Thus saith Pharaoh, I will not give you straw. Go ye, get you straw where ye can find it: yet not ought of your work shall be diminished. So the people were scattered abroad throughout all the land of Egypt to gather stubble instead of straw. And the taskmasters hasted them, saying, Fulfil your works, your daily tasks, as when there was straw.*

And the officers of the children of Israel, which Pharaoh's taskmasters had set over them, were beaten, and demanded, Wherefore have ye not fulfilled your task in making brick both yesterday and to day, as heretofore? Then the officers of the children of Israel came and cried unto Pharaoh, saying, Wherefore dealest thou thus with thy servants? There is no straw given unto thy servants, and they say to us, Make brick: and, behold, thy servants are beaten; but the fault is in thine own people.

But he said, Ye are idle, ye are idle: therefore ye say, Let us go and do sacrifice to the Lord. Go therefore now, and work; for there shall no straw be given you, yet shall ye deliver the tale of bricks. And the officers of the children of Israel did see that they were in evil case, after it was said, Ye shall not minish ought from your bricks of your daily task. And they met Moses and Aaron, who stood in the way, as they came forth from Pharaoh: And they said unto them, The Lord look upon you, and judge; because ye have made our savour to be abhorred in the eyes of Pharaoh, and in the eyes of his servants, to put a sword in their hand to slay us.

However, the account did not end there. After many vexations, Pharaoh gradually and in stages agreed to (1) let the people rest and worship God but only if they stayed in Egypt, (2) let them leave Egypt but not to wander too far away, (3) let them leave but their livestock had to stay behind, and (4) a complete release of the people and all they had.

We read of these stages in *Exodus 8:25-28, And Pharaoh called for Moses and for Aaron, and said, Go ye, sacrifice to your God in the land. And Moses said, It is not meet so to do; for we shall sacrifice the abomination of the Egyptians to the Lord our God: lo, shall we sacrifice the abomination of the Egyptians before*

their eyes, and will they not stone us? We will go three days'
journey into the wilderness, and sacrifice to the Lord our God, as
he shall command us. And Pharaoh said, I will let you go, that ye
may sacrifice to the Lord your God in the wilderness; only ye shall
not go very far away: intreat for me. Then in *Exodus 10:24-26,*
And Pharaoh called unto Moses, and said, Go ye, serve the Lord;
only let your flocks and your herds be stayed: let your little ones
also go with you. And Moses said, Thou must give us also
sacrifices and burnt offerings, that we may sacrifice unto the Lord
our God. Our cattle also shall go with us; there shall not an hoof
be left behind; for thereof must we take to serve the Lord our God;
and we know not with what we must serve the Lord, until we come
thither.

We are saved by Grace alone plus nothing else. It was
Jesus' sacrifice for us that enabled us to have a new life. We did
nothing to deserve salvation but received it as a free gift. There
were no works or sacrifices on our part at all.

However, once we become saved, there is a teaching that it
now depends entirely upon us to maintain that salvation that was
freely given in the first place. What we had nothing to do with
initially now becomes central. By our works, we maintain our
salvation. The problem with this teaching is that since we can lose
our salvation by our own works then, corollary, we can also earn
our salvation back again by more good works. This cannot be so as
salvation comes only by resting in the finished work of Jesus!

God desired His people to come to Mount Sinai to worship
Him and to experience His goodness to them. God wanted them to
cease from their works of brick making which would ultimately,
kill them. Instead, God wanted them to rest in Him so they could
receive life. However, in order to do that, they had to give up their
livelihood of making bricks. This was no easy task as the people
wanted to make bricks!

When God told Moses to take His people out of Egypt, He
meant rest in Himself first and only later, to rest in the Promised
Land. Moses misunderstood and asked for just a few days rest.
After all, the people had to make bricks. However, Pharaoh,
representing the world and the devil, flatly rejected it. He wanted

the people to work, not to rest. The devil acts in much the same way today. Work is elevated and worshipped to such an extent that we find our identity in our work. If we make a lot of money or 'bricks', we are lauded. If we make few bricks, we are shamed and made to feel guilty. We are also, many times, punished and rebuked for poor performance.

Since the devil cannot stop Jesus from rescuing sinners, he uses this same technique even after we become saved. He tells us that we will be rejected by Jesus if we do not do enough good works after our salvation. He lies to us and tells us that we are idle and lazy and therefore, must do more works to satisfy Jesus. He takes away our straw and forces us to go out and gather stubble. He demands that we produce more bricks even though more work does not equal better bricks. More bricks crumbled as more work to find more stubble was added. And he punishes us when we cannot perform. He declares that since we did not fulfill our quota of bricks we are now in danger of losing our salvation. When we try to rest in Jesus as the sole way to salvation, we are labeled slothful and indolent, prone to sinning. The prescription is more and more work to maintain our salvation. The devil wants us to focus on our own works and not on Jesus.

And should the Grace of God, Jesus, be preached, let the people agree with the message but to stay in their works. They must worship God in Egypt. But as Jesus becomes more and more prominent in the peoples' lives, they may demand more of Jesus. In that case, let them go a little ways off Egypt - a little Grace mixed with a lot of law. And if they choose to leave altogether, then let them leave their livestock behind. Frighten these people with loss of blessings. After all, you cannot just trust Jesus blindly, you have to take control. What happens if Jesus does not move? It is like a person who hears about Grace but is yet caught up in the law. The person may desire Jesus but the devil tricks the person to settle for 80% law and 20% grace. Then 50% law and 50% grace. As a last resort, the devil will allow the person to have 99% grace and 1% law. After all, a person must do some good, even if it is only a drop, to be accepted by God, right?

The wiles or cunning strategy of the devil is to keep you in varying levels of works or various mixtures of works with Grace. *Ephesians 6:11* says to *Put on the whole armour of God, that ye may be able to stand against the wiles of the devil.* We do not fight with the devil but to stand up to his lies. We should quote scripture back to the devil. In *Exodus 7:16*, we read, *And thou shalt say unto him, The Lord God of the Hebrews hath sent me unto thee, saying, Let my people go, that they may serve me in the wilderness.* Moses was told to say with clarity that His people were to be let go completely so that they would serve Him alone. **We should not be fooled any longer by the devil and his mixtures. For there should be no works on our part. Just God alone! 100% Jesus, 0% works!**

And when the Israelites finally went one hundred percent into the wilderness to serve God and to see His goodness, God blessed them abundantly. In *Exodus 12:35-36*, we read, *And the children of Israel did according to the word of Moses; and they borrowed of the Egyptians jewels of silver, and jewels of gold, and raiment: And the Lord gave the people favour in the sight of the Egyptians, so that they lent unto them such things as they required. And they spoiled the Egyptians.* Without having to earn it by their efforts, they received jewels of silver, jewels of gold and fine raiment. When they were working day and night before, by their own efforts, they could never afford such things. But now, everything they required was provided by God. **When we rest in the presence of the Provider, everything we need is provided for.**

❧ 29 ❧

JESUS AND DYING TO SELF

There are many writings in the bible where Jesus taught us lessons about law versus grace. Some of them are found in the parables of Jesus, one of which is found in *Luke 10:25-37, And, behold, a certain lawyer stood up, and tempted him, saying, Master, what shall I do to inherit eternal life? He said unto him, What is written in the law? how readest thou? And he answering said, Thou shalt love the Lord thy God with all thy heart, and with all thy soul, and with all thy strength, and with all thy mind; and thy neighbour as thyself. And he said unto him, Thou hast answered right: this do, and thou shalt live. But he, willing to justify himself, said unto Jesus, And who is my neighbour?*

And Jesus answering said, A certain man went down from Jerusalem to Jericho, and fell among thieves, which stripped him of his raiment, and wounded him, and departed, leaving him half dead. And by chance there came down a certain priest that way: and when he saw him, he passed by on the other side. And likewise a Levite, when he was at the place, came and looked on him, and passed by on the other side.

But a certain Samaritan, as he journeyed, came where he was: and when he saw him, he had compassion on him, And went to him, and bound up his wounds, pouring in oil and wine, and set him on his own beast, and brought him to an inn, and took care of him. And on the morrow when he departed, he took out two pence,

*and gave them to the host, and said unto him, Take care of him;
and whatsoever thou spendest more, when I come again, I will
repay thee.*

*Which now of these three, thinkest thou, was neighbour
unto him that fell among the thieves? And he said, He that shewed
mercy on him. Then said Jesus unto him, Go, and do thou likewise.*

Many teachers use this parable to illustrate the need for us
to be altruistic and charitable to others. When others fall onto hard
times, it is our duty to be unselfish and to help them. We should be
self-sacrificing and generous in our help. That way, God will be
pleased with us when we get to heaven.

However, the intent and purpose of the parable is actually
completely different. It has no magnanimous qualities in it as it
was spoken by Jesus to a Jewish lawyer who religiously adhered to
and practiced the law of Moses. The lawyer challenged Jesus with
the familiar question of what he must do to inherit eternal life.
Before he asked Jesus the question, he had already researched,
compiled, and written down his answer. It was about loving God
with all your mind, soul, and strength; and to love your neighbor as
yourself. It was all about him and his works. When Jesus agreed
with him, he asked Jesus for a definition of the word 'neighbor',
confident that he had qualified.

This famous parable was Jesus' response. Jerusalem was
the seat of the temple and employed many people. Jericho was a
suburb of Jerusalem and the road to and from Jerusalem was
sometimes fraught with hazards such as thieves, swindlers, and
crooks. A certain man was robbed and severely beaten to an inch
of his life on this road by thieves. A priest came by but when he
saw the man half dead decided to cross the street and pass this man
on the other side. Then a Levite passed by, looked on the battered
man and also passed by on the other side. Finally, a Samaritan
passed by and helped the Jew. Samaritans and Jews hate each
other, the feud dating back to the hatred that Joseph's brothers had
against Joseph. But as the Samaritan was the only person who
assisted the Jew, the lawyer grudgingly admitted that the Samaritan
sounded most like the neighbor mentioned in the law. The Jewish
lawyer's hatred for the Samaritans was so deep that he could not

even say the word but called the Samaritan 'he that showed mercy on him'. It was an untenable parable as it required the lawyer to love the Samaritan, his neighbor, as much as he loved himself. It was impossible for him, as the Samaritan did not merit such love.

The half- dead man represented us. We were without hope, beaten up by sin and left to die. The priest and the Levite, just like the lawyer, personified the law. If we are beaten up, then the law must have required it. The law is unbending and has no grace in it. As far as the priest and the Levite were concerned, the half-dead Jew deserved his beating, as he must have sinned. The Samaritan, who was free from the law, symbolized Grace. Seeing the man mortally wounded, he tore up his own clothes to make swaths of bandages to bind up the man's wounds. We are clothed with Grace. Only Jesus would sacrifice Himself to make us whole again. The oil and the wine poured into the man signified Jesus and the Holy Spirit being poured into us. Jesus healed us, rescued us, carried us to a safe place, paid the price for us and continued to maintain us in His Grace. What was impossible to do under the law was perfectly possible under Grace. It was possible because Jesus did it for us.

A few chapters later in the book of Luke, the parable above came to life. A rich ruler asked Jesus what he must do to inherit eternal life! We read of this in *Luke 18:18-30, And a certain ruler asked him, saying, Good Master, what shall I do to inherit eternal life? And Jesus said unto him, Why callest thou me good? none is good, save one, that is, God. Thou knowest the commandments, Do not commit adultery, Do not kill, Do not steal, Do not bear false witness, Honour thy father and thy mother. And he said, All these have I kept from my youth up.*

Now when Jesus heard these things, he said unto him, Yet lackest thou one thing: sell all that thou hast, and distribute unto the poor, and thou shalt have treasure in heaven: and come, follow me. And when he heard this, he was very sorrowful: for he was very rich. And when Jesus saw that he was very sorrowful, he said, How hardly shall they that have riches enter into the kingdom of God! For it is easier for a camel to go through a needle's eye, than for a rich man to enter into the kingdom of God. And they that

heard it said, Who then can be saved? And he said, The things
which are impossible with men are possible with God.

Since the rich ruler wanted the law, Jesus gave him the law
and its commandments. The man replied with pride that he had
kept all the commandments, and not only that but he had kept them
since he was a youth. Seeing the pride that came from following
the letter of the law, Jesus asked the ruler to sell all that he had and
to distribute the proceeds to the poor. Of course, the rich ruler
could not do that, as the poor were undeserving of his riches. To
him they were poor because of sin in their lives. God was
punishing them with poverty. He could not comprehend such an
outrageous request. He felt sorrow not because he lost the
opportunity to follow Jesus but because he could not do what Jesus
asked him to do. He thought he could do it all but he could not. He
thought he deserved eternal life because of his works but he was
sorely disappointed.

To the rich ruler, money was his god. He said he had kept
all the commandments yet he could not even keep the first
commandment. This scripture had nothing to do with riches. It had
to do with the law. The law showed that the man could not save
himself. When asked by his disciples, Jesus replied that it was
impossible for men to save themselves. Salvation is only possible
with God because only Jesus could fulfill all the points of the law.

Following the scripture of the rich ruler, we have the well-
known scripture of an undeserving rich conniver by the name of
Zacchaeus. Because of his short stature, he could not catch a
glimpse of Jesus. Therefore, by his own hands and feet, he climbed
up a sycamore tree to see Jesus. However, there was no need to
climb up the tree for Jesus is not up in the tree. He came down the
tree a long time ago.

In *Luke 19:1-10*, we read, *And Jesus entered and passed*
through Jericho. And, behold, there was a man named Zacchaeus,
which was the chief among the publicans, and he was rich. And he
sought to see Jesus who he was; and could not for the press,
because he was little of stature. And he ran before, and climbed up
into a sycamore tree to see him: for he was to pass that way. And
when Jesus came to the place, he looked up, and saw him, and said

unto him, Zacchaeus, make haste, and come down; for to day I must abide at thy house. And he made haste, and came down, and received him joyfully.

And when they saw it, they all murmured, saying, That he was gone to be guest with a man that is a sinner. And Zacchaeus stood, and said unto the Lord; Behold, Lord, the half of my goods I give to the poor; and if I have taken any thing from any man by false accusation, I restore him fourfold. And Jesus said unto him, This day is salvation come to this house, forsomuch as he also is a son of Abraham. For the Son of man is come to seek and to save that which was lost.

In this scripture, Zacchaeus quickly climbed down from his works and received Jesus joyfully into his house and his life. We see in *Romans 2:4, Or despisest thou the riches of his goodness and forbearance and longsuffering; not knowing that the goodness of God leadeth thee to repentance?* It is indeed the goodness of God that led him to repentance. Repentance comes when we see the goodness of God towards us. Grace entered him that day and he began his radical grace life by giving away half of his possessions. Zacchaeus did not encounter punishment, judgment, condemnation, guilt, blame, accusation, or finger pointing on that memorable day. He saw none of the law so he became radically changed. All he saw was Jesus' love, so he could not help himself but to love others back! Jesus came to seek and save those who are lost. Whether we admit to it or not, every one of us is lost and in need of Jesus.

While we may all agree that we need Jesus, many of us are clueless on how the process actually works. We fall into the trap of believing that that in order to deny ourselves and take up our cross daily, we have to practice self-denial. Thus, the more we deny our flesh and self-desires, the holier we become. The process is full of insecurity as there are no standards for how much self-denial is needed before it is enough. If we do not feel secure, then we have to deny ourselves some more until we feel that we have denied ourselves enough. That feeling of having done enough lasts for only a short while until the whole cycle of self-denial starts again.

In the history of mankind, there was a Syrian, Simeon Stylites, who reportedly spent more than forty years on a small platform atop a high pillar to feel worthy before God, self denying himself daily. The initial pillar of Simeon stood nine feet from the ground but successive pillars grew taller and taller until the final pillar stood about fifty feet from the ground. For many of us, we may need much higher pillars. We can deny ourselves, practice asceticism, on ever-growing pillars until we reach the moon only to find that God's holiness is much higher than that. No amount of self-righteousness and self-discipline can ever save us.

In *Luke 9:23-26,* we read, *And he said to them all, If any man will come after me, let him deny himself, and take up his cross daily, and follow me. For whosoever will save his life shall lose it: but whosoever will lose his life for my sake, the same shall save it. For what is a man advantaged, if he gain the whole world, and lose himself, or be cast away? For whosoever shall be ashamed of me and of my words, of him shall the Son of man be ashamed, when he shall come in his own glory, and in his Father's, and of the holy angels.* The real meaning of denying ourselves and taking up our cross daily is to be Jesus conscious daily. We are to deny as in reminding ourselves that we are dead and crucified in Christ daily. We are to esteem and prize the finished work of Jesus on the cross daily. **The more we focus on Jesus and what He did for us on the cross the more we die to self. It ultimately becomes all about Him and nothing about us.**

⮞ 30 ⮜

JESUS AND TREASURE

In many societies, our value is based upon the work that we do. For example, when two friends meet and talk, their conversation may sound something like this:

Friend 1: "Long time no see! How are you doing?"

Friend 2: "I'm fine! It's so good to see you after all this time. So what are you doing now?"

Friend 1: "Nothing much. I'm working at the mall as a security guard. How 'bout you?"

Friend 2: "Well, I graduated from Harvard and am now a doctor at Beth Sinai hospital!"

Friend1: "Wow! That's so cool! You must be making a ton of money!"

The conclusion is that Friend 2 is of much higher value than Friend 1 because of the fact that he/she is a doctor and that he/she is, presumably, making a ton of money. While there is some truth in the hypothetical conversation above, how true is this from Jesus' perspective? Are we valued more because of our work? Is our identity in our achievements? Are we defined by our failures? What is our value?

In the Old Testament, there is a system of valuation. It is found in *Leviticus 27:1-8, And **the Lord spake unto Moses**, saying, Speak unto the children of Israel, and say unto them, When a man shall make a singular vow, the persons shall be for the Lord by thy* *estimation. And thy estimation shall be of the male from twenty years old even unto sixty years old, even thy estimation shall be fifty shekels of silver, after the shekel of the sanctuary. And if it be a female, then thy estimation shall be thirty shekels. And if it be from five years old even unto twenty years old, then thy estimation shall be of the male twenty shekels, and for the female ten shekels. And if it be from a month old even unto five years old, then thy estimation shall be of the male five shekels of silver, and for the female thy estimation shall be three shekels of silver. And if it be from sixty years old and above; if it be a male, then thy estimation shall be fifteen shekels, and for the female ten shekels. But if he be poorer than thy estimation, then he shall present himself before the priest, and the priest shall value him; according to his ability that vowed shall the priest value him.*

This chapter in Leviticus dealt with people who had made vows to God – to serve in the temple for life. Verses 1 to 8 dealt specifically with people. The rest of the chapter covered animals, houses, fields and land vowed to God. At that time, an Israelite could make a vow to God to dedicate his life in service to God. He could also dedicate his wife, son or daughter as well. To find out the value of his work, he would go before Moses who would put a valuation upon him. The value differed from person to person depending on their age and what they could do. It ranged from fifty shekels to three shekels of silver.

After some time had passed, the man may change his mind. Maybe his farm is not doing too well and he would like to break his vow. He may want to redeem himself (or his wife or his son or daughter) back. Now, Moses has fixed his valuation beforehand. As the man does not have that much money now, he cannot go before Moses because Moses, who represented the law, is inflexible. The price is set and cannot be changed. Therefore, he cannot redeem himself before Moses.

However, God in His grace provided a way out for all the Israelites who had become poorer but still wanted to redeem themselves or their family. They did not have to go before Moses but could present themselves before the priest. The priest would then value the man according to his ability. If the man was worth

50 shekels of silver before, the priest could now say that the man is worth only 5 shekels of silver now. Thus, the man only has to pay 5 shekels of silver to redeem himself. Similarly, to redeem his wife, the priest could pronounce that the wife was now worth 1 shekel of silver. That is good news too but the sad fact is that his wife is now worth only 1 shekel of silver. He has a 1-shekel wife! That is not so good news! In fact, both of them are now worth considerably less.

However, in the New Testament, when a man cannot pay his debt for sin and go before Jesus, Jesus does the reverse of the Old Testament priest. He sets a high price for the man to be redeemed! How high is this price you might ask? Let us see from one of Jesus' parables. In *Matthew 13:44*, we read, *Again, the kingdom of heaven is like unto treasure hid in a field; the which when a man hath found, he hideth, and for joy thereof goeth and selleth all that he hath, and buyeth that field.*

The face value explanation is simple enough. A man has leased a field to plant in. As he is ploughing the field, the plough hits a metal box. He quickly digs up the box, opens it and finds treasure inside. Knowing that by law he has to cede the treasure to the rightful owner, he quickly decides to hide it. He puts it back in the box and buries it again. Then he goes and sells all that he has. With that sum of money, he goes back to the landowner, and asks to buy the land. The landowner may have inquired as to the reason for the purchase as the man had already leased the land. The man lies, hiding the find of the treasure from its legal owner, concocts up a plausible reason for breaking the lease, and finally buys up the field at the lowest possible cost. It is a story of greed, lies, nefarious schemes, and detestable illegal cover-ups!

Then I heard an explanation of this parable from a traditional viewpoint. It goes like this: the treasure in the field is Jesus. When you find Jesus, you should sell all that you have and buy Him because Jesus is worth any price. No matter how much it costs you, you must pay the price because Jesus is worth it. Pay everything you have to buy Jesus and hide Him in your heart!

Both explanations above seem incorrect. The first one cannot be correct, as Jesus would never tell us to lie to and cheat

the correct owner. The second one cannot be correct because
sinners never seek Jesus, only Jesus seeks sinners! Furthermore,
and more importantly, we cannot have anything that valuable that
we can afford to buy Jesus. Of course, even if we have something
of that value, Jesus is still not for sale! He is a free gift! And Jesus
is not something which you hide but is someone whom you share
and shout about.

So the parable can only be understood when explained by
Jesus, not man. In *Mark 4:13, 33-34*, we read, *And he said unto
them, Know ye not this parable? and how then will ye know all
parables? 33 And with many such parables spake he the word
unto them, as they were able to hear it. 34 But without a parable
spake he not unto them: and when they were alone, he expounded
all things to his disciples.* Jesus took time to explain to his
disciples the meaning of his parables. He explained in depth the
first parable, the parable of the sower, so that the meaning of the
rest of the parables could be clear.

The field represents the world. There are treasures hidden
within this world. The treasures are extremely expensive. Jesus is
seeking these treasures. In *Luke 19:10*, it states, *For the Son of
man is come to seek and to save that which was lost.* Jesus seeks
and seeks until He eventually finds a treasure. He is joyous over
His find. In *Luke 15:10*, we read that *there is joy in the presence
of the angels of God over one sinner that repenteth.* Even the
angels in heaven rejoice that another treasure has been found by
Jesus. The treasure is so valuable and precious that it must be
hidden from thieves who would like nothing more than to steal it.
But like Noah, no enemy or storm can ever snatch us away from
Jesus. In *Colossians 3:3*, we read, *your life is hid with Christ in
God.* We are hid by Christ in Christ and with Christ. No thief can
ever steal you away from Jesus.

**The treasure is you! You are that one treasure that He
found in this world. But you are very expensive. An angel
cannot redeem you for you are worth more than an angel. A
cherubim and a seraphim cannot redeem you for you are
worth more than them. In order to buy you God had to give up
everything, which is Jesus Christ - who is worth everything to**

the Father. If we were any cheaper, then we would have been redeemed with and angel, a cherubim, or a seraphim. But our price is too high. In *1 Corinthians 6:20,* we read, ***For ye are bought with a price*** **and that price is Jesus. Jesus is of inestimable worth to God. He is priceless! And in order to buy you, God gave up Jesus. Your price is Jesus. Your worth is Jesus. And because Jesus is priceless, you are priceless. You are invaluable because Jesus is invaluable.**

If we reject our true value and put a low valuation upon ourselves, we are in effect saying to Jesus that He is of comparable low value. At the same time, we also say to God that He had not sent anything valuable to redeem us. **We insult both Jesus and God by not valuing ourselves according to His valuation.**

In the Old Testament, the priest sets a low valuation for us according to our ability to pay. In the New Testament, Jesus sets a high valuation for us according to His ability to pay. That is why you and I are priceless!

❧ 31 ❧

JESUS AND FAITH

I remember an incident in my church when a woman was brought up for healing. She had a cancer growing on her liver and the doctors had told her that she was going to die in three months time. She had prayed and fasted for healing but to no avail. All her friends from a legalistic church had chided her for not having enough faith to be healed. Listening to her friends had made her feel condemned and guilty for not having enough faith. But she continued trying and went through a works program that reminded me of world class athletes preparing for the Olympics. She was exhausted by the time she came to my church. I explained to her that Jesus had already healed her and all that she had to do was to claim by faith what had already been done. There was no need for big faith or even bigger faith should the first 'big faith' fails. We claimed the healing that Jesus had already provided for her and she became healed of the cancer. Nine years later, she is still completely healed.

There are two types of faith being taught today. The first type is called 'law-based' faith. When we pray to God for a miracle or for a change in our circumstance, God does nothing until we first jump through faith hoops. When we finally attain a standard of faith that pleases God, He will nod His head in satisfaction and then, and only then, will He release the miracle that we had been seeking. If we fail to achieve the required level of faith, then we have to continue trying until we succeed. There is no guarantee of success and there is no clear standard as to when we have achieved enough faith to please God. After all, no pain, no gain! The main emphasis is for us to do as much as possible to gain favor with God. The only way to grow our faith is through our own abilities and efforts.

The second type of faith is called 'Grace-based faith'. First, we acknowledge that Jesus has done it all for us by His finished work on the cross. Our faith gymnastics do not move, influence, or add to what God has already provided through Jesus. We cannot persuade or cajole God to move because of the faith-works that we are doing. **Grace has no works in it; otherwise, it is no longer grace. Similarly, works has no grace in it; otherwise, it is no longer works.** There are also no mixtures of grace and works. It is all of grace and none of works or vice versa. In *Romans 11:6*, we read, *And if by grace, then is it no more of works: otherwise grace is no more grace. But if it be of works, then is it no more grace: otherwise work is no more work.*

The definition of grace is 'an unmerited gift or blessing brought to man by Jesus Christ'. The gift is actually Jesus Himself and the love, favor and kindness from Jesus towards us. Our response to grace is gratitude and thankfulness. Grace has nothing to do with us. Grace is one hundred percent God and from God. Grace existed before time began and was provided before the law was given. It is impossible to understand 'grace-based faith' without understanding that faith comes after grace.

We read in *Romans 4:16-22, Therefore it is of faith, that it might be by grace; to the end the promise might be sure to all the seed; not to that only which is of the law, but to that also which is of the faith of Abraham; who is the father of us all, (As it is written, I have made thee a father of many nations,) before him whom he believed, even God, who quickeneth the dead, and calleth those things which be not as though they were. Who against hope believed in hope, that he might become the father of many nations; according to that which was spoken, So shall thy seed be. And being not weak in faith, he considered not his own body now dead, when he was about an hundred years old, neither yet the deadness of Sara's womb: He staggered not at the promise of God through unbelief; but was strong in faith, giving glory to God; And being fully persuaded that, what he had promised, he was able also to perform. And therefore it was imputed to him for righteousness.*

When God promised a son to Abraham, it was all favor from God's part. Abraham by faith believed and accepted what God had promised and did not look at his old weakened body. Grace was given first. Then God saw Abraham's faith in what He had promised. This faith in God was imputed to Abraham for righteousness.

Even our salvation is Grace-based faith. In *Ephesians 2:8,* we read, *For by grace are ye saved through faith; and that not of yourselves: it is the gift of God.* Grace was provided for us first. Jesus was the free gift offering given to us first. Then by saving-faith, we believe in Him and receive the free gift of salvation. However, we did not only receive salvation but all that Jesus did for us on the cross. New life, healing, freedom from sin, victory over circumstances, prosperity and blessings, righteousness and holiness are all free gifts for us and we can appropriate each and every one of them by faith. Therefore, our faith rests squarely upon what Jesus did for us. Our faith to appropriate the free gifts is by itself a free gift from God. God gives us the faith to receive His blessings that He provided. *Romans 10:17* states that *faith cometh by hearing, and hearing by the word of God.* Faith came by hearing the Word of God, Jesus. Without Jesus, we cannot have grace-based faith.

There are many accounts in the bible whereby the people heard of Jesus and His grace, then approached or called out to Jesus. In every instance, Grace came first. In *Matthew 20:29-34, And as they departed from Jericho, a great multitude followed him. And, behold, two blind men sitting by the way side, when they heard that Jesus passed by, cried out, saying, Have mercy on us, O Lord, thou Son of David. And the multitude rebuked them, because they should hold their peace: but they cried the more, saying, Have mercy on us, O Lord, thou Son of David. And Jesus stood still, and called them, and said, What will ye that I shall do unto you? They say unto him, Lord, that our eyes may be opened. So Jesus had compassion on them, and touched their eyes: and immediately their eyes received sight, and they followed him.* The two blind men sitting by the way side heard about Jesus long before Jesus passed by them. God deposited faith in their hearts to receive their blessings. Jesus saw their faith and healed them. Now they could see their Faith, Jesus.

Again in *Matthew 9:20-22*, we read, *And, behold, a woman, which was diseased with an issue of blood twelve years, came behind him, and touched the hem of his garment: For she said within herself, If I may but touch his garment, I shall be whole. But Jesus turned him about, and when he saw her, he said, Daughter, be of good comfort; thy faith hath made thee whole. And the woman was made whole from that hour.* The woman with the issue of blood heard about Jesus and pressed in to touch His garment. Jesus turned around and saw her faith, the faith deposited by Him in her. And with this faith, she was made whole.

The people in Capernaum brought the paralytic to Jesus through a hole cut in the roof because they heard that Grace had come. *Mark 2:1-5, And again he entered into Capernaum, after some days; and it was noised that he was in the house. And straightway many were gathered together, insomuch that there was no room to receive them, no, not so much as about the door: and he preached the word unto them. And they come unto him, bringing one sick of the palsy, which was borne of four. And when they could not come nigh unto him for the press, they uncovered the roof where he was: and when they had broken it up, they let down the bed wherein the sick of the palsy lay. When Jesus saw their faith, he said unto the sick of the palsy, Son, thy sins be forgiven thee.* When the bed was lowered through the ceiling, Jesus saw their faith and the paralytic was made whole.

In *Deuteronomy 22:10*, we read that *Thou shalt not plow with an ox and an ass together.* Law-based faith and Grace-based faith cannot be yoked together like an ox and an ass. When we strive to increase our faith by our own efforts, it nullifies the grace of God that gave the faith to us in the first place. As it is entirely the Grace of God, no works can be added to it. **The faith that we have derives itself entirely from Jesus, and then He blesses us**

when he sees this faith in us. All His blessings and benefits fall upon us because of faith supplied by Jesus. *Psalm 103:1-5* states, *Bless the Lord, O my soul: and all that is within me, bless his holy name. Bless the Lord, O my soul, and forget not all his benefits: Who forgiveth all thine iniquities; who healeth all thy diseases; Who redeemeth thy life from destruction; who crowneth thee with lovingkindness and tender mercies; Who satisfieth thy mouth with good things; so that thy youth is renewed like the eagle's.* Forgiveness, healings, redemption, crowns, loving kindness, tender mercies, rich provisions, and youth are just a small part of His blessings. Faith is acknowledging that Jesus did it all and simply claiming His benefits by faith.

❧ 32 ❧

JESUS AND UNMERITED BLESSING

Isaac had two sons born seconds apart. The first son's name was Esau and the second was Jacob. Esau grew up to be a hunter and an outdoorsman while Jacob was plain and spent most of his time indoors. While Esau worked and toiled in the fields and forests, Jacob did not do much at all but honed his scheming skills. After all, his name meant 'grabber' or 'supplanter'. One day, he tricked his twin brother Esau to sell him his birthright with a thick stew of lentils and some bread. Although he was not the eldest, he managed to supplant his brother to all the privileges accorded to a first-born son. The elder began to serve the younger just as God had said to Rebekah, their mother, when they were born.

We read of this in *Genesis 25:23-34, And the Lord said unto her, Two nations are in thy womb, and two manner of people shall be separated from thy bowels; and the one people shall be stronger than the other people; and the elder shall serve the younger. And when her days to be delivered were fulfilled, behold, there were twins in her womb. And the first came out red, all over like an hairy garment; and they called his name Esau. And after that came his brother out, and his hand took hold on Esau's heel; and his name was called Jacob: and Isaac was threescore years old when she bare them.*

And the boys grew: and Esau was a cunning hunter, a man of the field; and Jacob was a plain man, dwelling in tents. And

Isaac loved Esau, because he did eat of his venison: but Rebekah loved Jacob. And Jacob sod pottage: and Esau came from the field, and he was faint: And Esau said to Jacob, Feed me, I pray thee, with that same red pottage; for I am faint: therefore was his name called Edom. And Jacob said, Sell me this day thy birthright. And Esau said, Behold, I am at the point to die: and what profit shall this birthright do to me? And Jacob said, Swear to me this day; and he sware unto him: and he sold his birthright unto Jacob. Then Jacob gave Esau bread and pottage of lentiles; and he did eat and drink, and rose up, and went his way: thus Esau despised his birthright.

Jacob's devious ways did not stop there. In *Genesis 27:9-29*, we read, *Go now to the flock, and fetch me from thence two good kids of the goats; and I will make them savoury meat for thy father, such as he loveth: And thou shalt bring it to thy father, that he may eat, and that he may bless thee before his death. And Jacob said to Rebekah his mother, Behold, Esau my brother is a hairy man, and I am a smooth man: My father peradventure will feel me, and I shall seem to him as a deceiver; and I shall bring a curse upon me, and not a blessing. And his mother said unto him, Upon me be thy curse, my son: only obey my voice, and go fetch me them. And he went, and fetched, and brought them to his mother: and his mother made savoury meat, such as his father loved.*

And Rebekah took goodly raiment of her eldest son Esau, which were with her in the house, and put them upon Jacob her younger son: And she put the skins of the kids of the goats upon his hands, and upon the smooth of his neck: And she gave the savoury meat and the bread, which she had prepared, into the hand of her son Jacob.

And he came unto his father, and said, My father: and he said, Here am I; who art thou, my son? And Jacob said unto his father, I am Esau thy firstborn; I have done according as thou badest me: arise, I pray thee, sit and eat of my venison, that thy soul may bless me. And Isaac said unto his son, How is it that thou hast found it so quickly, my son? And he said, Because the Lord thy God brought it to me. And Isaac said unto Jacob, Come near, I pray thee, that I may feel thee, my son, whether thou be my very son Esau or not. And Jacob went near unto Isaac his father; and he felt him, and said, The voice is Jacob's voice, but the hands are the hands of Esau. And he discerned him not, because his hands were hairy, as his brother Esau's hands: so he blessed him. And he said, Art thou my very son Esau? And he said, I am. And he said, Bring it near to me, and I will eat of my son's venison, that my soul may bless thee. And he brought it near to him, and he did eat: and he brought him wine, and he drank.

And his father Isaac said unto him, Come near now, and kiss me, my son. And he came near, and kissed him: and he smelled the smell of his raiment, and blessed him, and said, See, the smell of my son is as the smell of a field which the Lord hath blessed: Therefore God give thee of the dew of heaven, and the fatness of the earth, and plenty of corn and wine: Let people serve thee, and nations bow down to thee: be lord over thy brethren, and let thy mother's sons bow down to thee: cursed be every one that curseth thee, and blessed be he that blesseth thee.

As Isaac, their father, grew older, he wanted to bestow a family blessing upon Esau. However, Rebekah heard about it and quickly hatched a scheme with Jacob to steal the blessing of Isaac. Jacob was to steal two young goats from his father's flock from which Rebekah would prepare a meal that Isaac loved. Then Rebekah stole one of Esau's garments and put it on Jacob. Jacob must have been snickering by the time the hair from the goats was stuck onto his skin. He rehearsed his lines before going into his father's abode. Then by lying and conniving, Jacob got his father to believe that he was Esau. Isaac blessed Jacob thinking that he was blessing Esau.

Reading through Jacob's colorful roguish life, anyone would conclude that he deserved nothing but punishment from God. He was not the first born, he was not gifted in hunting nor had any affinity for hard work, he was not qualified, he was a plain man, he was a trickster, he was a liar and a smooth talker, he was a schemer and a colluder, and he was a supplanter taking what did not rightfully belonged to him. He deserved chastisement, maybe even death! Yet he did not get what he deserved. It was all very unfair.

But God never promised us that He would be fair to us. What He did promise was that He would be unfairly good to Abraham, then to Isaac, and then to Jacob. The unconditional covenant that God made with Abraham meant that Jacob had God on his side, blessing him where he did not deserve and favoring him to Esau's detriment. He had an unfair advantage over his elder brother. Grace is always unfair, as it does not look right to our natural eyes. Our natural mind cannot understand it. It cannot be understood, as it is not possible for us to understand how good God is! Even when Jacob was lying through his teeth to his father, he unconsciously met Grace and said 'because the Lord brought it to me'. Jacob deserved nothing but because of Jesus, he received the dew of heaven, the fatness of the earth, and plenty of corn and wine. People would serve him, nations would bow down before him, his brother would bow down before him, and he would be very blessed all the days of his life. But he did not earn it, you may scream. You are absolutely correct – he did not. That is why it is called Grace!

Surely God does not bless sinners, you may ask. Well, in *Ephesians 2:1-7*, we read, *And you hath he quickened, who were dead in trespasses and sins; Wherein in time past ye walked according to the course of this world, according to the prince of the power of the air, the spirit that now worketh in the children of disobedience: Among whom also we all had our conversation in times past in the lusts of our flesh, fulfilling the desires of the flesh and of the mind; and were by nature the children of wrath, even as others. But God, who is rich in mercy, for his great love wherewith he loved us, Even when we were dead in sins, hath quickened us together with Christ, (by grace ye are saved;) And hath raised us up together, and made us sit together in heavenly places in Christ Jesus: That in the ages to come he might shew the exceeding riches of his grace in his kindness toward us through Christ Jesus.* God does not bless sin but He does bless sinners who were dead in trespasses and sins. He blesses them with Jesus! We become believers and when we sin, God still shows us the exceeding riches of His grace and His kindness towards us. It is not that we suddenly became worthy but it is because of Jesus, who now lives in us, who is worthy.

Jacob should know for he saw Grace at work again in his old age through his son Joseph. When Joseph was a young teenager, he had a dream that his sheaf would stand upright and that his brothers' sheaves would bow down before his sheaf. We see this in *Genesis 37:7-10, For, behold, we were binding sheaves in the field, and, lo, my sheaf arose, and also stood upright; and, behold, your sheaves stood round about, and made obeisance to my sheaf. And his brethren said to him, Shalt thou indeed reign over us? or shalt thou indeed have dominion over us? And they hated him yet the more for his dreams, and for his words. And he dreamed yet another dream, and told it his brethren, and said, Behold, I have dreamed a dream more; and, behold, the sun and the moon and the eleven stars made obeisance to me. And he told it to his father, and to his brethren: and his father rebuked him, and said unto him, What is this dream that thou hast dreamed? Shall I and thy mother and thy brethren indeed come to bow down ourselves to thee to the earth?*

Then his next dream involved the sun, moon, and the eleven stars making obeisance to him again. Joseph represented Grace while his brothers and parents, the law. The law always bows down before Grace. Through his many trials, God gave Joseph favor until he became the right hand man of Pharaoh. When the seven-year famine hit, all the countries around Egypt came to Joseph to buy food. This is found in *Genesis 41:56-57, And the famine was over all the face of the earth: and Joseph opened all the storehouses, and sold unto the Egyptians; and the famine waxed sore in the land of Egypt. And all countries came into Egypt to Joseph for to buy corn; because that the famine was so sore in all lands.*

Included in this horde of people coming to purchase grain from Joseph were his ten brothers. His brothers did not recognize him but Joseph knew who they were and had them imprisoned temporarily. In *Genesis 42:7-9, 20, we read, And Joseph saw his brethren, and he knew them, but made himself strange unto them, and spake roughly unto them; and he said unto them, Whence*

come ye? And they said, From the land of Canaan to buy food. And
Joseph knew his brethren, but they knew not him. And Joseph
remembered the dreams which he dreamed of them, and said unto
them, Ye are spies; to see the nakedness of the land ye are come.
But bring your youngest brother unto me; so shall your words be
verified, and ye shall not die. And they did so.

The price for setting them free was to return with their
youngest brother, Benjamin. Benjamin was special as he had the
same mother as Joseph while the other brothers had different
mothers. Joseph represented grace and he was going to bless
Benjamin disproportionately. It was not because Benjamin was
disproportionately good as compared to the other brothers but the
blessings from Joseph came from his goodness. When the law as
symbolized by his brothers bowed down before Grace, blessings
flowed. All the ten brothers and their families were blessed but
special blessings went to Benjamin as he was of the same
bloodline and therefore, inherited the abundant unconditional
blessings.

Genesis 43:16, 34, reads And when Joseph saw Benjamin
with them, he said to the ruler of his house, Bring these men home,
and slay, and make ready; for these men shall dine with me at
noon. And he took and sent messes unto them from before him: but
Benjamin's mess was five times so much as any of theirs. And they
drank, and were merry with him. When Benjamin appeared, a feast
was thrown for him. At the feast, he had five times more food
brought for him and later, he had five changes of fine garments
given to him as compared to his brothers. Five represents grace, as
unmerited blessings were poured out upon him. We read this in
Genesis 45:10-11, 22, And thou shalt dwell in the land of Goshen,
and thou shalt be near unto me, thou, and thy children, and thy
children's children, and thy flocks, and thy herds, and all that thou
hast: And there will I nourish thee; for yet there are five years of
famine; lest thou, and thy household, and all that thou hast, come
to poverty. To all of them he gave each man changes of raiment;
but to Benjamin he gave three hundred pieces of silver, and five
changes of raiment. Also in Genesis 44:2, 17, we read, And put my
cup, the silver cup, in the sack's mouth of the youngest, and his

corn money. And he did according to the word that Joseph had
spoken. And he said, God forbid that I should do so: but the man
in whose hand the cup is found, he shall be my servant; and as for
you, get you up in peace unto your father. The silver cup was given
and then found in Benjamin's bag. Silver represented redemption
and Benjamin was given a position in the palace because Grace
redeemed him. He did not have to earn it but received it freely. His
position in the palace set him up for even more blessings. All the
brothers were nourished but none had any position in the palace.
Then Benjamin was given three hundred pieces of silver that
represented his debt paid in full by Joseph.

Jesus our Grace has done the same for us. **He has blessed**
us not based upon our poverty and lack but based upon His
position as King and possessor of all. We are of His blood. We
may be thankful with a little blessing but from His position, it
is not enough. The blessing may be enough for us but
thankfully, the bible is not about us. It is all about Jesus!
Therefore, Jesus, based upon His riches, disproportionately
blesses us. It is unmerited and once again, that is why it is
called Grace or the unmerited love and favor from God.

❧ 33 ❧

JESUS AND UNMERITED HEALING

One of the names of God is Jehovah Rapha meaning God Is Healer. Note that it does not translate God will Heal or God had Healed but in the present tense, God Is Healer. When we spend time with Jesus, we are spending time with Healer. **As we spend time with Healer, we are healed. There is no other possible outcome. We cannot help but be healed.** Even if we have weak faith, even if we have wavering faith, even if we do not know Him well or at all, even if we are ignorant of His goodness, we are still healed because Jesus is Healer. Healing is a person and his name is Jesus.

In my time as a missionary, I heard the strangest teaching twist on healing. Many churches actually promote the belief that if you have a disease or physical ailment; it is because God has sent you the disease. Therefore, you should embrace the disease! The purpose of the suffering is to make you humble and holy. Suffering bringing holiness makes as much sense as communism bringing freedom to the people. It makes no sense at all. Instead, if we have a physical ailment, let us continue to rejoice in hope of the Glory of God, Jesus Christ, Healer of all.

In *2 Kings 5:1-9*, we read, *Now Naaman, captain of the host of the king of Syria, was a great man with his master, and honourable, because by him the Lord had given deliverance unto Syria: he was also a mighty man in valour, but he was a leper. And the Syrians had gone out by companies, and had brought away captive out of the land of Israel a little maid; and she waited on Naaman's wife. And she said unto her mistress, Would God my lord were with the prophet that is in Samaria! for he would recover him of his leprosy. And one went in, and told his lord, saying, Thus and thus said the maid that is of the land of Israel.*

And the king of Syria said, Go to, go, and I will send a letter unto the king of Israel. And he departed, and took with him ten talents of silver, and six thousand pieces of gold, and ten changes of raiment. And he brought the letter to the king of Israel, saying, Now when this letter is come unto thee, behold, I have therewith sent Naaman my servant to thee, that thou mayest recover him of his leprosy. And it came to pass, when the king of Israel had read the letter, that he rent his clothes, and said, Am I God, to kill and to make alive, that this man doth send unto me to recover a man of his leprosy? wherefore consider, I pray you, and see how he seeketh a quarrel against me. And it was so, when Elisha the man of God had heard that the king of Israel had rent his clothes, that he sent to the king, saying, Wherefore hast thou rent thy clothes? let him come now to me, and he shall know that there is a prophet in Israel. So Naaman came with his horses and with his chariot, and stood at the door of the house of Elisha.

Naaman, a great general, had leprosy. Word reached him through his wife's maid that God could heal him of his disease. Being unaware of God's unmerited favor, he came bearing gifts of silver, gold, and fine raiment. The silver was to buy his redemption; the gold, which symbolizes divinity, was to be exchanged for holiness; and the fine raiments were gifts for cleansing and healing. He was going to buy his redemption, holiness, and healing by the works of his hands. He arrived at the house of Elisha, with his horses and chariot - symbolizing his own strength and might. He arrived with his works, carried by his might and his strength to earn and buy God's favor and blessings!

Elisha's answer to Naaman's display of wealth and power was shocking. He asked Naaman to dip and wash himself in the muddy waters of the Jordan river seven times. We see in *2 Kings 5:10-14, And Elisha sent a messenger unto him, saying, Go and wash in the Jordan seven times, and thy flesh shall come again to thee, and thou shalt be clean. But Naaman was wroth, and went away, and said, Behold, I thought, He will surely come out to me, and stand, and call on the name of the Lord his God, and strike his hand over the place, and recover the leper. Are not Abana and Pharpar, rivers of Damascus, better than all the waters of Israel? may I not wash in them, and be clean? So he turned and went away in a rage. And his servants came near, and spake unto him, and said, My father, if the prophet had bid thee do some great thing, wouldest thou not have done it? how much rather then, when he saith to thee, Wash, and be clean? Then went he down, and dipped himself seven times in Jordan, according to the saying of the man of God: and his flesh came again like unto the flesh of a little child, and he was clean.* Naaman replied in his wisdom that the rivers back home in Syria were much cleaner. He left in anger but later at the urging of his retinue, dipped and washed himself in the dirty Jordan river. His flesh became new like the flesh of a little child and he became clean.

Not understanding God's goodness, he tried to reward Elisha who flatly refused the offer. Naaman left unable to pay God for services rendered. However, he did turn his face away from Rimmon, the false Syrian god, to God Himself. On the other hand, Gehazi the servant of Elisha, ran after Naaman, lied to him, and requested compensation for what God had done. Naaman, only too glad to pay God back, acquiesced willingly. Gehazi, now plump with silver and fine garments, tried to lie to Elisha about his gains and was struck with leprosy himself.

We see this in *2 Kings 5:15-27, And he returned to the man of God, he and all his company, and came, and stood before him: and he said, Behold, now I know that there is no God in all earth, but in Israel: now therefore, I pray thee, take a blessing of thy servant. But he said, As the Lord liveth, before whom I stand, I will receive none. And he urged him to take it; but he refused. And Naaman said, Shall there not then, I pray thee, be given to thy servant two mules' burden of earth? for thy servant will henceforth offer neither burnt offering nor sacrifice unto other gods, but unto the Lord. In this thing the Lord pardon thy servant, that when my master goeth into the house of Rimmon to worship there, and he leaneth on my hand, and I bow myself in the house of Rimmon: when I bow down myself in the house of Rimmon, the Lord pardon thy servant in this thing. And he said unto him, Go in peace. So he departed from him a little way.*

But Gehazi, the servant of Elisha the man of God, said, Behold, my master hath spared Naaman this Syrian, in not receiving at his hands that which he brought: but, as the Lord liveth, I will run after him, and take somewhat of him. So Gehazi followed after Naaman. And when Naaman saw him running after him, he lighted down from the chariot to meet him, and said, Is all well? And he said, All is well. My master hath sent me, saying, Behold, even now there be come to me from mount Ephraim two young men of the sons of the prophets: give them, I pray thee, a talent of silver, and two changes of garments.

And Naaman said, Be content, take two talents. And he urged him, and bound two talents of silver in two bags, with two changes of garments, and laid them upon two of his servants; and they bare them before him. And when he came to the tower, he took them from their hand, and bestowed them in the house: and he let the men go, and they departed. But he went in, and stood before his master. And Elisha said unto him, Whence comest thou, Gehazi? And he said, Thy servant went no whither. And he said unto him, Went not mine heart with thee, when the man turned again from his chariot to meet thee? Is it a time to receive money, and to receive garments, and oliveyards, and vineyards, and sheep, and oxen, and menservants, and maidservants? The leprosy therefore of Naaman shall cleave unto thee, and unto thy seed for ever. And he went out from his presence a leper as white as snow.

Naaman was called to dip and wash himself in the river Jordan because his healing could only come from Jesus. We are baptized into His death and resurrected with Him into new life. *Romans 6:3-5* states, *Know ye not, that so many of us as were baptized into Jesus Christ were baptized into his death? Therefore we are buried with him by baptism into death: that like as Christ was raised up from the dead by the glory of the Father, even so we also should walk in newness of life. For if we have been planted together in the likeness of his death, we shall be also in the likeness of his resurrection:*

We are immersed and washed by Him into newness of life. With this new life comes healing. It is a free gift and cannot be bought. We cannot earn it nor can we merit it. Naaman was the only leper who was healed in Elisha's time because he did not and was not allowed to buy it. When his leprous eyes and body turned to Jesus for healing, he was healed. When he wanted to pay with silver, gold, and fine raiment, he was rebuffed and repudiated. In lieu of payment, he was allowed to carry away two donkeys load of earth. The belief at that time was that the god of each land could only be worshipped on his own soil. However, this soil was more than just for building an altar to worship God with and on. *Matthew 13:23* states, *But he that received seed into the good ground is he that heareth the word, and understandeth it; which also beareth fruit, and bringeth forth, some an hundredfold, some sixty, some thirty.* This earth represented good soil which would bear fruit thirty, sixty, and a hundred times over. Naaman, as a general, had far and wide influence over many in Syria. Jesus is The Seed that had been sown into Naaman. Naaman did nothing but rested in Jesus for his healing. Then he was sown with Jesus.

We see this in *Luke 4:27-29, And many lepers were in Israel in the time of Eliseus the prophet; and none of them was cleansed, saving Naaman the Syrian. And all they in the synagogue, when they heard these things, were filled with wrath, And rose up, and thrust him out of the city, and led him unto the brow of the hill whereon their city was built, that they might cast him down headlong.* That was why the Jewish leaders were filled with wrath for Jesus who reminded them of Naaman, the Syrian gentile who did nothing but received everything freely. Not only did he do nothing but also that he, a gentile, would bear fruit in abundance infuriated the law abiding Jews. The Jews who did everything but received nothing thrust Jesus out of the city just like an unclean leper, to hurl him from a cliff, but He escaped. The Jews who made the law 'keepable' enforced merit for healing while Jesus offered healing freely.

Jesus is good to us even when we do not want to see Him. We seek the healing but we do not want The Healer. We try to buy His healing power not understanding that He is the Healer. Our eyes and heart are set upon the cure and we forget all about Jesus. Healing is not purchased by long fasts, diligent prayers, assiduous studies, or by steadfast tithes. **God does not move in proportion to our works, performance, and abilities. He moves unproportionately due to His goodness, love, and grace for us. Healing was purchased for us more than two thousand years ago by Jesus. He did it already and all we need to do is to claim by faith the healing that He already did for us.**

Under the law, the person with leprosy is pronounced unclean by the priest. In *Leviticus 13:24-25, 43-46*, we read, *Or if there be any flesh, in the skin whereof there is a hot burning, and the quick flesh that burneth have a white bright spot, somewhat reddish, or white; Then the priest shall look upon it: and, behold, if the hair in the bright spot be turned white, and it be in sight deeper than the skin; it is a leprosy broken out of the burning: wherefore the priest shall pronounce him unclean: it is the plague of leprosy. Then the priest shall look upon it: and, behold, if the rising of the sore be white reddish in his bald head, or in his bald forehead, as the leprosy appeareth in the skin of the flesh; He is a leprous man, he is unclean: the priest shall pronounce him utterly unclean; his plague is in his head. And the leper in whom the plague is, his clothes shall be rent, and his head bare, and he shall put a covering upon his upper lip, and shall cry, Unclean, unclean. All the days wherein the plague shall be in him he shall be defiled; he is unclean: he shall dwell alone; without the camp shall his habitation be.*

The leper becomes an untouchable. If the leprosy was on his head, he would be shorn, his clothes would be rent, and he would be made to pronounce the curse upon himself incessantly, 'Unclean! Unclean!' Then he would be thrust out of the city to live alone for the rest of his unclean life. It does not matter if he cannot stand or see. He would be thrust out, rejected, and condemned. As a leper, he has no merit whatsoever. If he appeared in public, the law stated that he be stoned. But Jesus offered unmerited favor to them. He approached lepers, reached out to them, touched them and healed them. They stood, they saw, they were accepted, they were cleaned, and they were made whole. He is Healer and all those whom He touched and spent time with were healed. We can rest in the goodness of Jesus.

৯ 34 ৎ

JESUS AND UNMERITED PROVISION

My God is a very great God. His thoughts are not my thoughts and His ways are not my ways. **When I have a need, He does not give to me based upon my need. He gives to me based upon His riches in glory by Jesus Christ. The gap between my demand and His supply is immeasurable as His supply far exceeds my demand.** My limited mind cannot and is unable to understand the unlimited mind of God. When He blesses me, He blesses me based upon His goodness and His riches, not upon my goodness or my need. I may deserve very little but He gives me an overabundance because He is rich and good. In *Philippians 4:18-19*, we read, *But I have all, and abound: I am full, having received of Epaphroditus the things which were sent from you, an odour of a sweet smell, a sacrifice acceptable, wellpleasing to God. But my God shall supply all your need according to his riches in glory by Christ Jesus.* All the needs of the people in the church in Philippi who blessed Paul were supplied back, not according to their needs, but according to His riches.

Another wonderful example of this can be found in *Matthew 14:20-21, And they did all eat, and were filled: and they took up of the fragments that remained twelve baskets full. And they that had eaten were about five thousand men, beside women and children.* His supply far exceeded the demands of tens of thousands of people. Moreover, there was plenty of leftovers as well after the demand was fully satisfied.

We see this unmerited provision clearly in *1 Kings 17:10-16, So he arose and went to Zarephath. And when he came to the gate of the city, behold, the widow woman was there gathering of sticks: and he called to her, and said, Fetch me, I pray thee, a little water in a vessel, that I may drink. And as she was going to fetch it, he called to her, and said, Bring me, I pray thee, a morsel of bread in thine hand. And she said, As the Lord thy God liveth, I have not a cake, but an handful of meal in a barrel, and a little oil in a cruse: and, behold, I am gathering two sticks, that I may go in and dress it for me and my son, that we may eat it, and die.*

And Elijah said unto her, Fear not; go and do as thou hast said: but make me thereof a little cake first, and bring it unto me, and after make for thee and for thy son. For thus saith the Lord God of Israel, The barrel of meal shall not waste, neither shall the cruse of oil fail, until the day that the Lord sendeth rain upon the earth. And she went and did according to the saying of Elijah: and she, and he, and her house, did eat many days. And the barrel of meal wasted not, neither did the cruse of oil fail, according to the word of the Lord, which he spake by Elijah.

Elijah was very cognizant of God's unmerited provision. When the famine and drought was at its zenith, Elijah asked a widow to first bring water for him to drink. Then he requested the widow to feed him the last morsel of food in her house. The woman looking at her needs told him that she just had enough meal and oil for a small loaf of bread, not enough even for herself and her son. Her lack did not impress Elijah, not because he was uncaring but because he knew that God would supply her from His abundant riches. There was no lack in heaven. She gave from her lack, from her position of poverty. God supplied her back from His position of abundance and riches. From a little meal and oil to an inexhaustible supply which was more than sufficient for her and her son. Because of the famine and drought in the land, they could do nothing from their own works to increase their stock of food. But as there was no famine and drought in heaven, God could supply them with endless provisions. All they had to do was rest in what Elijah had said. Resting in Jesus' finished work is a sure way to being blessed.

God is Jehovah Jireh meaning God Provider. It does not mean God will provide or that God had provided. God is Provider. Period. But it takes a long time for us to understand that as we spend time with Him we are provided for, as we are spending time in the presence of Provider. For it is His presence that changes the circumstances we find ourselves in. We cannot understand this because many times we want the gifts but not the Giver. We want the blessings but not the Blessor. We do not really want Jesus, just what He can give to us. The purpose of God for taking His people out of Egypt was to have a relationship with them and to show them His goodness. However, the people wanted the Promised Land, not God! They wanted to be blessed based upon their own works.

It got so bad that God wanted to send an angel to fulfill His promise to take them into the Promised Land but that He would not go with them. We read this in *Exodus 33:1-3, 14-17, And the Lord said unto Moses, Depart, and go up hence, thou and the people which thou hast brought up out of the land of Egypt, unto the land which I sware unto Abraham, to Isaac, and to Jacob, saying, Unto thy seed will I give it: And I will send an angel before thee; and I will drive out the Canaanite, the Amorite, and the Hittite, and the Perizzite, the Hivite, and the Jebusite: Unto a land flowing with milk and honey: for I will not go up in the midst of thee; for thou art a stiffnecked people: lest I consume thee in the way.*

They would get what they wanted. They would get the promises but not the Promiser. It would have been a disaster for the Israelites for they would have left their Provider behind. Thankfully, Moses saw clearly the need for God's goodness on this journey into the Promised Land. If God were not with them, they would rather not go into the new land. *Exodus 33:14-17*, states, *And he said, My presence shall go with thee, and I will give thee rest. And he said unto him, If thy presence go not with me, carry us not up hence. For wherein shall it be known here that I and thy people have found grace in thy sight? is it not in that thou goest with us? so shall we be separated, I and thy people, from all the people that are upon the face of the earth. And the Lord said unto Moses, I will do this thing also that thou hast spoken: for thou hast found grace in my sight, and I know thee by name.* For it is only when God goes with them, then Grace goes with them. Grace is a person and His name is Jesus. When Jesus is with you, all your provisions are taken care of. There is no need for worry, fear and misgivings. For Jesus is Provider. When He is with us, we are provided for.

Another familiar example can be found in *Genesis 26:1-16, And there was a famine in the land, beside the first famine that was in the days of Abraham. And Isaac went unto Abimelech king of the Philistines unto Gerar. And the Lord appeared unto him, and said, Go not down into Egypt; dwell in the land which I shall tell thee of: Sojourn in this land, and I will be with thee, and will bless thee; for unto thee, and unto thy seed, I will give all these countries, and I will perform the oath which I sware unto Abraham thy father; And I will make thy seed to multiply as the stars of heaven, and will give unto thy seed all these countries; and in thy seed shall all the nations of the earth be blessed; Because that Abraham obeyed my voice, and kept my charge, my commandments, my statutes, and my laws.*

And Isaac dwelt in Gerar: And the men of the place asked him of his wife; and he said, She is my sister: for he feared to say, She is my wife; lest, said he, the men of the place should kill me for Rebekah; because she was fair to look upon. And it came to pass, when he had been there a long time, that Abimelech king of the Philistines looked out at a window, and saw, and, behold, Isaac was sporting with Rebekah his wife. And Abimelech called Isaac, and said, Behold, of a surety she is thy wife: and how saidst thou, She is my sister? And Isaac said unto him, Because I said, Lest I die for her. And Abimelech said, What is this thou hast done unto us? one of the people might lightly have lien with thy wife, and thou shouldest have brought guiltiness upon us. And Abimelech charged all his people, saying, He that toucheth this man or his wife shall surely be put to death.

Then Isaac sowed in that land, and received in the same year an hundredfold: and the Lord blessed him. And the man

waxed great, and went forward, and grew until he became very
great: For he had possession of flocks, and possessions of herds,
and great store of servants: and the Philistines envied him. For all
the wells which his father's servants had digged in the days of
Abraham his father, the Philistines had stopped them, and filled
them with earth. And Abimelech said unto Isaac, Go from us; for
thou art much mightier than we.

When Isaac went through a famine, God asked him to stay
behind in Gerar and not to go to Egypt. Egypt represented the
world and its works. God promised that His presence would be
with Isaac. When we stay with God, we are staying with Grace.
When we have Jesus, we have everything. Once again, there is
nothing we can do in a famine but rest in the Provider. As the
people moved into Egypt, Isaac moved closer into Jesus. Whatever
Isaac touched, Jesus blessed it a hundred times over. He sowed and
received back a hundred times over. His animals, servants, and
possessions multiplied as well. His wells were always full. He
became great, then very great in wealth. He became so wealthy
that the king envied him and had him leave the land for he was
now mightier than the king. Even when he made mistakes and lied
about Rebekah, his wife, God still blessed him unconditionally. **He**
was blessed solely because Jesus was with him. Jehovah Jireh,
God Provider, Jesus Christ was with him! His hundredfold
blessing was based upon God's goodness and riches, not on the
state of his righteousness or the state of the land.

Famine and drought was a curse and a consequence from
the sin of Adam and Eve. All of creation fell and became cursed
when sin entered the world. But because of Jesus, this curse has
been removed from us. **We cannot ever be under the curse of sin**
again as Jesus has been judged for our sins. It was not because
of mercy that God lifted this curse away from us. It was
righteous judgment. But the judgment that was meant for us
fell on Jesus. Judgment was pronounced, the penalty was paid,
and the curse of sin was removed. There is no need to pay for
what has already been paid in full. We cannot earn the blessings
of God. We can only receive it as someone else paid for it already.
We enjoy the right to the blessings as Jesus bought it for us.

The great famine in Samaria illustrates this beautifully. We read in *2 Kings 6:24-30, And it came to pass after this, that Ben-hadad king of Syria gathered all his host, and went up, and besieged Samaria. And there was a great famine in Samaria: and, behold, they besieged it, until an ass's head was sold for fourscore pieces of silver, and the fourth part of a cab of dove's dung for five pieces of silver. And as the king of Israel was passing by upon the wall, there cried a woman unto him, saying, Help, my lord, O king. And he said, If the Lord do not help thee, whence shall I help thee? out of the barnfloor, or out of the winepress? And the king said unto her, What aileth thee? And she answered, This woman said unto me, Give thy son, that we may eat him to day, and we will eat my son to morrow. So we boiled my son, and did eat him: and I said unto her on the next day, Give thy son, that we may eat him: and she hath hid her son. And it came to pass, when the king heard the words of the woman, that he rent his clothes; and he passed by upon the wall, and the people looked, and, behold, he had sackcloth within upon his flesh.*

During the long siege, food became so scarce that ass's heads, dove's dung (literal or otherwise), and babies were sold, bartered and eaten. The prices were exorbitant and the payment brutal, deadly, and cannibalistic. That was what they deserved living under sin.

However, because of Jesus, all food and provisions would be provided. We read of this account in *2 Kings 7:1-13, Then Elisha said, Hear ye the word of the Lord; Thus saith the Lord, To morrow about this time shall a measure of fine flour be sold for a shekel, and two measures of barley for a shekel, in the gate of Samaria. Then a lord on whose hand the king leaned answered the man of God, and said, Behold, if the Lord would make windows in heaven, might this thing be? And he said, Behold, thou shalt see it with thine eyes, but shalt not eat thereof.*

And there were four leprous men at the entering in of the gate: and they said one to another, Why sit we here until we die? If we say, We will enter into the city, then the famine is in the city, and we shall die there: and if we sit still here, we die also. Now therefore come, and let us fall unto the host of the Syrians: if they save us alive, we shall live; and if they kill us, we shall but die. And they rose up in the twilight, to go unto the camp of the Syrians: and when they were come to the uttermost part of the camp of Syria, behold, there was no man there. For the Lord had made the host of the Syrians to hear a noise of chariots, and a noise of horses, even the noise of a great host: and they said one to another, Lo, the king of Israel hath hired against us the kings of the Hittites, and the kings of the Egyptians, to come upon us. Wherefore they arose and fled in the twilight, and left their tents, and their horses, and their asses, even the camp as it was, and fled for their life. And when these lepers came to the uttermost part of the camp, they went into one tent, and did eat and drink, and carried thence silver, and gold, and raiment, and went and hid it; and came again, and entered into another tent, and carried thence also, and went and hid it.

Then they said one to another, We do not well: this day is a day of good tidings, and we hold our peace: if we tarry till the morning light, some mischief will come upon us: now therefore come, that we may go and tell the king's household. So they came and called unto the porter of the city: and they told them, saying, We came to the camp of the Syrians, and, behold, there was no man there, neither voice of man, but horses tied, and asses tied, and the tents as they were. And he called the porters; and they told it to the king's house within.

And the king arose in the night, and said unto his servants, I will now shew you what the Syrians have done to us. They know that we be hungry; therefore are they gone out of the camp to hide themselves in the field, saying, When they come out of the city, we shall catch them alive, and get into the city. And one of his servants answered and said, Let some take, I pray thee, five of the horses that remain, which are left in the city, (behold, they are as all the multitude of Israel that are left in it: behold, I say, they are even as all the multitude of the Israelites that are consumed:) and let us send and see. They took therefore two chariot horses; and the king sent after the host of the Syrians, saying, Go and see. And they went after them unto Jordan: and, lo, all the way was full of garments and vessels, which the Syrians had cast away in their

haste. And the messengers returned, and told the king. And the
people went out, and spoiled the tents of the Syrians. So a measure
of fine flour was sold for a shekel, and two measures of barley for
a shekel, according to the word of the Lord.

And the king appointed the lord on whose hand he leaned
to have the charge of the gate: and the people trode upon him in
the gate, and he died, as the man of God had said, who spake when
the king came down to him. And it came to pass as the man of God
had spoken to the king, saying, Two measures of barley for a
shekel, and a measure of fine flour for a shekel, shall be to morrow
about this time in the gate of Samaria: And that lord answered the
man of God, and said, Now, behold, if the Lord should make
windows in heaven, might such a thing be? And he said, Behold,
thou shalt see it with thine eyes, but shalt not eat thereof. And so it
fell out unto him: for the people trode upon him in the gate, and he
died.

Elisha, representing God, stated that God would provide all
the food they needed. They would not have to earn it or to work for
it. It either would be free or sold at ridiculously low prices. It was
too good to be true!

But many people could not accept that God could be so
good. They reasoned in their heads that they had to earn the right
to such abundance. They reasoned from their wisdom, not from the
Holy Spirit's wisdom, making them like the head of the ass. The
complete absence of the Holy Spirit in them is like the absence of
the dove, leaving behind only its lifeless dung. And rather than
feeding on the Son of man, they fed on each other. Much suffering
and death ensued. Trusting in their works and their wisdom, the
sons of men died, not knowing that the Son of man was their
Provider.

On the other hand, there were four leprous men sitting at
the entrance gate to the city. Under the law, they had been
banished, put out of the city. Therefore, they behaved like law-less
men. None of them deserved grace but all of them received Grace.
Jesus is superior to any sin resulting from the law. When they rose
up in the twilight to go into the enemy's camp, God had already
provided for them by making the enemy desert their camp earlier,

also in the twilight. They found unmerited blessings in the form of silver, gold, raiments, food, and drinks. Those who were thrown out got in first. Those who merited nothing were rewarded with everything. For Jesus had already paid the price and they rightfully received what Jesus had paid for. They received bountiful provisions from The Provider. They received Grace, the unmerited favor of God.

Because of the goodness of God, His supply far exceeded our demand. His unconditional supply transcends our understanding. *Amos 9:13* states, *Behold, the days come, saith the Lord, that the plowman shall overtake the reaper, and the treader of grapes him that soweth seed; and the mountains shall drop sweet wine, and all the hills shall melt.* The ploughman shall overtake the reaper. There is so much goodness and abundance from God that we are still reaping this year's harvest when we find the next season for planting and sowing upon us. Another crop will soon be on its way as we are still busily gathering in the crop from this season. His blessings outstrip our ability to receive all of it. In *Leviticus 26:4-5*, we read, *Then I will give you rain in due season, and the land shall yield her increase, and the trees of the field shall yield their fruit. And your threshing shall reach unto the vintage, and the vintage shall reach unto the sowing time.* The grape harvest is so bountiful that we are still treading them when the next season to sow seed arrives. The threshing shall reach unto the vintage and the vintage shall reach into the sowing time.

The sweetness of Jesus, our Provider, surpasses our vats and holding tanks. The never-ending supply defeats our effort to store it. There is so much affluence in Jesus that it goes beyond our imagination. *Joel 3:18* states, *And it shall come to pass in that day, that the mountains shall drop down new wine, and the hills shall flow with milk, and all the rivers of Judah shall flow with waters, and a fountain shall come forth of the house of the Lord, and shall water the valley of Shittim.* The mountains shall drop new wine. The old wine of the law is gone to be replaced by the new wine of Grace. It has already started and would flow as a river of Grace, watering the whole valley. There would be so many vines with so many clusters of grapes on it that the mountains would be covered with it. It would resemble a waterfall, flowing and dropping sweet new wine of the new covenant. There would be such an outpouring of Grace that the hills would melt with milk and honey. Rivers and fountains of goodness and provisions would overtake us. We would be watered, immersed, and saturated in His goodness and riches. **We cannot outrun His Grace, Jesus Christ.**

God blesses us unproportionately out of His abundance and riches. The land that we possess is not like the old land. *Deuteronomy 11:10-11* states, *For the land, whither thou goest in to possess it, is not as the land of Egypt, from whence ye came out, where thou sowedst thy seed, and wateredst it with thy foot, as a garden of herbs: But the land, whither ye go to possess it, is a land of hills and valleys, and drinketh water of the rain of heaven.* In the old land, we had to sow the seeds and we had to water it with foot pumps. However, in this new land that God had given to us, the whole land is replenished by God's supply. We cannot outrun nor can we outdistance His blessings. He drenches us while we drink from the water of the rain of heaven. He overtakes and soaks us with His blessings from heaven.

God is a very great God. *Acts 20:35* tells us to *remember the words of the Lord Jesus, how he said, It is more blessed to give than to receive.* **God being always on the 'more' side, wants to bless and give us abundantly. The more He blesses us, the more we receive. The more we receive, the 'more' blessed He becomes. We cannot receive too much from God as with each giving He becomes even more blessed. The only way to bless God back is to receive more blessings from Him, which makes Him even more blessed, ad infinitum.**

❧ 35 ❧

JESUS AND UNMERITED VICTORY

Every Sunday, for many years now, my closing prayer to my congregation is that because Jesus was victorious we are similarly victorious. As He is so are we! It is not because we merit victory but it is because He was victorious over the enemy, over sin, and over every circumstance in this world. Even if we do not merit it, we still get to enjoy these victories He wrought for us.

The war was won in the heavenly realm before it even started on earth. Jesus was provided as the cure before sin ever came into the world. Throughout the bible, we see this foregone unmerited victory. Before the law was given to Moses, we saw this victory of the Israelites against the Amalekites. The Israelites did not deserve to win but because of Jesus, they did. The Amalekites were Israel's enemies from time immemorial. They represented evil and confronted the Israelites repeatedly. King Saul was told by God to eliminate them but he did not. There was always a remnant of the Amalekites left until the reign of King Hezekiah.

In *Exodus 17:8-15,* we read, *Then came Amalek, and fought with Israel in Rephidim. And Moses said unto Joshua, Choose us out men, and go out, fight with Amalek: to morrow I will stand on the top of the hill with the rod of God in mine hand. So Joshua did as Moses had said to him, and fought with Amalek: and Moses, Aaron, and Hur went up to the top of the hill. And it came to pass, when Moses held up his hand, that Israel prevailed: and when he let down his hand, Amalek prevailed. But Moses' hands were heavy; and they took a stone, and put it under him, and he sat thereon; and Aaron and Hur stayed up his hands, the one on the one side, and the other on the other side; and his hands were steady until the going down of the sun. And Joshua discomfited Amalek and his people with the edge of the sword. And the Lord said unto Moses, Write this for a memorial in a book, and rehearse it in the ears of Joshua: for I will utterly put out the remembrance of Amalek from under heaven. And Moses built an altar, and called the name of it Jehovah-nissi:*

When the Israelites first fought with the Amalekites in Rephidim, meaning 'a place in the desert', a very strange event took place on the top of the hill overlooking the battlefield. While Joshua was fighting with the Amalekites, Moses would stand on the top of the hill with the rod of God in his hand. When Moses held up his hands, Israel would prevail. When Moses let his hands down, the Amalekites would prevail.

What Moses did was senseless until we see Jesus in the battle. Rephidim was a place in the desert, an uncluttered place, where the glory of Jesus could shine for all to see. Moses on the hilltop holding up the rod of God with his hands up high represented Jesus on the cross at Calvary. As long as the army of Israel saw the symbol of Jesus, the battle went their way. When Moses' hands went down, they could no longer see this symbol and the battle went against them. Aaron and Hur then had to sit Moses down on the stone, which represented resting on Jesus as our solid foundation. From this position of rest, Aaron would hold up one of Moses' arms while Hur would hold up the other. Aaron meant 'exalted' while Hur meant 'liberty'. **Up on the hill in clear sight of all, the war was won as the Exalted One, Jesus, defeated the enemy and gave us liberty.** He did it as we could not do it by our own strength. On the battlefield, Joshua discomfited the Amalekites because of Jesus.

Later on, the Israelites wanted to conquer in their own strength. The law had then been established. Failing to believe that God could give them the promised land, they turned back and encountered their old enemy, the Amalekites, who had now teamed

up with the Canaanites. We read this in *Numbers 14:27-31, 41-45,
How long shall I bear with this evil congregation, which murmur
against me? I have heard the murmurings of the children of Israel,
which they murmur against me. Say unto them, As truly as I live,
saith the Lord, as ye have spoken in mine ears, so will I do to you:
Your carcases shall fall in this wilderness; and all that were
numbered of you, according to your whole number, from twenty
years old and upward, which have murmured against me,
Doubtless ye shall not come into the land, concerning which I
sware to make you dwell therein, save Caleb the son of Jephunneh,
and Joshua the son of Nun. But your little ones, which ye said
should be a prey, them will I bring in, and they shall know the land
which ye have despised*

*And Moses said, Wherefore now do ye transgress the
commandment of the Lord? but it shall not prosper. Go not up, for
the Lord is not among you; that ye be not smitten before your
enemies. For the Amalekites and the Canaanites are there before
you, and ye shall fall by the sword: because ye are turned away
from the Lord, therefore the Lord will not be with you. But they
presumed to go up unto the hill top: nevertheless the ark of the
covenant of the Lord, and Moses, departed not out of the camp.
Then the Amalekites came down, and the Canaanites which dwelt
in that hill, and smote them, and discomfited them, even unto
Hormah.*

As Jesus was not with them now, the Amalekites
discomfited them now. Their carcasses, from twenty years and up,
would eventually fall in the desert. Without Jesus, there could be
no victory.

Another unmerited victory was wrought by God for King
Hezekiah. We read of this in *2 Kings 18:13-18, Now in the
fourteenth year of king Hezekiah did Sennacherib king of Assyria
come up against all the fenced cities of Judah, and took them. And
Hezekiah king of Judah sent to the king of Assyria to Lachish,
saying, I have offended; return from me: that which thou puttest on
me will I bear. And the king of Assyria appointed unto Hezekiah
king of Judah three hundred talents of silver and thirty talents of
gold. And Hezekiah gave him all the silver that was found in the*

house of the Lord, and in the treasures of the king's house. At that time did Hezekiah cut off the gold from the doors of the temple of the Lord, and from the pillars which Hezekiah king of Judah had overlaid, and gave it to the king of Assyria.

And the king of Assyria sent Tartan and Rabsaris and Rabshakeh from Lachish to king Hezekiah with a great host against Jerusalem. And they went up and came to Jerusalem. And when they were come up, they came and stood by the conduit of the upper pool, which is in the highway of the fuller's field. And when they had called to the king, there came out to them Eliakim the son of Hilkiah, which was over the household, and Shebna the scribe, and Joah the son of Asaph the recorder.

King Hezekiah was a righteous king but far from perfect. He was the southern king in the divided nation of Israel. Israel had split into two kingdoms at that time - Israel to the north and Judah in the south. The king of Assyria conquered all the surrounding kingdoms, including Israel, and all that remained was the kingdom of Judah. Instead of resting in God, King Hezekiah immediately paid tribute to the king of Assyria. The price would be three hundred talents of silver and thirty talents of gold. All the silver and gold from the king's house plus the gold from the temple went to the king of Assyria. At the same time, Hezekiah made a pact with Egypt to protect them from any invasion. By his own works, King Hezekiah not only bowed down before the king of Assyria but also made a pact with Pharaoh. All of these were to no avail as the king of Assyria prepared to attack Jerusalem, the capital of Judah.

Before conquering Jerusalem, the last bastion of Hezekiah, the Assyrian generals mocked Hezekiah's men. They laughed at his pact with the Egyptians and they ridiculed their trust in God. They mistakenly assumed that since Hezekiah had destroyed all the high places and altars of idol worship, there would be less of God to worship. They taunted Hezekiah and his small army for not being able to provide enough equestrians to ride two thousand gift horses. Then they lied, said that God was with them, and had commanded them to destroy Jerusalem as well. After all, had not God given them all their victories? God was on their side as mightier kingdoms than Judah had fallen before. They mocked Hezekiah and his trust in God. After all, had he not paid tribute to the king of Assyria and had he not trusted the Egyptians more than God for his well-being?

We read of this in *2 Kings 18:19-37, And Rab-shakeh said unto them, Speak ye now to Hezekiah, Thus saith the great king, the king of Assyria, What confidence is this wherein thou trustest? Thou sayest, (but they are but vain words,) I have counsel and strength for the war. Now on whom dost thou trust, that thou rebellest against me? Now, behold, thou trustest upon the staff of this bruised reed, even upon Egypt, on which if a man lean, it will go into his hand, and pierce it: so is Pharaoh king of Egypt unto all that trust on him.*

But if ye say unto me, We trust in the Lord our God: is not that he, whose high places and whose altars Hezekiah hath taken away, and hath said to Judah and Jerusalem, Ye shall worship before this altar in Jerusalem? Now therefore, I pray thee, give pledges to my lord the king of Assyria, and I will deliver thee two thousand horses, if thou be able on thy part to set riders upon them. How then wilt thou turn away the face of one captain of the least of my master's servants, and put thy trust on Egypt for chariots and for horsemen? Am I now come up without the Lord against this place to destroy it? The Lord said to me, Go up against this land, and destroy it.

Then said Eliakim the son of Hilkiah, and Shebna, and Joah, unto Rab-shakeh, Speak, I pray thee, to thy servants in the Syrian language; for we understand it: and talk not with us in the Jews' language in the ears of the people that are on the wall. But Rab-shakeh said unto them, Hath my master sent me to thy master, and to thee, to speak these words? hath he not sent me to the men which sit on the wall, that they may eat their own dung, and drink their own piss with you. Then Rab-shakeh stood and cried with a loud voice in the Jews' language, and spake, saying, Hear the word of the great king, the king of Assyria: Thus saith the king, Let not Hezekiah deceive you: for he shall not be able to deliver you out of his hand: Neither let Hezekiah make you trust in the Lord, saying,

The Lord will surely deliver us, and this city shall not be delivered into the hand of the king of Assyria.

Hearken not to Hezekiah: for thus saith the king of Assyria, Make an agreement with me by a present, and come out to me, and then eat ye every man of his own vine, and every one of his fig tree, and drink ye every one the waters of his cistern: Until I come and take you away to a land like your own land, a land of corn and wine, a land of bread and vineyards, a land of oil olive and of honey, that ye may live, and not die: and hearken not unto Hezekiah, when he persuadeth you, saying, The Lord will deliver us.

Hath any of the gods of the nations delivered at all his land out of the hand of the king of Assyria? Where are the gods of Hamath, and of Arpad? where are the gods of Sepharvaim, Hena, and Ivah? have they delivered Samaria out of mine hand? Who are they among all the gods of the countries, that have delivered their country out of mine hand, that the Lord should deliver Jerusalem out of mine hand?But the people held their peace, and answered him not a word: for the king's commandment was, saying, Answer him not.

By the law of Moses, King Hezekiah did not deserve any mercy from God. By his own works, he had sinned by paying obeisance to the king of Assyria. He had also trusted in Egypt, a symbol of the world and satan. However, Hezekiah was part of the lineage that would bring forth the Promised Seed, Jesus. God Himself would defend the city of Jerusalem from the Assyrians for His own sake and for His promise to David. The promise was Jesus! We read this in *2 Kings 19:6-7, 27-28, 32-35, And Isaiah said unto them, Thus shall ye say to your master, Thus saith the Lord, Be not afraid of the words which thou hast heard, with which the servants of the king of Assyria have blasphemed me.Behold, I will send a blast upon him, and he shall hear a rumour, and shall return to his own land; and I will cause him to fall by the sword in his own land.*

But I know thy abode, and thy going out, and thy coming in, and thy rage against me. Because thy rage against me and thy tumult is come up into mine ears, therefore I will put my hook in thy nose, and my bridle in thy lips, and I will turn thee back by the way by which thou camest.

Therefore thus saith the Lord concerning the king of Assyria, He shall not come into this city, nor shoot an arrow there, nor come before it with shield, nor cast a bank against it. By the way that he came, by the same shall he return, and shall not come into this city, saith the Lord. For I will defend this city, to save it, for mine own sake, and for my servant David's sake. And it came to pass that night, that the angel of the Lord went out, and smote in the camp of the Assyrians an hundred fourscore and five thousand: and when they arose early in the morning, behold, they were all dead corpses.

Hezekiah's righteousness came not from his own works but from his faith in God's promise. Although Hezekiah did not merit it, God defeated the mighty Assyrian army with a blast or the ruacH of God! The same breath of the Spirit that gave life to Abraham and Sarah in their old age defeated the enemy. One hundred and eighty five thousand fell that night. The rest of the army hobbled back like prisoners, with hooks in their noses and bridles in their lips, in utter defeat.

Our performance or non-performance does not affect God one iota. He does not move according to our works but according to His Grace. His Grace is Jesus. All those of us who have faith in Jesus are counted as righteous. Righteous means we have right standing with God. *Psalm 5:11-12* states, *But let all those that put their trust in thee rejoice: let them ever shout for joy, because thou defendest them: let them also that love thy name be joyful in thee. For thou, Lord, wilt bless the righteous; with favour wilt thou compass him as with a shield.* As righteous people, favor will compass us like a shield. We will be victorious even if we do not deserve it. It is not about us. It is all about Jesus! We will rejoice and shout for joy because Jesus Christ is victorious. And as He is victorious, so are we!

❧ 36 ❧

JESUS AND GOOD WORKS

There is a very simple answer to all the questions I receive about 'good works' that we do as Christians. Many people are afraid that doing good works would bring them back under the law. That is far from the truth. **Many people who rest in Jesus completely do many more 'good works' than anybody else.** This apparent conflict is easily resolved by scripture. Let us read from *Titus 2:11-14, For the grace of God that bringeth salvation hath appeared to all men, Teaching us that, denying ungodliness and worldly lusts, we should live soberly, righteously, and godly, in this present world; Looking for that blessed hope, and the glorious appearing of the great God and our Saviour Jesus Christ; Who gave himself for us, that he might redeem us from all iniquity, and purify unto himself a peculiar people, zealous of good works.*

It is the Grace of God, Jesus Christ, who gives salvation to all men and women. There is none other and there is no other way. There are no works involved and we cannot add our works to the finished work of Christ on the cross. There is only one Savior and His name is Jesus. He gave Himself for us and redeemed us from all iniquity and sin. Even if our sins mark us like scarlet and stain us crimson in color, yet when we come to Jesus, He un-marks and un-stains us. He makes us spotless and stainless. *Isaiah 1:18* states, *Come now, and let us reason together, saith the Lord: though your sins be as scarlet, they shall be as white as snow; though they be red like crimson, they shall be as wool.* He is our Blessed Hope. Because of Him, we are purified and washed white as snow.

The bible now calls us a peculiar people, a holy people, a chosen generation and a royal priesthood. In an instant, not in the process of time, we become peculiar, holy, chosen and priestly. We read this in *Deuteronomy 14:2, for thou art an holy people unto the Lord thy God, and the Lord hath chosen thee to be a peculiar people unto himself, above all the nations that are upon the earth.* And again in *1 Peter 2:6-10, Wherefore also it is contained in the scripture, Behold, I lay in Sion a chief corner stone, elect, precious: and he that believeth on him shall not be confounded. Unto you therefore which believe he is precious: but unto them which be disobedient, the stone which the builders disallowed, the same is made the head of the corner, And a stone of stumbling, and a rock of offence, even to them which stumble at the word, being disobedient: whereunto also they were appointed. But ye are a chosen generation, a royal priesthood, an holy nation, a peculiar people; that ye should shew forth the praises of him who hath called you out of darkness into his marvellous light: Which in time past were not a people, but are now the people of God: which had not obtained mercy, but now have obtained mercy.* This sounds too good to be true; especially when we look into the mirror and we see ourselves looking exactly the same as before. However, the bible is talking about our spirits here – the part of us that we cannot see.

Our spirits become instantaneously renewed when we believe in Jesus, the chief corner stone. We now have a brand new spirit! Because we now have Jesus living in us, who is completely holy, we become completely holy. Because Jesus is spotless, we become spotless. Because Jesus is perfectly acceptable to God, we become perfectly acceptable to God. Because of Jesus, we become adopted into the family of God. *Ephesians 1:3-7 states, Blessed be the God and Father of our Lord Jesus Christ, who hath blessed us with all spiritual blessings in heavenly places in Christ: According as he hath chosen us in him before the foundation of the world, that we should be holy and without blame before him in love:*

Having predestinated us unto the adoption of children by Jesus Christ to himself, according to the good pleasure of his will, To the praise of the glory of his grace, wherein he hath made us accepted in the beloved. In whom we have redemption through his blood, the forgiveness of sins, according to the riches of his grace. We can never lose this right as it was given to us by God through Jesus, who now lives in us. We are holy and without blame before Him because of Jesus.

As Jesus is, we become! We become like Him. We become pure, as He is pure. We become righteous, as He is righteous. We become sinless, as He is sinless. **Our new spirit cannot sin nor does it want to sin!** We cannot sin and does not want to sin in our spirit because Jesus abides in us. *1 John 3:1-9* states, *Behold, what manner of love the Father hath bestowed upon us, that we should be called the sons of God: therefore the world knoweth us not, because it knew him not. Beloved, now are we the sons of God, and it doth not yet appear what we shall be: but we know that, when he shall appear, we shall be like him; for we shall see him as he is. And every man that hath this hope in him purifieth himself, even as he is pure.*

Whosoever committeth sin transgresseth also the law: for sin is the transgression of the law. And ye know that he was manifested to take away our sins; and in him is no sin. Whosoever abideth in him sinneth not: whosoever sinneth hath not seen him, neither known him. Little children, let no man deceive you: he that doeth righteousness is righteous, even as he is righteous. He that committeth sin is of the devil; for the devil sinneth from the beginning. For this purpose the Son of God was manifested, that he might destroy the works of the devil.

Whosoever is born of God doth not commit sin; for his seed remaineth in him: and he cannot sin, because he is born of God.

But note again that it is our spirit that is born again, not our minds or our bodies. We have the same mind and the same body after we are born again in the spirit. Our minds and bodies can fall into sin but because of our new spirit nature, we are no longer dominated by sin. Sin has very little influence over us because we are new.

So what does a new, born-again in the spirit person want to do if he or she is no longer attracted nor influenced by sin? We read in Titus verse 14 above that they become zealous to good works! Because of Jesus' overwhelming love, they cannot help it but have a strong desire to share Jesus with the rest of the world and also to do other good works. However, their focus is not on their good works but on Jesus. Almost every believer I know who rest in Jesus absolutely accomplish great works! The fruit of focusing on Jesus is plenty of good works. The good works do not maintain their right standing before God. Their right standing come from faith in Jesus and is maintained by Jesus.

These good works come automatically, without thinking, because of their new spirit. Without thinking about it, people living under Grace can deny ungodliness and worldly lusts, live soberly, righteously, and godly in this present world. The more they rest on what Jesus did, the more they automatically and unconsciously accomplish good works. **As they recognize that Jesus, in the spirit, had already done everything, anything still undone on earth can be done in Jesus' name.** There is no doubt in their spirits that good works, no matter how difficult, can be done as Jesus already did it. It is never difficult, frustrating, or stressful to do mighty works when we realize that everything has already been done by Jesus. They work out of their rest in Jesus. Therefore, when Jesus calls a person who lives under Him to do a work, the person gladly responds with a 'Yes!' They do not have to say 'Yes'. They want to say 'Yes'. They delight in saying 'Yes'. **That is why people under Grace are usually loyal people as opposed to committed people. Committed people work from their own strength but loyalty can only come from a new spirit.** It comes from inside. For loyalty is spiritual and came from God first. He was loyal to us even when we did not know Him.

Every nation, which opposes Jesus, can be reached because Jesus had done it already. Every dead church can be revived and re-birthed because Jesus had done it. Every family, torn apart, can be restored fully because Jesus had done it. Every broken relationship can be mended because Jesus had done it. Every hurt and pain can be overcome because Jesus had done it. Every inequality can be righted because Jesus had done it. Every injustice can be corrected because Jesus had done it. Every addiction can be stopped because Jesus had done it. Every disease can be healed because Jesus had done it. Every financial and economic ruin can be reversed because Jesus had done it. Every destroyed life can be made whole again because Jesus had done it. No power on earth can stop the work of a believer because Jesus had done it. Everything still undone can be done as Jesus had done it!

The devil is fully aware of our new born again power in Jesus Christ. While he cannot prevent us from becoming Christians, he is extremely consistent and insistent that we lose our focus on Jesus and fall back on our works. He likes us to talk about commitment, not loyalty, for he knows that our commitment would only last for a period of time. Our commitment to good works can only last that long before we fail. Then he lies to us and tells us that Jesus would have loved us, if only we had stayed committed. Since we failed in our commitment, God no longer loves us.

When Jesus was baptized, the heavens opened and God declared that Jesus was His Beloved Son. *Matthew 3:16-17* states, *And Jesus, when he was baptized, went up straightway out of the water: and, lo, the heavens were opened unto him, and he saw the Spirit of God descending like a dove, and lighting upon him: And lo a voice from heaven, saying, This is my beloved Son, in whom I am well pleased.* This was before Jesus began His earthly ministry. He had not done a single thing yet. **God loved Jesus because of who Jesus was. He was His Son. He does not need to earn His position as a Son of God. He did not have to become. He already was.**

We read in *Matthew 4:1-11, Then was Jesus led up of the Spirit into the wilderness to be tempted of the devil. And when he had fasted forty days and forty nights, he was afterward an hungred. And when the tempter came to him, he said, If thou be the Son of God, command that these stones be made bread. But he answered and said, It is written, Man shall not live by bread alone, but by every word that proceedeth out of the mouth of God.*

Then the devil taketh him up into the holy city, and setteth him on a pinnacle of the temple, And saith unto him, If thou be the

Son of God, cast thyself down: for it is written, He shall give his angels charge concerning thee: and in their hands they shall bear thee up, lest at any time thou dash thy foot against a stone. Jesus said unto him, It is written again, Thou shalt not tempt the Lord thy God. Again, the devil taketh him up into an exceeding high mountain, and sheweth him all the kingdoms of the world, and the glory of them; And saith unto him, All these things will I give thee, if thou wilt fall down and worship me. Then saith Jesus unto him, Get thee hence, Satan: for it is written, Thou shalt worship the Lord thy God, and him only shalt thou serve. Then the devil leaveth him, and, behold, angels came and ministered unto him.

The devil came to tempt Jesus. He said to Jesus that if He was the Son of God, then he could command the stones to become bread. The word 'Beloved' is left out in the devil's statement. The temptation was to make Jesus do something to earn His father's love for Him. In this case, it was to convert the stones to bread. The next was for angels to bear Jesus up. Each time he prodded Jesus to do something to earn favor with His Father. Then and only then, would Jesus earn back the Beloved title. If Jesus did nothing, then he will not be the Beloved Son of God. But Jesus answered back pointedly that man will live by every word that proceeded out of God's mouth. God's mouth just spoke! He declared that Jesus was His Beloved Son. Period. Nothing to be added and nothing to be taken away. He was loved because he was the Son!

The devil in his third attempt asked Jesus to fall down and worship him. If Jesus would do this 'work' first, then the devil would reward Him with all the kingdoms of the world and the glories therein. God gave everything to Jesus first and called Him Beloved. In *Ephesians 1:19-23, And what is the exceeding greatness of his power to usward who believe, according to the working of his mighty power, Which he wrought in Christ, when he raised him from the dead, and set him at his own right hand in the heavenly places, Far above all principality, and power, and might, and dominion, and every name that is named, not only in this world, but also in that which is to come: And hath put all things under his feet, and gave him to be the head over all things to the church, Which is his body, the fulness of him that filleth all in all.*

God put Jesus at His own right hand and put all things under His feet. Jesus was to be the head of everything. He is the fullness that fills all in all. However, the devil will give you nothing until you 'work' for it first. He will tell you to give all your money to feed the poor and to give your body to be burnt. Only then you can become the devil's beloved. The devil responds to your 'holy' actions. God responds to Jesus' actions and our faith in Him.

It is senseless to try to buy God's favor. He is to be worshipped because of His goodness towards us. Similarly, we are sons and daughters of God in Jesus. Even if we do nothing at all, God would still love us exactly the same. That is loyalty. However, because of His abounding love towards us first, we are changed and transformed irrevocably; therefore we cannot help but do good works. We are new creatures and it is in our new nature to want to worship, praise, fellowship, read His word, and share Him. Not because we have to do it but because we want to do it. In fact, we would literally burst if we tried to contain our zeal for good works. Jesus is so good to us that we want to do everything possible back for Him!

However, good works are indistinguishable on the surface. Two people could be reading the bible. One has to do it while the other wants to do it. Two people may have raised hands worshiping God. One does it because of peer pressure, the other because he wants to. One of the common mistakes we make is to make assumptions about who is saved and who is not based upon outward works. For example, we assume that a person is saved because he/she goes to church. Many parents have assumed that their children, while growing up, were believers because they went to church, but were greatly disappointed when they discovered later on that their children had no relationship with Jesus at all. The outward action of going or not going to church does not make a person saved. A believer is one who has faith in Jesus, not one who goes to church. **Outward actions and works are never perfect indicators and as such, should not be used to judge people.** Going to church has tremendous benefits, as do other works, but does not give salvation.

This assumption of who is a believer and who is not based solely upon works has grave consequences. Since we are not God and cannot see into the hearts and spirits of people, we should avoid making over-generalized statements about whether people are saved or not. When I first ministered in Eastern Europe, I found that the legalistic churches had stamped people as believers, or not, based exclusively on outward appearances and works. Nothing else mattered. Everyone who did not act and looked like them were automatically repudiated. There was quick judgment, followed by severe and relentless condemnation. In a short time, almost all unbelievers wanted nothing to do with church. **Because the churches made them feel worse than their plight, they would rather go to hell than attend a legalistic church.** This was extremely sad and it continues to this present day. Whole populations choosing to go to hell because they were condemned by legalism are devastating to the kingdom of God. In my opinion, the correct way to reach out into the community is to always share Jesus and what He had done for them.

Let us look at another example from scripture. In this scripture, two people could be cutting wood but their motives could be completely different. In *2 Kings 6:1-7*, we read, *And the sons of the prophets said unto Elisha, Behold now, the place where we dwell with thee is too strait for us. Let us go, we pray thee, unto Jordan, and take thence every man a beam, and let us make us a place there, where we may dwell. And he answered, Go ye. And one said, Be content, I pray thee, and go with thy servants. And he answered, I will go. So he went with them. And when they came to Jordan, they cut down wood. But as one was felling a beam, the axe head fell into the water: and he cried, and said, Alas, master! for it was borrowed. And the man of God said, Where fell it? And he shewed him the place. And he cut down a stick, and cast it in thither; and the iron did swim. Therefore said he, Take it up to thee. And he put out his hand, and took it.*

In Elisha's school of prophecy, the students were hewing wood to build a new school building. They were all busily cutting wood when one of the axe heads slipped out and fell into the Jordan river. It would be an accident except for what follows. The man whose axe head fell into the river exclaimed that it was borrowed. He was in someone's debt now. In the bible, the axe represents works. It can even boast of its own works as we see in *Isaiah 10:15, Shall the axe boast itself against him that heweth therewith?* Elisha had a solution for the guilt-ridden woodcutter. He took a stick, symbolizing Jesus on the cross, and cast it into the exact spot where the axe head fell. As the stick sank, the axe head rose up! Jesus met us in the exact spot where we failed. He came down to lift us up. He did what we could not do. He paid the debt we could not pay.

In *Deuteronomy 19:5,* we read, *As when a man goeth into the wood with his neighbour to hew wood, and his hand fetcheth a stroke with the axe to cut down the tree, and the head slippeth from the helve, and lighteth upon his neighbour, that he die; he shall flee unto one of those cities, and live.* This is a similar account of an axe head that flew off but it killed another person. Our own works are deadly. We are guilty and indebted. We cannot pay off our guilt. The man described here ran into the city where he would be 'saved'. The city is Jesus and all those who run into Him would be saved.

Back to our woodcutter, who having procured the risen axe head, went back to chopping wood. But now, the axe represented Grace as it was given back freely. What was irredeemably lost was found by Grace. Now, all the good works that he did from that point forward was because of Grace. He cut wood as to the Lord, acknowledging the goodness of God that freed him from debt. Everything about God is good and He is good all the time. God is not good some of the time or most of the time. God is good all of the time as there is no badness in God at all. *James 1:17* states that *Every good gift and every perfect gift is from above, and cometh down from the Father of lights, with whom is no variableness, neither shadow of turning.* And in *Psalm 34:8, O taste and see that the Lord is good: blessed is the man that trusteth in him.* God is good. Period. And only because of His goodness towards us, we can also be good.

37

JESUS AND SIN

There is much confusion about some terms used by biblical scholars that some have resorted to calling their fellow brothers and sisters heretics! In *2 Corinthians 5:21,* we read, *For he hath made him to be sin for us, who knew no sin; that we might be made the righteousness of God in him.* The controversy surrounds whether Jesus actually became sin or whether He just became a sin offering.

There are two interpretations for the verse above. A literal interpretation suggests that Jesus became sin, even though for only a short period, during His crucifixion. The spotless lamb became spotted. The unblemished lamb became blemished. Jesus became the physical embodiment of all our sins. He became sin itself. He became what God hated. Jesus, for one moment, took on all the sins of the world, past present, and future. He became all the sins of mankind - condensed and viscous in evil. *Habakkuk 1:13* states, *Thou art of purer eyes than to behold evil, and canst not look on iniquity.* As God cannot look on sin or iniquity, he forsook His Son and turned His face and back on Him. Jesus, as sin, took the full brunt of the curse of sin - separation from God. The Trinity was broken for one brief moment. God separated Himself from Jesus, as Jesus became sin for us. That is why in *Matthew 27:46,* we read, *And about the ninth hour Jesus cried with a loud voice, saying, Eli,*

Eli, lama sabachthani? that is to say, My God, my God, why hast thou forsaken me?

The second explanation goes like this. As God is holy, He cannot sin. God cannot contradict Himself and be sinful. God's inherent holiness is unchanging. Jesus, as part of the Trinity, is inseparable from God. The Trinity cannot be broken. Therefore, Christ as God cannot become sin. Yes, it was Jesus that was crucified and not the Father, yet the Trinity is eternally inseparable. The Godhead is holy so Jesus cannot become sin; otherwise, the Godhead is no longer holy. There cannot be dissolution in the Trinity, no matter for how short a period. The Trinity is holy or it is not. Therefore, Jesus became a sin offering, not sin itself.

Also, in the sacrificial offerings, the animal must be without blemish. Even if it has a small blemish, it is unacceptable as a sacrifice. We see this clearly in *Leviticus 22:19-22*, which states, *Ye shall offer at your own will a male without blemish, of the beeves, of the sheep, or of the goats. But whatsoever hath a blemish, that shall ye not offer: for it shall not be acceptable for you. And whosoever offereth a sacrifice of peace offerings unto the Lord to accomplish his vow, or a freewill offering in beeves or sheep, it shall be perfect to be accepted; there shall be no blemish therein. Blind, or broken, or maimed, or having a wen, or scurvy, or scabbed, ye shall not offer these unto the Lord, nor make an offering by fire of them upon the altar unto the Lord.* Therefore, Jesus being our sacrificial Lamb had to be spotless. He cannot even for a brief period of time be tarnished. Hence, He cannot become sin, as that would render Him unacceptable as the spotless Lamb. Therefore, He did not become sin but a sin offering.

The two explanations above have divided great-learned men of God and have caused innumerable divisions within the body of Christ. Which explanation is correct or can both be correct? Let me be the first to say that both explanations are correct! But both explanations are also inadequate.

In the whole New Testament, Jesus never spoke to His Father as My God. Jesus always called God as My Father. Therefore, when Jesus cried, 'My God, my God, why have you forsaken me?' Jesus was not calling out to God at the cross.

Otherwise, He would have cried, "My Father, my Father". Rather, when Jesus said, "My God, my God, why have you forsaken me?" he was actually quoting scripture. He was fulfilling prophecy as written by David in Psalm 22.

Psalm 22:1-21, My God, my God, why hast thou forsaken me? why art thou so far from helping me, and from the words of my roaring? O my God, I cry in the daytime, but thou hearest not; and in the night season, and am not silent. But thou art holy, O thou that inhabitest the praises of Israel. Our fathers trusted in thee: they trusted, and thou didst deliver them. They cried unto thee, and were delivered: they trusted in thee, and were not confounded. But I am a worm, and no man; a reproach of men, and despised of the people. All they that see me laugh me to scorn: they shoot out the lip, they shake the head saying, He trusted on the Lord that he would deliver him: let him deliver him, seeing he delighted in him. But thou art he that took me out of the womb: thou didst make me hope when I was upon my mother's breasts. I was cast upon thee from the womb: thou art my God from my mother's belly. Be not far from me; for trouble is near; for there is none to help. Many bulls have compassed me: strong bulls of Bashan have beset me round. They gaped upon me with their mouths, as a ravening and a roaring lion. I am poured out like water, and all my bones are out of joint: my heart is like wax; it is melted in the midst of my bowels. My strength is dried up like a potsherd; and my tongue cleaveth to my jaws; and thou hast brought me into the dust of death. For dogs have compassed me: the assembly of the wicked have inclosed me: they pierced my hands and my feet, I may tell all my bones: they look and stare upon me. They part my garments among them, and cast lots upon my vesture. But be not thou far from me, O Lord: O my strength, haste thee to help me. Deliver my soul from the sword; my darling from the power of the dog. Save me from the lion's mouth: for thou hast heard me from the horns of the unicorns.

All the verses in Psalm 22 refer to Jesus. Psalm 22 was a psalm that every Israelite knew by rote. Every Jew around the cross that day could recite the psalm effortlessly. Therefore, when Jesus started quoting it, everybody knew exactly what He was talking about. He referred to the High Priest, the Roman soldiers, His bones protruding out from His skin, His heart melting like wax in His bowels, the piercings on His hands and feet, His garments being parted, His thirst and His ebbing strength.

He was telling them that He really was their Messiah. He was the One whom the prophets prophesied and spoke about. He was the One who was sent to redeem them. He was really their Savior. Even as He died, He gave them one more chance to believe in Him. He showed them grace as they crucified Him. In that moment, He took on the sins of the world in His flesh. He was made sin but only in the flesh. *Romans 8:3-5* states, *For what the law could not do, in that it was weak through the flesh, God sending his own Son in the likeness of sinful flesh, and for sin, condemned sin in the flesh: That the righteousness of the law might be fulfilled in us, who walk not after the flesh, but after the Spirit. For they that are after the flesh do mind the things of the flesh; but they that are after the Spirit the things of the Spirit.* **God sent His Son in the likeness of sinful flesh. He was made flesh to be condemned for sin in the flesh. As He was made sin in the flesh, He conquered sin in the flesh. That is also why sin has no dominion over our flesh.**

But Jesus was never made sin in His spirit. As God is spirit, Jesus was never made sin in the spirit. There was no separation of the Trinity in the spirit. Jesus in the spirit did not become sin. He was the Perfect sin offering. The tone from verse 22, in Psalm 22, onwards depicts this. From despair and rejection in the flesh to jubilation and praise in the spirit. In the midst of the congregation and throughout all nations, God would be praised and worshiped. For His plan of salvation through His Son Jesus has been accomplished. The Spotless Lamb of God had been sacrificed and all who has faith in Him would be made righteous. His righteousness was declared and imputed to a people that were re-born. All born again saints would point to Jesus and say that He has done it! It is finished and continues to be finished for eternity.

God has never turned His back on a sinner. He loved us while we were yet sinners. We read in *Psalm 22:24 , For he hath not despised nor abhorred the affliction of the afflicted; neither hath he hid his face from him; but when he cried unto him, he heard.* He heard us. As a sin offering, God would never turn His face away from His Son as He does not even turn His face away from us. This was what His Son was sent to do from the foundations of the earth. As God cannot look at sin, He may have averted His eyes away from His Son in the flesh. However, in the spirit, He did not turn His face away from His Son nor hid His face from Him. He heard Jesus' cries. He heard the pain that sin brought upon Jesus. He never for one moment rejected His own Son. In Jesus' pain, God could not have been closer to His Son. As Jesus took on the sins of the world in His flesh, He became sin. In that moment, God could not look at Jesus in the flesh. But in His spirit, His Father was close to Him. They were never separated in the spirit.

๛ 38 ๛

JESUS AND THE HOLY SPIRIT

All of us are composed of three parts, namely body, soul, and spirit. We see this clearly in *1 Thessalonians 5:23, And the very God of peace sanctify you wholly; and I pray God your whole spirit and soul and body be preserved blameless unto the coming of our Lord Jesus Christ.* The body is our physical self; the soul is our mind and our emotions; and the spirit is the part of us that we cannot see. The part that we cannot see is actually the most important part as this is how we were made. God is a spirit and when He made us in His image, He made us after the likeness of His Spirit. Therefore, we are actually spiritual beings living in a physical body and possessing minds with emotions. The spirit and the soul are so much alike that people usually confuse the two. *Hebrews 4:12* states, *For the word of God is quick, and powerful, and sharper than any two edged sword, piercing even to the dividing asunder of soul and spirit.* Many times, only the Word of God can discern between the two. This distinction is important because God talks to us through our spirit, rarely if ever through our mind or body.

When we become born again, our spirit that was dead because of Adam, becomes alive again. In *John 3:5-6,* we read, *Jesus answered, Verily, verily, I say unto thee, Except a man be born of water and of the Spirit, he cannot enter into the kingdom of God. That which is born of the flesh is flesh; and that which is born of the Spirit is spirit.* Because it is born again of the Holy Spirit, our new spirit is completely different from the old spirit.

1 Peter 1:23 states, *Being born again, not of corruptible seed, but of incorruptible, by the word of God, which liveth and abideth for ever.* **It is not born again from corruptible seed but by an Incorruptible Seed. This new spirit of ours cannot sin and does not want to sin. But our souls and our bodies were not born again. Our intellect, our emotions, and our flesh are not born again like our spirit. Unlike our spirit, which can never sin because it was reborn, our flesh can sin. Our flesh is contrary to our born again spirit.** *Galatians 5:17-18* states, *For the flesh lusteth against the Spirit, and the Spirit against the flesh: and these are contrary the one to the other: so that ye cannot do the things that ye would. But if ye be led of the Spirit, ye are not under the law.*

However, just like sinners cannot enter into God's spiritual presence and live, our fleshly sins cannot enter into our re-born spirit and live. Our spirit is unaffected by our flesh. However, our minds are not. This struggle between our spirit and our flesh is fought out in our minds. Sometimes we would do something, which we do not want to do and other times, we would not do something, which we should do. Paul talks at length about this struggle in *Romans 7:19-25, For the good that I would I do not: but the evil which I would not, that I do. Now if I do that I would not, it is no more I that do it, but sin that dwelleth in me. I find then a law, that, when I would do good, evil is present with me. For I delight in the law of God after the inward man: But I see another law in my members, warring against the law of my mind, and bringing me into captivity to the law of sin which is in my members. O wretched man that I am! who shall deliver me from the body of this death? I thank God through Jesus Christ our Lord. So then with the mind I myself serve the law of God; but with the flesh the law of sin.*

Even though this struggle exists and is very real, something has changed radically within us. When we became born again, God comes to live within us. God the Father, God the Son, and God the Holy Spirit actually comes and lives inside of us, in our spirit. We read this in many scriptures. *Galatians 2:20* states, *I am crucified with Christ: nevertheless I live; yet not I, but Christ liveth in me: and the life which I now live in the flesh I live by the faith of the Son of God, who loved me, and gave himself for me.* In *John 14:23, Jesus answered and said unto him, If a man love me, he will keep my words: and my Father will love him, and we will come unto him, and make our abode with him. 1 Corinthians 3:16* states, *Know ye not that ye are the temple of God, and that the Spirit of God dwelleth in you?* Then in *Romans 8:11, But if the Spirit of him that raised up Jesus from the dead dwell in you, he that raised up Christ from the dead shall also quicken your mortal bodies by his Spirit that dwelleth in you.* We read further in *1 John 4:12, No man hath seen God at any time. If we love one another, God dwelleth in us, and his love is perfected in us.* Again in *Ephesians 2:22, In whom ye also are builded together for an habitation of God through the Spirit.*

The actions of our flesh cannot affect our spirit, as it has been reborn with a new identity. Our new identity is Jesus. Because of the power of the Trinity inside our spirit, when we choose to follow our spirit and not our flesh, we easily win the war in our mind. The battle has been won by His perfect love for us. The war may still happen from time to time but it cannot win over us. **We always win, even if we stumble in the flesh, as our spirit is preserved sinless by Jesus Christ.** As we become more and more aware of our new reborn spirit in Jesus, the desire to sin from our flesh becomes less and less. Jesus is my justification and my sanctification. And even if we do sin, we still maintain our spotless nature because of Jesus. It is as though we did not sin. God always sees us through Jesus. And as Jesus is always spotless, we remain spotless because He is our new identity. Our old spotted identity is dead and crucified. We are clothed in His perfect righteousness. Jesus lives in me and therefore, I am spotless. Jesus lives in you and therefore, you are spotless.

The Holy Spirit who lives in us knows all things, as He is God. He not only imparts spiritual life to us and seals the believer but He baptizes us into our position in Christ and bears witness to our Sonship. He knows the deep things of God and He wants to reveal it to us. He is not only our Comforter but He is also our Teacher. He testifies the truth to the believer. He does not teach us man's wisdom but only spiritual truths. The Holy Spirit witness is the primary way whereby God leads and teaches us.

But what does the Holy Spirit actually teach us? This is very clear in scripture. We read in *1 Corinthians 2:9-14, But as it is written, Eye hath not seen, nor ear heard, neither have entered into the heart of man, the things which God hath prepared for them that love him. But God hath revealed them unto us by his Spirit: for the Spirit searcheth all things, yea, the deep things of God. For what man knoweth the things of a man, save the spirit of man which is in him? even so the things of God knoweth no man, but the Spirit of God. Now we have received, not the spirit of the world, but the spirit which is of God; that we might know the things that are freely given to us of God. Which things also we speak, not in the words which man's wisdom teacheth, but which the Holy Ghost teacheth; comparing spiritual things with spiritual. But the natural man receiveth not the things of the Spirit of God: for they are foolishness unto him: neither can he know them, because they are spiritually discerned. In John 14:26, But the Comforter, which is the Holy Ghost, whom the Father will send in my name, he shall teach you all things, and bring all things to your remembrance, whatsoever I have said unto you. Again in John 16:12-15, I have yet many things to say unto you, but ye cannot bear them now. Howbeit when he, the Spirit of truth, is come, he will guide you into all truth: for he shall not speak of himself; but whatsoever he shall hear, that shall he speak: and he will shew you things to come. He shall glorify me: for he shall receive of mine, and shall shew it unto you. All things that the Father hath are mine: therefore said I, that he shall take of mine, and shall shew it unto you. Also, in 1 John 2:27, But the anointing which ye have received of him abideth in you, and ye need not that any man teach you: but as the same anointing teacheth you of all things, and is truth, and is no lie, and even as it hath taught you, ye shall abide in him.*

The Holy Spirit teaches us all things pertaining to Jesus Christ. He brings to our remembrance all that Jesus had taught and said. Even Jesus' disciples could not understand some of Jesus' teachings in His day but we can, because the Holy Spirit has revealed these deep things to us.

Jesus laid out with clarity the purpose of the Holy Spirit. *John 16:7-11* states, *Nevertheless I tell you the truth; It is expedient for you that I go away: for if I go not away, the Comforter will not come unto you; but if I depart, I will send him unto you. And when he is come, he will reprove the world of sin, and of righteousness, and of judgment: Of sin, because they believe not on me; Of righteousness, because I go to my Father, and ye see me no more; Of judgment, because the prince of this world is judged.*

The Holy Spirit will reprove sinners for not believing in Jesus; He will remind believers of their eternal righteous position in Christ; and He will recall to our minds that satan is a defeated foe and has been judged. In *Ephesians 3:16-19*, we read, *That he would grant you, according to the riches of his glory, to be strengthened with might by his Spirit in the inner man; That Christ may dwell in your hearts by faith; that ye, being rooted and grounded in love, May be able to comprehend with all saints what is the breadth, and length, and depth, and height; And to know the love of Christ, which passeth knowledge, that ye might be filled with all the fulness of God.* **As believers, the Holy Spirit reminds us every day that Jesus has made us righteous and that it is not through our own works lest we boast.** The Holy Spirit's objective is to glorify Jesus. The Holy Spirit wants us to understand how much Christ loved us as this love is simply beyond our human knowledge. The breadth, length, depth, and height of Jesus' love for us is infinite. When we are filled with all the fullness of Jesus and strengthened with might by the Holy Spirit in the inner man, then the Holy Spirit has fulfilled His purpose in glorifying Jesus.

❧ 39 ❦

JESUS AND SANCTIFICATION

Justification and Sanctification (positional and progressive) are two biblical words that need clarification. They are actually very simple in their meanings and I have alluded to them in other chapters.

Justification is the work of God where the righteousness of Jesus is imputed to the sinner, so the sinner is declared by God as being righteous under the law. *Romans 3:24-28* states, *Being justified freely by his grace through the redemption that is in Christ Jesus: Whom God hath set forth to be a propitiation through faith in his blood, to declare his righteousness for the remission of sins that are past, through the forbearance of God; To declare, I say, at this time his righteousness: that he might be just, and the justifier of him which believeth in Jesus. Where is boasting then? It is excluded. By what law? of works? Nay: but by the law of faith. Therefore we conclude that a man is justified by faith without the deeds of the law.* Also, in *Ephesians 2:8-9, For by grace are ye saved through faith; and that not of yourselves: it is the gift of God: Not of works, lest any man should boast.* It is by His Grace through the redemption that is in Christ that we are declared righteous. Jesus is righteous, therefore we are righteous. This is unmerited righteousness as it is not earned or merited by any effort on the part of the person saved. It is a free gift from God and no works are required nor accepted.

We see this further in *1 Peter 2:24, Who his own self bare our sins in his own body on the tree, that we, being dead to sins, should live unto righteousness: by whose stripes ye were healed.* And also in *2 Corinthians 5:21, For he hath made him to be sin for us, who knew no sin; that we might be made the righteousness of God in him.*

We can do nothing and add nothing as Jesus paid and did it all for us. We can never be justified by the deeds of the law. In *Isaiah 64:6, But we are all as an unclean thing, and all our righteousnesses are as filthy rags; and we all do fade as a leaf; and our iniquities, like the wind, have taken us away.* We can never be justified by our own works, which are like filthy rags before God. If we try to be justified by our works, then we are fallen from Grace and do not know Jesus. We read in *Galatians 5:1-5, Stand fast therefore in the liberty wherewith Christ hath made us free, and be not entangled again with the yoke of bondage. Behold, I Paul say unto you, that if ye be circumcised, Christ shall profit you nothing. For I testify again to every man that is circumcised, that he is a debtor to do the whole law. Christ is become of no effect unto you, whosoever of you are justified by the law; ye are fallen from grace. For we through the Spirit wait for the hope of righteousness by faith.* It is not of ourselves otherwise we would boast of our good works and Christ would have become of no effect to us.

Justification is instantaneous and it is eternal as it gives us eternal life. Saving-faith in Jesus and His completed work on the cross is the basis of justification. We can say that we are justified by faith in Jesus. We read in *Romans 6:23, For the wages of sin is death; but the gift of God is eternal life through Jesus Christ our Lord.* Then in *Romans 5:1-2, 9-11, Therefore being justified by faith, we have peace with God through our Lord Jesus Christ: By whom also we have access by faith into this grace wherein we stand, and rejoice in hope of the glory of God. Much more then, being now justified by his blood, we shall be saved from wrath through him. For if, when we were enemies, we were reconciled to God by the death of his Son, much more, being reconciled, we shall be saved by his life. And not only so, but we also joy in God through our Lord Jesus Christ, by whom we have now received the atonement.*

Again in *Galatians 3:11, 22-27, But that no man is justified by the law in the sight of God, it is evident: for, The just shall live by faith. But the scripture hath concluded all under sin, that the promise by faith of Jesus Christ might be given to them that believe. But before faith came, we were kept under the law, shut up unto the faith which should afterwards be revealed. Wherefore the law was our schoolmaster to bring us unto Christ, that we might be justified by faith. But after that faith is come, we are no longer under a schoolmaster. For ye are all the children of God by faith in Christ Jesus. For as many of you as have been baptized into Christ have put on Christ.*

Continuing in *Galatians 2:16, 20-21, Knowing that a man is not justified by the works of the law, but by the faith of Jesus Christ, even we have believed in Jesus Christ, that we might be justified by the faith of Christ, and not by the works of the law: for by the works of the law shall no flesh be justified. I am crucified with Christ: nevertheless I live; yet not I, but Christ liveth in me: and the life which I now live in the flesh I live by the faith of the Son of God, who loved me, and gave himself for me. I do not frustrate the grace of God: for if righteousness come by the law, then Christ is dead in vain.* And in *Hebrews 10:19-23, Having therefore, brethren, boldness to enter into the holiest by the blood of Jesus, By a new and living way, which he hath consecrated for us, through the veil, that is to say, his flesh; And having an high priest over the house of God; Let us draw near with a true heart in full assurance of faith, having our hearts sprinkled from an evil conscience, and our bodies washed with pure water. Let us hold fast the profession of our faith without wavering; (for he is faithful that promised;)*

Because of what Jesus did on the cross for us, we can enter into the Holiest Place with boldness. We can draw near to God with a true heart in full assurance of faith. This is our born-again experience when we become the new man. The new man cannot become the old man again. The transformation is irreversible, just like the butterfly cannot become a caterpillar again. We are saved by grace and maintained by grace. Our salvation is never maintained by works. We did nothing to get in and we cannot do anything to get out.

However, many preachers mistakenly assume that justification covers the whole man – spirit, soul and body. Justification only covers the spirit man, not the soul or the body. *1 John 3:9* states, *Whosoever is born of God doth not commit sin; for his seed remaineth in him: and he cannot sin, because he is born of God.* Our new spirit man cannot sin and does not want to sin as it is completely born again and has nothing in common with the old, now dead, spirit. Whosoever is born of God does not commit sin nor can he sin because he is born of God. It is impossible to sin in our spirit once we are born again of God.

Justification is also called Positional Righteousness as Jesus grants us this position of righteousness freely. It can also be called Positional Sanctification. In many parts of the bible, sanctification refers to positional sanctification, not progressive sanctification. This position of perfect status is given to us freely as we have been redeemed and cleansed by the blood of Jesus. As God did not spare His own Son but delivered Him up for us all, how shall he not also freely give us justification or positional sanctification?

There are many scriptures describing positional sanctification. Some of them are as follows. *Hebrews 10:10, 14, By the which will we are sanctified through the offering of the body of Jesus Christ once for all. For by one offering he hath perfected for ever them that are sanctified.*
John 17:22-23, And the glory which thou gavest me I have given them; that they may be one, even as we are one: I in them, and thou in me, that they may be made perfect in one; and that the world may know that thou hast sent me, and hast loved them, as thou hast loved me.
1 Corinthians 6:11, And such were some of you: but ye are washed, but ye are sanctified, but ye are justified in the name of the Lord Jesus, and by the Spirit of our God.
Ephesians 5:26-27, That he might sanctify and cleanse it with the washing of water by the word, That he might present it to himself a

glorious church, not having spot, or wrinkle, or any such thing; but that it should be holy and without blemish.
Romans 8:30-34, Moreover whom he did predestinate, them he also called: and whom he called, them he also justified: and whom he justified, them he also glorified. What shall we then say to these things? If God be for us, who can be against us? He that spared not his own Son, but delivered him up for us all, how shall he not with him also freely give us all things? Who shall lay any thing to the charge of God's elect? It is God that justifieth. Who is he that condemneth? It is Christ that died, yea rather, that is risen again, who is even at the right hand of God, who also maketh intercession for us.
1 John 2:1, My little children, these things write I unto you, that ye sin not. And if any man sin, we have an advocate with the Father, Jesus Christ the righteous:
Hebrews 7:24-26, But this man, because he continueth ever, hath an unchangeable priesthood. Wherefore he is able also to save them to the uttermost that come unto God by him, seeing he ever liveth to make intercession for them. For such an high priest became us, who is holy, harmless, undefiled, separate from sinners, and made higher than the heavens;
Hebrews 13:12, Wherefore Jesus also, that he might sanctify the people with his own blood, suffered without the gate.

All our sins have been forgiven and we are put into this position permanently through the offering of Jesus who became our sacrifice once and for all time. We are sanctified and made perfect forever through the offering of the body of Jesus. God sanctifies us definitely and He declares us holy before Him, and then He places and separates us in a position of holiness. If any accusation by the devil comes up against us, Jesus as our Advocate makes intercession for us. He is our unchanging High Priest as he is forever. And forever He intercedes for us. We are fully accepted, washed, sanctified, justified, and made spotless and holy because of Jesus. We belong to Him and nothing will ever separate us from His love.

We read in *1 Corinthians 1:2, 30, Unto the church of God which is at Corinth, to them that are sanctified in Christ Jesus,*

called to be saints, with all that in every place call upon the name
of Jesus Christ our Lord, both theirs and ours: But of him are ye
in Christ Jesus, who of God is made unto us wisdom, and
righteousness, and sanctification, and redemption. Then in
Colossians 2:3, 9-10, In whom are hid all the treasures of wisdom
and knowledge. For in him dwelleth all the fulness of the
Godhead bodily. And ye are complete in him, which is the head of
all principality and power. We have wisdom, knowledge,
righteousness, sanctification, and redemption because of Jesus. **We
are complete in Jesus. We do not become progressively
complete. We are already complete in the spirit.**

Then we read in Ezekiel 36:26-27, A new heart also will I
give you, and a new spirit will I put within you: and I will take
away the stony heart out of your flesh, and I will give you an heart
of flesh. And I will put my spirit within you, and cause you to walk
in my statutes, and ye shall keep my judgments, and do them. We
have received a new heart and a new spirit. Our spiritual walk
begins from a point of completeness. Because of this positional
sanctification, we are set apart for His holy use.

From this point of completeness in Jesus, we no longer
perform dead works but serve the living God. Hebrews 9:13-14
states, For if the blood of bulls and of goats, and the ashes of an
heifer sprinkling the unclean, sanctifieth to the purifying of the
flesh: How much more shall the blood of Christ, who through the
eternal Spirit offered himself without spot to God, purge your
conscience from dead works to serve the living God? We serve
God from our new position of righteousness. We read in Exodus
19:6, And ye shall be unto me a kingdom of priests, and an holy
nation. And in 1 Peter 2:9-10, But ye are a chosen generation, a
royal priesthood, an holy nation, a peculiar people; that ye should
shew forth the praises of him who hath called you out of darkness
into his marvellous light: Which in time past were not a people, but
are now the people of God: which had not obtained mercy, but
now have obtained mercy. Again in Hebrews 2:11, For both he
that sanctifieth and they who are sanctified are all of one: for
which cause he is not ashamed to call them brethren.

We are called saints, not partial, progressive or work-in-progress saints. In Exodus, the Israelites were to be a kingdom of priests and a holy nation. They were either that or they were not. There were no progressive priests. Similarly, we are the chosen generation, the royal priesthood, the holy nation, and the peculiar people. As fully completed saints, sanctified by Jesus and the Holy Spirit, we can minister the gospel of Jesus Christ with boldness. We see this in *Romans 15:15-16, Nevertheless, brethren, I have written the more boldly unto you in some sort, as putting you in mind, because of the grace that is given to me of God, That I should be the minister of Jesus Christ to the Gentiles, ministering the gospel of God, that the offering up of the Gentiles might be acceptable, being sanctified by the Holy Ghost.*

Due to our Positional Sanctification, we are now as perfect as Christ is. Because God sees us only through Jesus, all His righteousness, purity, perfection, and loveliness is imputed upon us. It was not our keeping but Jesus' delivering that mattered. It was not our falling but Jesus' raising that counted. Because of Jesus, God becomes our father and we become His children, adopted into His family. God also says that we become kings, priests, saints, heirs, and joint-heirs with Jesus. Because of Jesus, we become heirs to Abraham's promises. It becomes part of our inheritance. And if we were to look into the book of life, we will see that our names are written therein as we sit with Him in the heavenly realms.

Some of the supporting scriptures are as follows: *Romans 4:24-25, But for us also, to whom it shall be imputed, if we believe on him that raised up Jesus our Lord from the dead; Who was delivered for our offences, and was raised again for our justification.*
Galatians 3:26, For ye are all the children of God by faith in Christ Jesus.
John 1:12-13, But as many as received him, to them gave he power to become the sons of God, even to them that believe on his name: Which were born, not of blood, nor of the will of the flesh, nor of the will of man, but of God.

Galatians 4:5-7, To redeem them that were under the law, that we might receive the adoption of sons. And because ye are sons, God hath sent forth the Spirit of his Son into your hearts, crying, Abba, Father. Wherefore thou art no more a servant, but a son; and if a son, then an heir of God through Christ.

Ephesians 1:4-6, According as he hath chosen us in him before the foundation of the world, that we should be holy and without blame before him in love: Having predestinated us unto the adoption of children by Jesus Christ to himself, according to the good pleasure of his will, To the praise of the glory of his grace, wherein he hath made us accepted in the beloved.

1 John 3:1-2, Behold, what manner of love the Father hath bestowed upon us, that we should be called the sons of God: therefore the world knoweth us not, because it knew him not. Beloved, now are we the sons of God, and it doth not yet appear what we shall be: but we know that, when he shall appear, we shall be like him; for we shall see him as he is.

Revelation 1:5-6, And from Jesus Christ, who is the faithful witness, and the first begotten of the dead, and the prince of the kings of the earth. Unto him that loved us, and washed us from our sins in his own blood, And hath made us kings and priests unto God and his Father; to him be glory and dominion for ever and ever. Amen.

Romans 8:16-17, The Spirit itself beareth witness with our spirit, that we are the children of God: And if children, then heirs; heirs of God, and joint-heirs with Christ; if so be that we suffer with him, that we may be also glorified together.

Galatians 3:29, And if ye be Christ's, then are ye Abraham's seed, and heirs according to the promise.

Ephesians 1:11-12, In whom also we have obtained an inheritance, being predestinated according to the purpose of him who worketh all things after the counsel of his own will: That we should be to the praise of his glory, who first trusted in Christ.

Ephesains 2:6, And hath raised us up together, and made us sit together in heavenly places in Christ Jesus:

Luke 10:20, Notwithstanding in this rejoice not, that the spirits are subject unto you; but rather rejoice, because your names are written in heaven.

Now, let us see what the scriptures say about progressive sanctification. We read this in *Romans 6:3-7, 11-18, Know ye not, that so many of us as were baptized into Jesus Christ were baptized into his death? Therefore we are buried with him by baptism into death: that like as Christ was raised up from the dead by the glory of the Father, even so we also should walk in newness of life. For if we have been planted together in the likeness of his death, we shall be also in the likeness of his resurrection: Knowing this, that our old man is crucified with him, that the body of sin might be destroyed, that henceforth we should not serve sin. For he that is dead is freed from sin.*

Likewise reckon ye also yourselves to be dead indeed unto sin, but alive unto God through Jesus Christ our Lord. Let not sin therefore reign in your mortal body, that ye should obey it in the lusts thereof. Neither yield ye your members as instruments of unrighteousness unto sin: but yield yourselves unto God, as those that are alive from the dead, and your members as instruments of righteousness unto God.

For sin shall not have dominion over you: for ye are not under the law, but under grace. What then? shall we sin, because we are not under the law, but under grace? God forbid. Know ye not, that to whom ye yield yourselves servants to obey, his servants ye are to whom ye obey; whether of sin unto death, or of obedience unto righteousness? But God be thanked, that ye were the servants of sin, but ye have obeyed from the heart that form of doctrine which was delivered you. Being then made free from sin, ye became the servants of righteousness.

It is very important to understand that progressive sanctification is for the soul and the body, not the spirit. Progressive sanctification means to be conformed or transformed to the image of Christ. It has nothing to do with our spirit that has been permanently justified and sanctified by Jesus. This sanctification is not instantaneous as evidenced by our still fleshly desires both in our minds and in our bodies. The easiest way to illustrate this is to imagine a new born again believer looking at himself in a mirror. As he cannot see his own spirit, which is entirely new, he sees only his body which is the same as before. He looks physically the same as he was before he was born again, but on the inside, he has irrevocably changed. His old spirit died with Jesus and his new spirit has been resurrected with Jesus. As his old spirit died, he was freed from sin. He cannot serve sin anymore. His spirit is now dead to sin and alive unto God. His new spirit is much stronger than his mind and body that still has a propensity to sin. His new spirit is stronger not only because it is new but because Jesus indwells that spirit now. Because of Jesus' power, sin now has no dominion over his mind and body. He finds it easy to not let sin reign in his body and mind because he is now under Grace. The allure of sins and evil desires no longer has control over him. Instead of leaning towards sin, his mind and body now has a tendency to lean towards righteousness. The power of sin wanes and dies as Grace takes over.

We see this in the following scriptures. *2 Corinthians 7:1, Having therefore these promises, dearly beloved, let us cleanse ourselves from all filthiness of the flesh and spirit, perfecting holiness in the fear of God.*
1 Thessalonians 4:7, For God hath not called us unto uncleanness, but unto holiness.
1 John 3:1-8, Behold, what manner of love the Father hath bestowed upon us, that we should be called the sons of God: therefore the world knoweth us not, because it knew him not. Beloved, now are we the sons of God, and it doth not yet appear what we shall be: but we know that, when he shall appear, we shall be like him; for we shall see him as he is. And every man that hath this hope in him purifieth himself, even as he is pure. Whosoever committeth sin transgresseth also the law: for sin is the transgression of the law. And ye know that he was manifested to take away our sins; and in him is no sin. Whosoever abideth in him sinneth not: whosoever sinneth hath not seen him, neither known him. Little children, let no man deceive you: he that doeth righteousness is righteous, even as he is righteous. He that committeth sin is of the devil; for the devil sinneth from the

beginning. For this purpose the Son of God was manifested, that he might destroy the works of the devil.

While progressive sanctification is a process, it is not a striving, sweaty process. We read in *Philippians 3:12-16, Not as though I had already attained, either were already perfect: but I follow after, if that I may apprehend that for which also I am apprehended of Christ Jesus. Brethren, I count not myself to have apprehended: but this one thing I do, forgetting those things which are behind, and reaching forth unto those things which are before, I press toward the mark for the prize of the high calling of God in Christ Jesus. Let us therefore, as many as be perfect, be thus minded: and if in any thing ye be otherwise minded, God shall reveal even this unto you. Nevertheless, whereto we have already attained, let us walk by the same rule, let us mind the same thing.*

It is the faith that we have in Jesus at work in us as we press towards Him. It is justifying faith at work. There is no endeavoring to be holy, working to be more godly, diligently confessing sins, actively fighting and resisting sin, and daily, even hourly, contending and submitting to God's will. The process is effortless because Jesus is now living inside our spirit. To say that we are fighting a great battle every day, the battle between our spirit and our flesh is a misnomer. Jesus has already won the war and all the battles and we just have to effortlessly let our soul and body be led by Jesus and the Spirit of God who also resides within us. The work we have to do in our sanctification process is to let go and let God rule over our minds and our bodies. It is very important that we let go completely and quickly. Let Him cleanse and purify us. That is the prize of the high calling of God in our lives. We want this prize because only then can we begin to cleanse and purify ourselves to become more and more like Jesus. This occurs when we spend time with Jesus and spend time in the Word of God. Meditate on His goodness and on His unconditional love towards us. I encourage every person to spend as much time as possible with Jesus every day. However, note that no matter how much time we spent with Jesus, we can never achieve this sanctification and arrive at sinless perfection like Jesus. We can go on towards perfection but we can never become perfect in our minds and body, otherwise we would no longer need Jesus. We can never stand before a holy God in our flesh. Although we never arrive, we are still saved as our spirit is saved and justified by Jesus. Our salvation is assured. To say that we can lose our salvation because we are not sanctified is to not understand the justification of Christ and His completed work.

All the works we do here come from our absolute rest in Jesus and His finished work on the cross. Our faith in Jesus produces works. *James 2:17*, states, *Even so faith, if it hath not works, is dead, being alone.* **This is often called practical righteousness but it does not make us righteous. Without justification, all of our practical righteousness comes to nought.** However, with a correct understanding of the finished work of Christ, we can do more practical righteousness than we can imagine. Good works, not dead works, are what the Holy Spirit asks us to do. We can of course say 'No' to the Holy Spirit. He would then just call someone else to do the good work that He originally called us to do. He does not condemn or make us feel guilty for saying 'No'. But every believer who knows Jesus cannot wait to say 'Yes' as his spirit has been renewed and his mind and body has been yielded to Jesus.

Many times, we can do the impossible because of what He has done for us. We can achieve things which are deemed unachievable, we can access places deemed inaccessible with the gospel, we can conceive the inconceivable, and attain the unattainable. Unimaginable fivefold ministries, church buildings, helps, and giving have occurred because of the rest we have in Him.

As we become 'more and more' filled with Jesus, there would be 'less and less' of us. The more focused we are on Christ; the less focused we are on our own progressive sanctification and the more fruits we would produce effortlessly. **John the Baptist puts it best – Jesus must increase and he must decrease.** We read this in *John 3:30, He must increase, but I must decrease.* **The more of Jesus we have, the holier we become.** Why? Because only Jesus is holy! Our holiness comes entirely from Him and not from our practical righteousness.

Legalism often creeps in when talking about the progressive sanctification process. Instead of relying on Jesus and the Holy Spirit to sanctify us first, legalists depend entirely on their own ability to sanctify themselves. However, in *1 Thessalonians 5:23-24*, it states, *And the very God of peace sanctify you wholly; and I pray God your whole spirit and soul and body be preserved blameless unto the coming of our Lord Jesus Christ. Faithful is he that calleth you, who also will do it.* It is very clear that the whole progressive sanctification process is to be done by Jesus Himself. He calls us to do it and then He does it for us. This is repeated in *Philippians 2:13,For it is God which worketh in you both to will and to do of his good pleasure.* God is at work within us, helping us obey Him, and then helping us do what He wants.

In *1 John 2:5-6*, we read, *But whoso keepeth his word, in him verily is the love of God perfected: hereby know we that we are in him.He that saith he abideth in him ought himself also so to walk, even as he walked.* We should walk correctly even as Jesus walked but only with Him helping us all the way. It is called the love of God perfecting us. **The power to do right and to behave right is not in the power of our flesh but in the power of God within us enabling us to do right.**

The legalists miss this and they gravitate back to self-works to please God. Their messages are full of self and always place unnecessary demands on self and others. If they achieve their self-works, they exalt themselves and feel superior but when they fail, they feel guilty and condemned. They are usually highly critical and judgmental of others who fall behind in the sanctification process, making them feel guilty and condemned. The entire progressive sanctification process is turned into a 'better than you' process leading to fear, insecurity, confusion, frustration, anger, and control. They will be the ones who teach that you will lose your salvation because you did not finish your sanctification process. You started the process but you did not stay in the process, therefore you are disqualified! Note that it is all about self and has nothing to do with Jesus, nothing with being Holy Spirit led, and nothing to do with honoring God. Legalists are obsessed with the law, which is all about self.

These are the teachers who may say that grace is a license to sin. **Of course, Grace is never a license to sin as a person living in grace does not want to sin!** *Romans 6:1-2* states, *What shall we say then? Shall we continue in sin, that grace may abound? God forbid. How shall we, that are dead to sin, live any longer therein?* Because he is dead to sin in his spirit and alive to Christ, and as he is led by the Holy Spirit, he has no desire to sin even when his mind and body are still carnal and susceptible to sin and temptation. Occasionally he may stumble and make a mistake, but the Holy Spirit immediately reminds him of his justified and righteous position in Christ. We see this clearly in *John 16:13-14, Howbeit when he, the Spirit of truth, is come, he will guide you into all truth: for he shall not speak of himself; but whatsoever he shall hear, that shall he speak: and he will shew you things to come. He shall glorify me: for he shall receive of mine, and shall shew it unto you.* The Holy Spirit always points us back towards Christ, to glorify Him. Despite our mistakes, we are still justified and sanctified by Jesus Christ. *Romans 8:38-39* states, *For I am persuaded, that neither death, nor life, nor angels, nor principalities, nor powers, nor things present, nor things to come, Nor height, nor depth, nor any other creature, shall be able to separate us from the love of God, which is in Christ Jesus our Lord.* **Sinning does have adverse consequences but it cannot and will never ever tear us apart from the love of Jesus.**

❧ 40 ❧

JESUS AND OUR HOME

It has always amazed me that God could love us so much first that He sent His Son to die for us while we were yet sinners. It was never about Jesus dying for us first and that is why we are loved by God or that we are loved by God because we loved Him first. We are loved by God first. Period! In *1 John 4:10*, we read, *Herein is love, not that we loved God, but that he loved us, and sent his Son to be the propitiation for our sins.*

Because of what Jesus did on the cross, our home is no longer on Mount Sinai. *Hebrews 12:18-21* states, *For ye are not come unto the mount that might be touched, and that burned with fire, nor unto blackness, and darkness, and tempest, And the sound of a trumpet, and the voice of words; which voice they that heard intreated that the word should not be spoken to them any more: (For they could not endure that which was commanded, And if so much as a beast touch the mountain, it shall be stoned, or thrust through with a dart: And so terrible was the sight, that Moses said, I exceedingly fear and quake:)* On Mount Sinai, there was fire, blackness, darkness, earthquakes, tempest, judgments, fear, and trembling. Now, we have a new home on another mountain called Mount Zion. However, the devil does not want us to get there so he continues to roar and lie like a toothless lion. He continues to shift our focus away from Jesus, to our works and ourselves.

I have drawn a simple matrix that summarizes the truths that has been the central theme of this book.

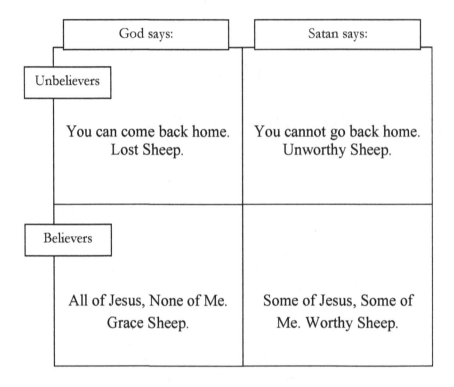

God says:	Satan says:
Unbelievers	
You can come back home. Lost Sheep.	You cannot go back home. Unworthy Sheep.
Believers	
All of Jesus, None of Me. Grace Sheep.	Some of Jesus, Some of Me. Worthy Sheep.

Billy's Matrix of Sheep

1. In the top left hand corner, God says to all unbelievers that their sins have already been forgiven. Every unbeliever can come back home to God by faith in Jesus. God says that these unbelievers are lost and calls them Lost Sheep.

2. In the top right hand corner, Satan says to all unbelievers that their sins would never be forgiven. No unbeliever can go back home to God because they will not be accepted. Because of what they had done, they no longer deserve the love and grace of God. Satan calls them Unworthy Sheep.

3. In the bottom left hand corner, God says to all believers that what Jesus did on the cross was more than sufficient to pay the debt for their sins. It is all of Jesus and none of self-works. Everything we need God has already provided. Our identity is in Jesus and what he did for us. We were given this position freely. We do not need to perform to earn this position. Our worth is Jesus. We are worthy because of Jesus. We are good and faithful because of Jesus. God calls these sheep Grace Sheep.

4. In the bottom right hand corner, Satan says to all believers that what Jesus did on the cross was insufficient to pay the debt for their sins. As Jesus' work is not finished, all believers must add their works to what Jesus did. Our achievements, performances, and attainments matter. We must continue to honor Him, please Him, and impress Him by our works just in case God gets angry with us and forfeits our salvation. It is some of Jesus and some of self. The more of self the more deserving we become to God. We are good and faithful because of us. Satan calls these sheep Worthy Sheep because of their works. This is a lie that many people believe in.

     The basic strategy of the devil is always the same. He wants us to question the merit of our worth before God. He shifts the focus away from God, onto ourselves. In the garden of Eden, he pointed to the only tree in the garden which God told Adam not to eat from and managed to pervert God's goodness as a Giver to a Taker. 'If you are truly worthy, why would God not allow you to eat from that tree? If you eat from that tree, you will be like god!' Therefore, when we look at ourselves, we would say, 'Yes, why does God not allow me to eat from that tree? We want to be like God!' And we forget about all the thousands of other trees that God said we could eat from. We also forget that we do not have to do something to become like God for we are already created in the image of God. In the matrix above, the devil still uses the same strategy. He calls us unworthy and worthy based upon our own works. If we fail, we are condemned and made to feel guilty. He wants us to forget about Jesus. He says that we are defined by our failures and Jesus does not accept failures.

But the truth is that God never forgets about us despite our failures and mistakes. He wants to take all who are lost, back home with Him. **God has no unworthy sheep, just lost sheep**. He made it easy for us to be with Him. That is why He gave us by grace His only begotten Son, Jesus, to die for us so that all of us who have faith in Jesus can go back home. There is no effort on our part. God provides even the faith in Jesus to believe in Him. By grace, He provided Jesus who accomplished it all. Jesus did it all for me! Jesus did it all for you!

Our new home is on another mountain called Mount Zion or the New Jerusalem. We read of this new home in many scriptures. Some of these are as follows: *Psalms 9:11, Sing praises to the Lord, which dwelleth in Zion: declare among the people his doings.*

Psalms 132:13-14, For the Lord hath chosen Zion; he hath desired it for his habitation. This is my rest for ever: here will I dwell; for I have desired it.

Psalms 50:2, Out of Zion, the perfection of beauty, God hath shined.

Hebrews 12:22-24, But ye are come unto mount Sion, and unto the city of the living God, the heavenly Jerusalem, and to an innumerable company of angels, To the general assembly and church of the firstborn, which are written in heaven, and to God the Judge of all, and to the spirits of just men made perfect, And to Jesus the mediator of the new covenant, and to the blood of sprinkling, that speaketh better things than that of Abel.

Psalms 16:11, Thou wilt shew me the path of life: in thy presence is fulness of joy; at thy right hand there are pleasures for evermore.

Psalms 48:1-3, Great is the Lord, and greatly to be praised in the city of our God, in the mountain of his holiness. Beautiful for situation, the joy of the whole earth, is mount Zion, on the sides of the north, the city of the great King. God is known in her palaces for a refuge.

Psalms 133:1-3, Behold, how good and how pleasant it is for brethren to dwell together in unity! It is like the precious ointment upon the head, that ran down upon the beard, even Aaron's beard:

*that went down to the skirts of his garments; As the dew of
Hermon, and as the dew that descended upon the mountains of
Zion: for there the Lord commanded the blessing, even life for
evermore.*
*Revelation 21:1-6, 21-23, And I saw a new heaven and a new
earth: for the first heaven and the first earth were passed away;
and there was no more sea. And I John saw the holy city, new
Jerusalem, coming down from God out of heaven, prepared as a
bride adorned for her husband. And I heard a great voice out of
heaven saying, Behold, the tabernacle of God is with men, and he
will dwell with them, and they shall be his people, and God himself
shall be with them, and be their God. And God shall wipe away all
tears from their eyes; and there shall be no more death, neither
sorrow, nor crying, neither shall there be any more pain: for the
former things are passed away. And he that sat upon the throne
said, Behold, I make all things new. And he said unto me, Write:
for these words are true and faithful. And he said unto me, It is
done. I am Alpha and Omega, the beginning and the end.*
*And the twelve gates were twelve pearls; every several gate was of
one pearl: and the street of the city was pure gold, as it were
transparent glass. And I saw no temple therein: for the Lord God
Almighty and the Lamb are the temple of it. And the city had no
need of the sun, neither of the moon, to shine in it: for the glory of
God did lighten it, and the Lamb is the light thereof.*

In our new home, there are no tears, no sorrow, no pain, no
crying, and no death. There is no moon and no sun. Everything is
new and made new in our new home. In Zion, there is eternal life,
perfect light, singing of songs of praise, rest, refuge, perfection of
beauty, joy, unity, angels, and our family and friends. There will be
pleasures forevermore and fullness of joy. Most importantly, in our
new home there will be God the Father, God the Son, and God the
Holy Spirit. Jesus Himself will welcome us home. We finally get
to meet Him face to face, the One who did it all for you and me.
Jesus is the alpha and the omega. He is A to Z. He is Aleph to Tav.
Jesus is the beginning, the middle, and the end. It is truly all about
Jesus!

APPENDIX A

The following are the 613 commandments. The source of their derivation is from the Hebrew Bible as enumerated by Maimonides: Moses Maimonides, translation by Charles Ber Chavel and Moses ibn Tibbon. *The book of divine commandments (the Sefer Ha-mitzvoth of Moses Maimonides)* London: Soncino Press, 1940. This list is reprinted here under the terms of the Creative Commons Attribution Share-Alike license (CC-BY-SA). The URL is at http://en.wikipedia.org/wiki/613_commandments.

1. To know there is a God — Ex. 20:2
2. Not to even think that there are other gods besides Him — Standard->Ex. 20:3 Yemenite->Ex. 20:2
3. To know that He is One — Deut. 6:4
4. To love Him —Deut. 6:5
5. To fear Him — Deut. 10:20
6. To sanctify His Name — Lev. 22:32
7. Not to profane His Name — Lev. 22:32
8. Not to destroy objects associated with His Name — Deut. 12:4
9. To listen to the prophet speaking in His Name — Deut. 18:15
10. Not to try the LORD unduly — Deut. 6:16
11. To emulate His ways — Deut. 28:9
12. To cleave to those who know Him — Deut. 10:20
13. To love other Jews — Lev. 19:18
14. To love converts — Deut. 10:19
15. Not to hate fellow Jews — Lev. 19:17
16. To reprove a sinner — Lev. 19:17
17. Not to embarrass others — Lev. 19:17
18. Not to oppress the weak — Ex. 22:21
19. Not to speak derogatorily of others — Lev. 19:16
20. Not to take revenge — Lev. 19:18
21. Not to bear a grudge — Lev. 19:18
22. To learn Torah — Deut. 6:7
23. To honor those who teach and know Torah — Lev. 19:32
24. Not to inquire into idolatry — Lev. 19:4
25. Not to follow the whims of your heart or what your eyes see — Num. 15:39
26. Not to blaspheme — Ex. 22:27
27. Not to worship idols in the manner they are worshiped — Standard->Ex. 20:6 Yemenite->Ex. 20:5
28. Not to worship idols in the four ways we worship God — Standard->Ex. 20:6 Yemenite->Ex. 20:5

29. Not to make an idol for yourself — Standard->Ex. 20:5 Yemenite->Ex. 20:4
30. Not to make an idol for others — Lev. 19:4
31. Not to make human forms even for decorative purposes — Standard->Ex. 20:21 Yemenite->Ex. 20:20
32. Not to turn a city to idolatry — Deut. 13:14
33. To burn a city that has turned to idol worship — Deut. 13:17
34. Not to rebuild it as a city — Deut. 13:17
35. Not to derive benefit from it — Deut. 13:18
36. Not to missionize an individual to idol worship — Deut. 13:12
37. Not to love the idolater — Deut. 13:9
38. Not to cease hating the idolater — Deut. 13:9
39. Not to save the idolater — Deut. 13:9
40. Not to say anything in the idolater's defense — Deut. 13:9
41. Not to refrain from incriminating the idolater — Deut. 13:9
42. Not to prophesize in the name of idolatry — Deut. 13:14
43. Not to listen to a false prophet — Deut. 13:4
44. Not to prophesize falsely in the name of God — Deut. 18:20
45. Not to be afraid of the false prophet — Deut. 18:22
46. Not to swear in the name of an idol — Ex. 23:13
47. Not to perform ov (medium) — Lev. 19:31
48. Not to perform yidoni ("magical seer") — Lev. 19:31
49. Not to pass your children through the fire to Molech — Lev. 18:21
50. Not to erect a pillar in a public place of worship — Deut. 16:22
51. Not to bow down before a smooth stone — Lev. 26:1
52. Not to plant a tree in the Temple courtyard — Deut. 16:21
53. To destroy idols and their accessories — Deut. 12:2
54. Not to derive benefit from idols and their accessories — Deut. 7:26
55. Not to derive benefit from ornaments of idols — Deut. 7:25
56. Not to make a covenant with idolaters —Deut. 7:2
57. Not to show favor to them — Deut. 7:2
58. Not to let them dwell in the Land of Israel — Ex. 23:33
59. Not to imitate them in customs and clothing — Lev. 20:23
60. Not to be superstitious — Lev. 19:26
61. Not to go into a trance to foresee events, etc. — Deut. 18:10
62. Not to engage in divination or soothsaying — Lev. 19:26
63. Not to mutter incantations — Deut. 18:11
64. Not to attempt to contact the dead — Deut. 18:11
65. Not to consult the ov — Deut. 18:11
66. Not to consult the yidoni — Deut. 18:11
67. Not to perform acts of magic — Deut. 18:10
68. Men must not shave the hair off the sides of their head — Lev. 19:27
69. Men must not shave their beards with a razor — Lev. 19:27
70. Men must not wear women's clothing — Deut. 22:5
71. Women must not wear men's clothing — Deut. 22:5
72. Not to tattoo the skin — Lev. 19:28
73. Not to tear the skin in mourning — Deut. 14:1
74. Not to make a bald spot in mourning — Deut. 14:1
75. To repent and confess wrongdoings — Num. 5:7
76. To say the Shema twice daily — Deut. 6:7

77. To pray every day — Ex. 23:25
78. The *Kohanim* must bless the Jewish nation daily — Num. 6:23
79. To wear *tefillin* (phylacteries) on the head — Deut. 6:8
80. To bind *tefillin* on the arm — Deut. 6:8
81. To put a *mezuzah* on the door post — Deut. 6:9
82. Each male must write a Torah scroll — Deut. 31:19
83. The king must have a separate Torah scroll for himself — Deut. 17:18
84. To have *tzitzit* on four-cornered garments — Num. 15:38
85. To bless the Almighty after eating — Deut. 8:10
86. To circumcise all males on the eighth day after their birth — Gen. 17:10
87. To rest on the seventh day — Ex. 23:12
88. Not to do prohibited labor on the seventh day — Standard->Ex. 20:11
    Yemenite->Ex. 20:10
89. The court must not inflict punishment on Shabbat — Ex. 35:3
90. Not to walk outside the city boundary on Shabbat — Ex. 16:29
91. To sanctify Shabbat with *Kiddush* and *Havdalah* — Standard->Ex. 20:9
    Yemenite->Ex. 20:8
92. To rest from prohibited labor on Yom Kippur — Lev. 23:32
93. Not to do prohibited labor on Yom Kippur — Lev. 23:32
94. To afflict oneself on Yom Kippur — Lev. 16:29
95. Not to eat or drink on Yom Kippur — Lev. 23:29
96. To rest on the first day of Passover — Lev. 23:7
97. Not to do prohibited labor on the first day of Passover — Lev. 23:8
98. To rest on the seventh day of Passover — Lev. 23:8
99. Not to do prohibited labor on the seventh day of Passover — Lev. 23:8
100. To rest on Shavuot — Lev. 23:21
101. Not to do prohibited labor on Shavuot — Lev. 23:21
102. To rest on Rosh Hashanah — Lev. 23:24
103. Not to do prohibited labor on Rosh Hashanah — Lev. 23:25
104. To rest on Sukkot — Lev. 23:35
105. Not to do prohibited labor on Sukkot
106. To rest on Shemini Atzeret — Lev. 23:36
107. Not to do prohibited labor on Shemini Atzeret —Lev. 23:36
108. Not to eat *chametz* on the afternoon of the 14th day of Nissan — Deut. 16:3
109. To destroy all *chametz* on 14th day of Nissan — Ex. 12:15
110. Not to eat chametz all seven days of Passover —Ex. 13:3
111. Not to eat mixtures containing *chametz* all seven days of Passover — Ex. 12:20
112. Not to see *chametz* in your domain seven days — Ex. 13:7
113. Not to find *chametz* in your domain seven days — Ex. 12:19
114. To eat *matzah* on the first night of Passover — Ex. 12:18
115. To relate the Exodus from Egypt on that night — Ex. 13:8
116. To hear the *Shofar* on the first day of Tishrei (Rosh Hashanah) — Num. 9:1
117. To dwell in a *Sukkah* for the seven days of Sukkot — Lev. 23:42
118. To take up a *Lulav* and *Etrog* all seven days — Lev. 23:40
119. Each man must give a half shekel annually — Ex. 30:13
120. Courts must calculate to determine when a new month begins — Ex. 12:2
121. To afflict oneself and cry out before God in times of calamity — Num. 10:9
122. To marry a wife by means of *ketubah* and *kiddushin* — Deut. 22:13
123. Not to have sexual relations with women not thus married — Deut. 23:18

124. Not to withhold food, clothing, and sexual relations from your wife — Ex. 21:10
125. To have children with one's wife — Gen. 1:28
126. To issue a divorce by means of a *Get* document — Deut. 24:1
127. A man must not remarry his ex-wife after she has married someone else — Deut. 24:4
128. To perform *yibbum* (marry the widow of one's childless brother) — Deut. 25:5
129. To perform *halizah* (free the widow of one's childless brother from *yibbum*) — Deut. 25:9
130. The widow must not remarry until the ties with her brother-in-law are removed (by *halizah*) — Deut. 25:5
131. The court must fine one who sexually seduces a maiden — Ex. 22:15-16
132. The rapist must marry his victim if she is unwed — Deut. 22:29
133. He is never allowed to divorce her — Deut. 22:29
134. The slanderer must remain married to his wife — Deut 22:19
135. He must not divorce her — Deut. 22:19
136. To fulfill the laws of the Sotah — Num. 5:30
137. Not to put oil on her meal offering (as usual) — Num. 5:15
138. Not to put frankincense on her meal offering (as usual) — Num. 5:15
139. Not to have sexual relations with your mother — Lev. 18:7
140. Not to have sexual relations with your father's wife — Lev. 18:8
141. Not to have sexual relations with your sister — Lev. 18:9
142. Not to have sexual relations with your father's wife's daughter — Lev. 18:11
143. Not to have sexual relations with your son's daughter — Lev. 18:10
144. Not to have sexual relations with your daughter — Lev. 18:10
145. Not to have sexual relations with your daughter's daughter — Lev. 18:10
146. Not to have sexual relations with a woman and her daughter — Lev. 18:17
147. Not to have sexual relations with a woman and her son's daughter — Lev. 18:17
148. Not to have sexual relations with a woman and her daughter's daughter — Lev. 18:17
149. Not to have sexual relations with your father's sister — Lev. 18:12
150. Not to have sexual relations with your mother's sister — Lev. 18:13
151. Not to have sexual relations with your father's brother's wife — Lev. 18:14
152. Not to have sexual relations with your son's wife — Lev. 18:15
153. Not to have sexual relations with your brother's wife — Lev. 18:16
154. Not to have sexual relations with your wife's sister — Lev. 18:18
155. A man must not have sexual relations with an animal — Lev. 18:23
156. A woman must not have sexual relations with an animal — Lev. 18:23
157. A man must not have sexual relations with a man — Lev. 18:22
158. Not to have sexual relations with your father — Lev. 18:7
159. Not to have sexual relations with your father's brother — Lev. 18:14
160. Not to have sexual relations with someone else's wife — Lev. 18:20
161. Not to have sexual relations with a menstrually impure woman — Lev. 18:19
162. Not to marry non-Jews — Deut. 7:3
163. Not to let Moabite and Ammonite males marry into the Jewish people — Deut. 23:4
164. Not to *prevent* a third-generation Egyptian convert from marrying into the Jewish people — Deut. 23:8-9

165. Not to refrain from marrying[clarification needed] a third generation Edomite convert — Deut. 23:8-9
166. Not to let a mamzer (a child born due to an illegal relationship) marry into the Jewish people — Deut. 23:3
167. Not to let a eunuch marry into the Jewish people — Deut. 23:2
168. Not to offer to God any castrated male animals — Lev. 22:24
169. The High Priest must not marry a widow — Lev. 21:14
170. The High Priest must not have sexual relations with a widow even outside of marriage — Lev. 21:15
171. The High Priest must marry a virgin maiden — Lev. 21:13
172. A Kohen (priest) must not marry a divorcee — Lev. 21:7
173. A Kohen must not marry a zonah (a woman who has had a forbidden sexual relationship) — Lev. 21:7
174. A Kohen must not marry a chalalah ("a desecrated person") (party to or product of 169-172) — Lev. 21:7
175. Not to make pleasurable (sexual) contact with any forbidden woman — Lev. 18:6
176. To examine the signs of animals to distinguish between kosher and non-kosher — Lev. 11:2
177. To examine the signs of fowl to distinguish between kosher and non-kosher — Deut. 14:11
178. To examine the signs of fish to distinguish between kosher and non-kosher — Lev. 11:9
179. To examine the signs of locusts to distinguish between kosher and non-kosher — Lev. 11:21
180. Not to eat non-kosher animals — Lev. 11:4
181. Not to eat non-kosher fowl — Lev. 11:13
182. Not to eat non-kosher fish — Lev. 11:11
183. Not to eat non-kosher flying insects — Deut. 14:19
184. Not to eat non-kosher creatures that crawl on land — Lev. 11:41
185. Not to eat non-kosher maggots — Lev. 11:44
186. Not to eat worms found in fruit on the ground — Lev. 11:42
187. Not to eat creatures that live in water other than (kosher) fish — Lev. 11:43
188. Not to eat the meat of an animal that died without ritual slaughter — Deut. 14:21
189. Not to benefit from an ox condemned to be stoned — Ex. 21:2
190. Not to eat meat of an animal that was mortally wounded — Ex. 22:30
191. Not to eat a limb torn off a living creature — Deut. 12:23
192. Not to eat blood —Lev. 3:17
193. Not to eat certain fats of clean animals — Lev. 3:17
194. Not to eat the sinew of the thigh — Gen. 32:33
195. Not to eat mixtures of milk and meat cooked together — Ex. 23:19
196. Not to cook meat and milk together — Ex. 34:26
197. Not to eat bread from new grain before the Omer — Lev. 23:14
198. Not to eat parched grains from new grain before the Omer — Lev. 23:14
199. Not to eat ripened grains from new grain before the Omer — Lev. 23:14
200. Not to eat fruit of a tree during its first three years — Lev. 19:23
201. Not to eat diverse seeds planted in a vineyard — Deut. 22:9
202. Not to eat untithed fruits — Lev. 22:15

203. Not to drink wine poured in service to idols — Deut. 32:38
204. To ritually slaughter an animal before eating it — Deut. 12:21
205. Not to slaughter an animal and its offspring on the same day — Lev. 22:28
206. To cover the blood (of a slaughtered beast or fowl) with earth — Lev. 17:13
207. To send away the mother bird before taking its children — Deut. 22:6
208. To release the mother bird if she was taken from the nest — Deut. 22:7
209. Not to swear falsely in God's Name — Lev. 19:12
210. Not to take God's Name in vain — Standard->Ex. 20:7 Yemenite->Ex. 20:6
211. Not to deny possession of something entrusted to you — Lev. 19:11
212. Not to swear in denial of a monetary claim — Lev. 19:11
213. To swear in God's Name to confirm the truth when deemed necessary by court — Deut. 10:20
214. To fulfill what was uttered and to do what was avowed — Deut. 23:24
215. Not to break oaths or vows — Num. 30:3
216. For oaths and vows annulled, there are the laws of annulling vows explicit in the Torah — Num. 30:3
217. The Nazarite must let his hair grow — Num. 6:5
218. He must not cut his hair — Num. 6:5
219. He must not drink wine, wine mixtures, or wine vinegar — Num. 6:3
220. He must not eat fresh grapes — Num. 6:3
221. He must not eat raisins — Num. 6:3
222. He must not eat grape seeds — Num. 6:4
223. He must not eat grape skins — Num. 6:4
224. He must not be under the same roof as a corpse — Num. 6:6
225. He must not come into contact with the dead — Num. 6:7
226. He must shave his head after bringing sacrifices upon completion of his Nazarite period — Num. 6:9
227. To estimate the value of people as determined by the Torah —Lev. 27:2
228. To estimate the value of consecrated animals — Lev. 27:12-13
229. To estimate the value of consecrated houses — Lev. 27:14
230. To estimate the value of consecrated fields — Lev. 27:16
231. Carry out the laws of interdicting possessions (*cherem*) — Lev. 27:28
232. Not to sell the *cherem* — Lev. 27:28
233. Not to redeem the *cherem* — Lev. 27:28
234. Not to plant diverse seeds together — Lev. 19:19
235. Not to plant grains or greens in a vineyard — Deut. 22:9
236. Not to crossbreed animals — Lev. 19:19
237. Not to work different animals together — Deut. 22:10
238. Not to wear *shaatnez*, a cloth woven of wool and linen — Deut. 22:11
239. To leave a corner of the field uncut for the poor — Lev. 19:10
240. Not to reap that corner — Lev. 19:9
241. To leave gleanings — Lev. 19:9
242. Not to gather the gleanings — Lev. 19:9
243. To leave the unformed clusters of grapes — Lev. 19:10
244. Not to pick the unformed clusters of grapes — Lev. 19:10
245. To leave the gleanings of a vineyard — Lev. 19:10
246. Not to gather the gleanings of a vineyard — Lev. 19:10
247. To leave the forgotten sheaves in the field — Deut. 24:19
248. Not to retrieve them — Deut. 24:19

249. To separate the "tithe for the poor" — Deut. 14:28
250. To give charity — Deut. 15:8
251. Not to withhold charity from the poor — Deut. 15:7
252. To set aside *Terumah* (heave offering) *Gedolah* (gift for the *Kohen*) — Deut. 18:4
253. The Levite must set aside a tenth of his tithe — Num. 18:26
254. Not to preface one tithe to the next, but separate them in their proper order — Ex. 22:28
255. A non-*Kohen* must not eat *Terumah* — Lev. 22:10
256. A hired worker or a Jewish bondsman of a *Kohen* must not eat *Terumah* — Lev. 22:10
257. An uncircumcised *Kohen* must not eat *Terumah* — Ex. 12:48
258. An impure *Kohen* must not eat *Terumah* — Lev. 22:4
259. A *chalalah* (party to #s 169-172 above) must not eat *Terumah* — Lev. 22:12
260. To set aside *Ma'aser* (tithe) each planting year and give it to a Levite — Num. 18:24
261. To set aside the second tithe (*Ma'aser Sheni*) — Deut. 14:22
262. Not to spend its redemption money on anything but food, drink, or ointment — Deut. 26:14
263. Not to eat *Ma'aser Sheni* while impure — Deut. 26:14
264. A mourner on the first day after death must not eat *Ma'aser Sheni* — Deut. 26:14
265. Not to eat *Ma'aser Sheni* grains outside Jerusalem — Deut. 12:17
266. Not to eat *Ma'aser Sheni* wine products outside Jerusalem — Deut. 12:17
267. Not to eat *Ma'aser Sheni* oil outside Jerusalem — Deut. 12:17
268. The fourth year crops must be totally for holy purposes like *Ma'aser Sheni* — Lev. 19:24
269. To read the confession of tithes every fourth and seventh year — Deut. 26:13
270. To set aside the first fruits and bring them to the Temple — Ex. 23:19
271. The *Kohanim* must not eat the first fruits outside Jerusalem — Deut. 12:17
272. To read the Torah portion pertaining to their presentation — Deut. 26:5
273. To set aside a portion of dough for a *Kohen* — Num. 15:20
274. To give the foreleg, two cheeks, and abomasum of slaughtered animals to a *Kohen* — Deut. 18:3
275. To give the first shearing of sheep to a *Kohen* — Deut. 18:4
276. To redeem firstborn sons and give the money to a *Kohen* — Num. 18:15
277. To redeem the firstborn donkey by giving a lamb to a *Kohen* — Ex. 13:13
278. To break the neck of the donkey if the owner does not intend to redeem it — Ex. 13:13
279. To rest the land during the seventh year by not doing any work which enhances growth — Ex. 34:21
280. Not to work the land during the seventh year — Lev. 25:4
281. Not to work with trees to produce fruit during that year — Lev. 25:4
282. Not to reap crops that grow wild that year in the normal manner — Lev. 25:5
283. Not to gather grapes which grow wild that year in the normal way — Lev. 25:5
284. To leave free all produce which grew in that year — Ex. 23:11
285. To release all loans during the seventh year — Deut. 15:2
286. Not to pressure or claim from the borrower — Deut. 15:2

287. Not to refrain from lending immediately before the release of the loans for fear of monetary loss —Deut. 15:9
288. The Sanhedrin must count seven groups of seven years — Lev. 25:8
289. The Sanhedrin must sanctify the fiftieth year — Lev. 25:10
290. To blow the *Shofar* on the tenth of Tishrei to free the slaves — Lev. 25:9
291. Not to work the soil during the fiftieth year (Jubilee) — Lev. 25:11
292. Not to reap in the normal manner that which grows wild in the fiftieth year — Lev. 25:11
293. Not to pick grapes which grew wild in the normal manner in the fiftieth year — Lev. 25:11
294. Carry out the laws of sold family properties — Lev. 25:24
295. Not to sell the land in Israel indefinitely — Lev. 25:23
296. Carry out the laws of houses in walled cities — Lev. 25:29
297. The Tribe of Levi must not be given a portion of the land in Israel, rather they are given cities to dwell in — Deut. 18:1
298. The Levites must not take a share in the spoils of war — Deut. 18:1
299. To give the Levites cities to inhabit and their surrounding fields — Num. 35:2
300. Not to sell the fields but they shall remain the Levites' before and after the Jubilee year — Lev. 25:34
301. To build a Temple — Ex. 25:8
302. Not to build the altar with stones hewn by metal — Standard->Ex. 20:24 Yemenite->Ex. 20:23
303. Not to climb steps to the altar — Standard->Ex. 20:27 Yemenite->Ex. 20:26
304. To show reverence to the Temple — Lev. 19:30
305. To guard the Temple area — Num. 18:2
306. Not to leave the Temple unguarded — Num. 18:5
307. To prepare the anointing oil — Ex. 30:31
308. Not to reproduce the anointing oil — Ex. 30:32
309. Not to anoint with anointing oil — Ex. 30:32
310. Not to reproduce the incense formula — Ex. 30:37
311. Not to burn anything on the Golden Altar besides incense — Ex. 30:9
312. The Levites must transport the ark on their shoulders — Num. 7:9
313. Not to remove the staves from the ark — Ex. 25:15
314. The Levites must work in the Temple — Num. 18:23
315. No Levite must do another's work of either a *Kohen* or a Levite — Num. 18:3
316. To dedicate the *Kohen* for service — Lev. 21:8
317. The work of the *Kohanim's* shifts must be equal during holidays — Deut. 18:6-8
318. The *Kohanim* must wear their priestly garments during service — Ex. 28:2
319. Not to tear the priestly garments — Ex. 28:32
320. The *Kohen Gadol* 's (High Priest) breastplate must not be loosened from the *Efod* — Ex. 28:28
321. A *Kohen* must not enter the Temple intoxicated — Lev. 10:9
322. A *Kohen* must not enter the Temple with his head uncovered — Lev. 10:6
323. A *Kohen* must not enter the Temple with torn clothes — Lev. 10:6
324. A *Kohen* must not enter the Temple indiscriminately — Lev. 16:2
325. A *Kohen* must not leave the Temple during service — Lev. 10:7
326. To send the impure from the Temple — Num. 5:2
327. Impure people must not enter the Temple — Num. 5:3

328. Impure people must not enter the Temple Mount area — Deut. 23:11
329. Impure *Kohanim* must not do service in the temple — Lev. 22:2
330. An impure *Kohen*, following immersion, must wait until after sundown before returning to service — Lev. 22:7
331. A *Kohen* must wash his hands and feet before service — Ex. 30:19
332. A *Kohen* with a physical blemish must not enter the sanctuary or approach the altar — Lev. 21:23
333. A *Kohen* with a physical blemish must not serve — Lev. 21:17
334. A *Kohen* with a temporary blemish must not serve — Lev. 21:17
335. One who is not a *Kohen* must not serve — Num. 18:4
336. To offer only unblemished animals — Lev. 22:21
337. Not to dedicate a blemished animal for the altar — Lev. 22:20
338. Not to slaughter it — Lev. 22:22
339. Not to sprinkle its blood — Lev. 22:24
340. Not to burn its fat — Lev. 22:22
341. Not to offer a temporarily blemished animal — Deut. 17:1
342. Not to sacrifice blemished animals even if offered by non-Jews — Lev. 22:25
343. Not to inflict wounds upon dedicated animals — Lev. 22:21
344. To redeem dedicated animals which have become disqualified — Deut. 12:15
345. To offer only animals which are at least eight days old — Lev. 22:27
346. Not to offer animals bought with the wages of a harlot or the animal exchanged for a dog. Some interpret "exchange for a dog" as referring to wage of a male prostitute.[9][10] — Deut. 23:19
347. Not to burn honey or yeast on the altar — Lev. 2:11
348. To salt all sacrifices — Lev. 2:13
349. Not to omit the salt from sacrifices — Lev. 2:13
350. Carry out the procedure of the burnt offering as prescribed in the Torah — Lev. 1:3
351. Not to eat its meat — Deut. 12:17
352. Carry out the procedure of the sin offering — Lev. 6:18
353. Not to eat the meat of the inner sin offering — Lev. 6:23
354. Not to decapitate a fowl brought as a sin offering — Lev. 5:8
355. Carry out the procedure of the guilt offering — Lev. 7:1
356. The *Kohanim* must eat the sacrificial meat in the Temple — Ex. 29:33
357. The *Kohanim* must not eat the meat outside the Temple courtyard — Deut. 12:17
358. A non-*Kohen* must not eat sacrificial meat — Ex. 29:33
359. To follow the procedure of the peace offering — Lev. 7:11
360. Not to eat the meat of minor sacrifices before sprinkling the blood — Deut. 12:17
361. To bring meal offerings as prescribed in the Torah — Lev. 2:1
362. Not to put oil on the meal offerings of wrongdoers — Lev. 5:11
363. Not to put frankincense on the meal offerings of wrongdoers — Lev. 3:11
364. Not to eat the meal offering of the High Priest — Lev. 6:16
365. Not to bake a meal offering as leavened bread — Lev. 6:10
366. The Kohanim must eat the remains of the meal offerings — Lev. 6:9
367. To bring all avowed and freewill offerings to the Temple on the first subsequent festival — Deut. 12:5-6
368. Not to withhold payment incurred by any vow — Deut. 23:22

369. To offer all sacrifices in the Temple — Deut. 12:11
370. To bring all sacrifices from outside Israel to the Temple — Deut. 12:26
371. Not to slaughter sacrifices outside the courtyard — Lev. 17:4
372. Not to offer any sacrifices outside the courtyard — Deut. 12:13
373. To offer two lambs every day — Num. 28:3
374. To light a fire on the altar every day — Lev. 6:6
375. Not to extinguish this fire — Lev. 6:6
376. To remove the ashes from the altar every day — Lev. 6:3
377. To burn incense every day — Ex. 30:7
378. To light the Menorah every day — Ex. 27:21
379. The *Kohen Gadol* must bring a meal offering every day — Lev. 6:13
380. To bring two additional lambs as burnt offerings on Shabbat — Num. 28:9
381. To make the show bread — Ex. 25:30
382. To bring additional offerings on Rosh Chodesh (" The New Month") — Num. 28:11
383. To bring additional offerings on Passover — Num. 28:19
384. To offer the wave offering from the meal of the new wheat — Lev. 23:10
385. Each man must count the Omer - seven weeks from the day the new wheat offering was brought — Lev. 23:15
386. To bring additional offerings on Shavuot — Num. 28:26
387. To bring two leaves to accompany the above sacrifice — Lev. 23:17
388. To bring additional offerings on Rosh Hashana — Num. 29:2
389. To bring additional offerings on Yom Kippur — Num. 29:8
390. To bring additional offerings on Sukkot — Num. 29:13
391. To bring additional offerings on Shmini Atzeret — Num. 29:35
392. Not to eat sacrifices which have become unfit or blemished — Deut. 14:3
393. Not to eat from sacrifices offered with improper intentions — Lev. 7:18
394. Not to leave sacrifices past the time allowed for eating them — Lev. 22:30
395. Not to eat from that which was left over — Lev. 19:8
396. Not to eat from sacrifices which became impure — Lev. 7:19
397. An impure person must not eat from sacrifices — Lev. 7:20
398. To burn the leftover sacrifices — Lev. 7:17
399. To burn all impure sacrifices — Lev. 7:19
400. To follow the procedure of Yom Kippur in the sequence prescribed in Parshah *Acharei Mot* ("After the death of Aaron's sons...") — Lev. 16:3
401. One who profaned property must repay what he profaned plus a fifth and bring a sacrifice — Lev. 5:16
402. Not to work consecrated animals — Deut. 15:19
403. Not to shear the fleece of consecrated animals — Deut. 15:19
404. To slaughter the paschal sacrifice at the specified time — Ex. 12:6
405. Not to slaughter it while in possession of leaven — Ex. 23:18
406. Not to leave the fat overnight — Ex. 23:18
407. To slaughter the second Paschal Lamb — Num. 9:11
408. To eat the Paschal Lamb with matzah and Marror on the night of the fourteenth of Nissan — Ex. 12:8
409. To eat the second Paschal Lamb on the night of the 15th of Iyar — Num. 9:11
410. Not to eat the paschal meat raw or boiled — Ex. 12:9
411. Not to take the paschal meat from the confines of the group — Ex. 12:46
412. An apostate must not eat from it — Ex. 12:43

413. A permanent or temporary hired worker must not eat from it — Ex. 12:45
414. An uncircumcised male must not eat from it — Ex. 12:48
415. Not to break any bones from the paschal offering — Ex. 12:46 Ps. 34:20
416. Not to break any bones from the second paschal offering — Num. 9:12
417. Not to leave any meat from the paschal offering over until morning — Ex. 12:10
418. Not to leave the second paschal meat over until morning — Num. 9:12
419. Not to leave the meat of the holiday offering of the 14th until the 16th — Deut. 16:4
420. To be seen at the Temple on Passover, Shavuot, and Sukkot — Deut. 16:16
421. To celebrate on these three Festivals (bring a peace offering) — Ex. 23:14
422. To rejoice on these three Festivals (bring a peace offering) — Deut. 16:14
423. Not to appear at the Temple without offerings — Deut. 16:16
424. Not to refrain from rejoicing with, and giving gifts to, the Levites — Deut. 12:19
425. To assemble all the people on the Sukkot following the seventh year — Deut. 31:12
426. To set aside the firstborn animals — Ex. 13:12
427. The Kohanim must not eat unblemished firstborn animals outside Jerusalem — Deut. 12:17
428. Not to redeem the firstborn — Num. 18:17
429. Separate the tithe from animals — Lev. 27:32
430. Not to redeem the tithe — Lev. 27:33
431. Every person must bring a sin offering (in the temple) for his transgression — Lev. 4:27
432. Bring an *asham talui* (temple offering) when uncertain of guilt — Lev. 5:17-18
433. Bring an *asham vadai* (temple offering) when guilt is ascertained — Lev. 5:25
434. Bring an *oleh v'yored* (temple offering)(if the person is wealthy, an animal; if poor, a bird or meal offering) — Lev. 5:7-11
435. The Sanhedrin must bring an offering (in the Temple) when it rules in error — Lev. 4:13
436. A woman who had a running (vaginal) issue must bring an offering (in the Temple) after she goes to the Mikveh — Lev. 15:28-29
437. A woman who gave birth must bring an offering (in the Temple) after she goes to the Mikveh — Lev. 12:6
438. A man who had a running (unnatural urinary) issue must bring an offering (in the Temple) after he goes to the Mikveh — Lev. 15:13-14
439. A metzora (one having a skin disease) must bring an offering (in the Temple) after going to the Mikveh — Lev. 14:10
440. Not to substitute another beast for one set apart for sacrifice — Lev. 27:10
441. The new animal, in addition to the substituted one, retains consecration — Lev. 27:10
442. Not to change consecrated animals from one type of offering to another — Lev. 27:26
443. Carry out the laws of impurity of the dead — Num. 19:14
444. Carry out the procedure of the Red Heifer (*Para Aduma*) — Num. 19:2
445. Carry out the laws of the sprinkling water — Num. 19:21
446. Rule the laws of human tzara'at as prescribed in the Torah — Lev. 13:12
447. The metzora must not remove his signs of impurity — Deut. 24:8

448. The metzora must not shave signs of impurity in his hair — Lev. 13:33
449. The metzora must publicize his condition by tearing his garments, allowing his hair to grow and covering his lips — Lev. 13:45
450. Carry out the prescribed rules for purifying the *metzora* — Lev. 14:2
451. The metzora must shave off all his hair prior to purification — Lev. 14:9
452. Carry out the laws of tzara'at of clothing — Lev. 13:47
453. Carry out the laws of *tzara'at* of houses — Lev. 13:34
454. Observe the laws of menstrual impurity — Lev. 15:19
455. Observe the laws of impurity caused by childbirth — Lev. 12:2
456. Observe the laws of impurity caused by a woman's running issue — Lev. 15:25
457. Observe the laws of impurity caused by a man's running issue (irregular ejaculation of infected semen) — Lev. 15:3
458. Observe the laws of impurity caused by a dead beast — Lev. 11:39
459. Observe the laws of impurity caused by the eight shratzim (insects) — Lev. 11:29
460. Observe the laws of impurity of a seminal emission (regular ejaculation, with normal semen) — Lev. 15:16
461. Observe the laws of impurity concerning liquid and solid foods — Lev. 11:34
462. Every impure person must immerse himself in a Mikvah to become pure — Lev. 15:16
463. The court must judge the damages incurred by a goring ox — Ex. 21:28
464. The court must judge the damages incurred by an animal eating — Ex. 22:4
465. The court must judge the damages incurred by a pit — Ex. 21:33
466. The court must judge the damages incurred by fire — Ex. 22:5
467. Not to steal money stealthily — Lev. 19:11
468. The court must implement punitive measures against the thief — Ex. 21:37
469. Each individual must ensure that his scales and weights are accurate — Lev. 19:36
470. Not to commit injustice with scales and weights — Lev. 19:35
471. Not to possess inaccurate scales and weights even if they are not for use — Deut. 25:13
472. Not to move a boundary marker to steal someone's property — Deut. 19:14
473. Not to kidnap — Standard->Ex. 20:14 Yemenite->Ex. 20:13
474. Not to rob openly — Lev. 19:13
475. Not to withhold wages or fail to repay a debt — Lev. 19:13
476. Not to covet and scheme to acquire another's possession — Standard->Ex. 20:15 Yemenite->Ex. 20:14
477. Not to desire another's possession — Standard->Deut. 5:19 Yemenite->Deut. 5:18
478. Return the robbed object or its value — Lev. 5:23
479. Not to ignore a lost object — Deut. 22:3
480. Return the lost object — Deut. 22:1
481. The court must implement laws against the one who assaults another or damages another's property — Ex. 21:18
482. Not to murder — Standard->Ex. 20:13 Yemenite->Ex. 20:12
483. Not to accept monetary restitution to atone for the murderer — Num. 35:31
484. The court must send the accidental murderer to a city of refuge — Num. 35:25
485. Not to accept monetary restitution instead of being sent to a city of refuge — Num. 35:32

486. Not to kill the murderer before he stands trial — Num. 35:12
487. Save someone being pursued even by taking the life of the pursuer — Deut. 25:12
488. Not to pity the pursuer — Num. 35:12
489. Not to stand idly by if someone's life is in danger — Lev. 19:16
490. Designate cities of refuge and prepare routes of access — Deut. 19:3
491. Break the neck of a calf by the river valley following an unsolved murder — Deut. 21:4
492. Not to work nor plant that river valley — Deut. 21:4
493. Not to allow pitfalls and obstacles to remain on your property — Deut. 22:8
494. Make a guard rail around flat roofs — Deut. 22:8
495. Not to put a stumbling block before a blind man (nor give harmful advice) — Lev. 19:14
496. Help another remove the load from a beast which can no longer carry it — Ex. 23:5
497. Help others load their beast — Deut. 22:4
498. Not to leave others distraught with their burdens (but to help either load or unload) — Deut. 22:4
499. Conduct sales according to Torah law — Lev. 25:14
500. Not to overcharge or underpay for an article — Lev. 25:14
501. Not to insult or harm anybody with words — Lev. 25:17
502. Not to cheat a convert monetarily — Ex. 22:20
503. Not to insult or harm a convert with words — Ex. 22:20
504. Purchase a Hebrew slave in accordance with the prescribed laws — Ex. 21:2
505. Not to sell him as a slave is sold — Lev. 25:42
506. Not to work him oppressively — Lev. 25:43
507. Not to allow a non-Jew to work him oppressively — Lev. 25:53
508. Not to have him do menial slave labor — Lev. 25:39
509. Give him gifts when he goes free — Deut. 15:14
510. Not to send him away empty-handed — Deut. 15:13
511. Redeem Jewish maidservants — Ex. 21:8
512. Betroth the Jewish maidservant — Ex. 21:8
513. The master must not sell his maidservant — Ex. 21:8
514. Canaanite slaves must work forever unless injured in one of their limbs — Lev. 25:46
515. Not to extradite a slave who fled to (Biblical) Israel — Deut. 23:16
516. Not to wrong a slave who has come to Israel for refuge — Deut. 23:16
517. The courts must carry out the laws of a hired worker and hired guard — Ex. 22:9
518. Pay wages on the day they were earned — Deut. 24:15
519. Not to delay payment of wages past the agreed time — Lev. 19:13
520. The hired worker may eat from the unharvested crops where he works — Deut. 23:25
521. The worker must not eat while on hired time — Deut. 23:26
522. The worker must not take more than he can eat — Deut. 23:25
523. Not to muzzle an ox while plowing — Deut. 25:4
524. The courts must carry out the laws of a borrower — Ex. 22:13
525. The courts must carry out the laws of an unpaid guard — Ex. 22:6
526. Lend to the poor and destitute — Ex. 22:24

527. Not to press them for payment if you know they don't have it — Ex. 22:24
528. Press the idolater for payment — Deut. 15:3
529. The creditor must not forcibly take collateral — Deut. 24:10
530. Return the collateral to the debtor when needed — Deut. 24:13
531. Not to delay its return when needed — Deut. 24:12
532. Not to demand collateral from a widow — Deut. 24:17
533. Not to demand as collateral utensils needed for preparing food — Deut. 24:6
534. Not to lend with interest — Lev. 25:37
535. Not to borrow with interest — Deut. 23:20
536. Not to intermediate in an interest loan, guarantee, witness, or write the promissory note — Ex. 22:24
537. Lend to and borrow from idolaters with interest — Deut. 23:21
538. The courts must carry out the laws of the plaintiff, admitter, or denier — Ex. 22:8
539. Carry out the laws of the order of inheritance — Num. 27:8
540. Appoint judges — Deut. 16:18
541. Not to appoint judges who are not familiar with judicial procedure — Deut. 1:17
542. Decide by majority in case of disagreement — Ex. 23:2
543. The court must not execute through a majority of one; at least a majority of two is required — Ex. 23:2
544. A judge who presented an acquittal plea must not present an argument for conviction in capital cases — Deut. 23:2
545. The courts must carry out the death penalty of stoning — Deut. 22:24
546. The courts must carry out the death penalty of burning — Lev. 20:14
547. The courts must carry out the death penalty of the sword — Ex. 21:20
548. The courts must carry out the death penalty of strangulation — Lev. 20:10
549. The courts must hang those stoned for blasphemy or idolatry — Deut. 21:22
550. Bury the executed on the day they are killed — Deut. 21:23
551. Not to delay burial overnight — Deut. 21:23
552. The court must not let the sorcerer live — Ex. 22:17
553. The court must give lashes to the wrongdoer — Deut. 25:2
554. The court must not exceed the prescribed number of lashes — Deut. 25:3
555. The court must not kill anybody on circumstantial evidence — Ex. 23:7
556. The court must not punish anybody who was forced to do a crime — Deut. 22:26
557. A judge must not pity the murderer or assaulter at the trial — Deut. 19:13
558. A judge must not have mercy on the poor man at the trial — Lev. 19:15
559. A judge must not respect the great man at the trial — Lev. 19:15
560. A judge must not decide unjustly the case of the habitual transgressor — Ex. 23:6
561. A judge must not pervert justice — Lev. 19:15
562. A judge must not pervert a case involving a convert or orphan — Deut. 24:17
563. Judge righteously — Lev. 19:15
564. The judge must not fear a violent man in judgment — Deut. 1:17
565. Judges must not accept bribes — Ex. 23:8
566. Judges must not accept testimony unless both parties are present — Ex. 23:1
567. Not to curse judges — Ex. 22:27
568. Not to curse the head of state or leader of the Sanhedrin — Ex. 22:27

569. Not to curse any upstanding Jew — Lev. 19:14
570. Anybody who knows evidence must testify in court — Lev. 5:1
571. Carefully interrogate the witness — Deut. 13:15
572. A witness must not serve as a judge in capital crimes — Deut. 19:17
573. Not to accept testimony from a lone witness — Deut. 19:15
574. Transgressors must not testify — Ex. 23:1
575. Relatives of the litigants must not testify — Deut. 24:16
576. Not to testify falsely — Standard->Ex. 20:14 Yemenite->Ex. 20:13
577. Punish the false witnesses as they tried to punish the defendant — Deut. 19:19
578. Act according to the ruling of the Sanhedrin — Deut. 17:11
579. Not to deviate from the word of the Sanhedrin — Deut. 17:11
580. Not to add to the Torah commandments or their oral explanations — Deut. 13:1
581. Not to diminish from the Torah any commandments, in whole or in part — Deut. 13:1
582. Not to curse your father and mother — Ex. 21:17
583. Not to strike your father and mother — Ex. 21:15
584. Respect your father or mother — Standard->Ex. 20:13 Yemenite->Ex. 20:12
585. Fear your mother or father — Lev. 19:3
586. Not to be a rebellious son — Deut. 21:18
587. Mourn for relatives — Lev. 10:19
588. The High Priest must not defile himself for any relative — Lev. 21:11
589. The High Priest must not enter under the same roof as a corpse — Lev. 21:11
590. A Kohen must not defile himself (by going to funerals or cemeteries) for anyone except relatives — Lev. 21:1
591. Appoint a king from Israel — Deut. 17:15
592. Not to appoint a foreigner — Deut. 17:15
593. The king must not have too many wives — Deut. 17:17
594. The king must not have too many horses — Deut. 17:16
595. The king must not have too much silver and gold — Deut. 17:17
596. Destroy the seven Canaanite nations — Deut. 20:17
597. Not to let any of them remain alive — Deut. 20:16
598. Wipe out the descendants of Amalek — Deut. 25:19
599. Remember what Amalek did to the Jewish people — Deut. 25:17
600. Not to forget Amalek's atrocities and ambush on our journey from Egypt in the desert — Deut. 25:19
601. Not to dwell permanently in Egypt — Deut. 17:16
602. Offer peace terms to the inhabitants of a city while holding siege, and treat them according to the Torah if they accept the terms — Deut. 20:10
603. Not to offer peace to Ammon and Moab while besieging them — Deut. 23:7
604. Not to destroy food trees even during the siege — Deut. 20:19
605. Prepare latrines outside the camps — Deut. 23:13
606. Prepare a shovel for each soldier to dig with — Deut. 23:14
607. Appoint a priest to speak with the soldiers during the war — Deut. 20:2
608. He who has taken a wife, built a new home, or planted a vineyard is given a year to rejoice with his possessions — Deut. 24:5
609. Not to demand from the above any involvement, communal or military — Deut. 24:5
610. Not to panic and retreat during battle — Deut. 20:3
611. Keep the laws of the captive woman — Deut. 21:11

612. Not to sell her into slavery — Deut. 21:14
613. Not to retain her for servitude after having sexual relations with her — Deut. 21:14

APPENDIX B

The following are the 39 categories of work forbidden on Shabbat/Sabbath. The source of their derivation is from Ribiat, Rabbi Dovid (1999), *The 39 Melochos*. Jerusalem: Feldheim Publishers. ISBN 1-58330-368-5.This list is reprinted here under the terms of the Creative Commons Attribution Share-Alike license (CC-BY-SA). The URL is at http://en.wikipedia.org/wiki/Activities_prohibited_on_Shabbat. The thirty-nine creative activities are based on the Mishna Shabbat 7:2.

1.Planting - Not only planting is included in this category; other activities that promote plant growth are also prohibited. This includes watering, fertilizing, planting seeds, or planting grown plants.

2.Plowing - Included in this prohibition is any preparation or improvement of land for agricultural use. This includes dragging chair legs in soft soil thereby unintentionally making furrows. Pouring water on arable land that is not saturated. Making a hole in the soil would provide protection for a seed placed there from rain and runoff; even if no seed is ever placed there, the soil is now enhanced for the process of planting.

3.Reaping - Removing all or part of a plant from its source of growth is reaping. Rabbinically it is forbidden to climb a tree, for fear this may lead to one tearing off a branch. It is also forbidden rabbinically to ride an animal, as one may unthinkingly detach a stick to hit the animal with.

4.Gathering - E.g. After picking strawberries, forming a pile or collecting them into one's pockets, or a basket. Collecting rock salt or any mineral (from a mine or from the Earth) and making a pile of the produce. This can only occur in the place where the gathering should take place. So, a bowl of apples that falls in a house can be gathered as 1) they do not grow in that environment and 2) they have already undergone their initial gathering at the orchard.

5.Threshing/Extraction - It refers to any productive extraction and includes juicing of fruits and vegetables and wringing (desirable fluids) out of cloths, as the juice or water inside the fruit is considered 'desirable' for these purposes, while the pulp of the fruit would be the 'undesirable.' As such, squeezing (S'chita) is forbidden unless certain rules are applied. The wringing of undesirable water out of cloths may come under the law of Melabain (Scouring/Laundering)

6.Winnowing - In the Talmudic sense it usually refers exclusively to the separation of chaff from grain—i.e. to any separation of intermixed materials which renders edible that which was inedible. It also refers to separating things that are desirable from undesirable ones. Example: If one has a handful of peanuts, in their paper-thin brown skins, and one blows on the mixture of peanuts and skins, dispersing the unwanted skins from the peanuts, this would be an act of 'winnowing' according to both the Babylonian and Jerusalem Talmud. According to the Jerusalem Talmud's definition, the use of the Venturi tube spray system and spray painting would come under this prohibition, while butane or propane propelled sprays, which are common in deodorants and air fresheners, etc. are permissible to operate as the dispersal force generated isn't from air, rather from the propellent within the can. According to the Babylonian Talmud's definition, neither of the above spraying methods is involved in sorting undesirable from desirable and therefore not part of this heading. However, as mentioned, the Rema rules that, unusually, we[who?] are to accept the Jerusalem Talmud's definition in this case.

7.Sorting/Purification - In the Talmudic sense usually refers exclusively to the separation of debris from grain—i.e. to any separation of intermixed materials which renders edible that which was inedible. Thus, filtering undrinkable water to make it drinkable falls under this category, as does picking small bones from fish. (*Gefilte fish* is one solution to this problem.) Dosh & Borer contrasted. This activity differs from Dosh (Threshing/Extraction) as here there is a mixture of types. Sorting a mixture via the removal of undesirable elements leaving a purified, refined component is the key process of Borer. Dosh is the extraction of one desirable thing from within another which is not desired. "Dosh" does not entail sorting or purification, just extraction of the inner from the unwanted housing or outer component, such as squeezing a grape for its juice. The juice and the pulp have not undergone sorting, the juice has been extracted from the pulp.

For example, if there is a bowl of mixed peanuts & raisins and one desires the raisins and dislikes the peanuts: Removing (effectively sorting) the peanuts from the bowl, leaving a 'purified' pile of raisins free from unwanted peanuts, would be acts of Borer as the peanuts are removed. However, removing the *desirable* raisins from the peanuts does not purify the mixture, as one's left with undesirable peanuts (hence unrefined) not a refined component as before, and is thus permissible. Note that in this case there has not been any extraction of material from either the peanuts or raisins (Dosh), just the sorting of undesirable from desirable (Borer).

Examples of Permissible and Prohibited Types of Borer:

1. Peeling fruits: Peeling fruits is permissible with the understanding that the fruit will be eaten right away.
2. Sorting silverware: Sorting silverware is permitted when the sorter intends to eat the Shabbat meal immediately. Alternatively, if the sorter intends to set up the meal for a later point, it is prohibited.
3. Removing items from a mixture: If the desired item is being removed from the mix then this is permissible. If the non-desired item is being removed, the person removing is committing a serious transgression according to the laws of Shabbat.

8.Grinding - "Tochain" (grinding) can arise in simply cutting into pieces fruits or vegetables for a salad. Very small pieces would involve "tochain," therefore cutting into slightly larger than usual pieces would be in order, thus avoiding cutting the pieces into their final, most usable, state. All laws relating to the use of medicine on the shabbath are a *Toldah*, or sub-category, of this order, as most medicines require pulverization at some point and thus undergo tochain. The laws of medicine use on the sabbath are complex; they are based around the kind of illness the patient is suffering from and the type of medication or procedure that is required. Generally, the more severe the illness (from a halachic perspective) the further into the list the patient's situation is classed. As a patient is classed as more ill there are fewer restrictions and greater leniencies available for treating the illness on the Sabbath.

9.Sifting - This is essentially the same as the melochah of Borer, but performed with a utensil specifically designed for the purpose of sorting, such as a sieve, strainer, or the like. As such, Borer acts done with such a device, such as the netting of a tea bag, would be classed as an act of Merakaid (Sieving/Straining).

10.Kneading/Amalgamation - Kneading is not a very accurate translation of this activity. It may better be translated as 'amalgamation' or the like. The key principle of this creative activity is the combining of solid and liquid together to make a paste or dough-like substance.

There are four categories of substances produced: -

1. Blilah Aveh (a thick, dense mixture)
2. Blilah Racha (a thinner, pourable mixture)
3. Davar Nozel (a pourable liquid with a similar viscosity to water)
4. Chatichot Gedolot (large pieces mixed with a liquid)

Only a Blilah Aveh is biblically forbidden to be made on the Sabbath while Blilah Racha mixtures are rabbinically forbidden to make without the use of a "shinui", such as the reversing the adding of the ingredients or mixing in criss-cross motions to differentiate the task, in which case they are permitted. As Davar Nozel and Chatichot Gedolot are not really mixtures, even after adding the liquid to the solid, they are permitted to be made on the sabbath without any shinui (unusual mode) of production.

11.Cooking/Baking - Baking, cooking, frying, or any method of applying heat to food to prepare for eating is included in this prohibition. This is different from "preparing". For example, one can make a salad because the form of the vegetables doesn't change, only the size. However one cannot cook the vegetables to soften them for eating.

12.Shearing - Severing/uprooting any body-part of a creature.

13.Scouring/Laundering - Cleansing absorbent materials of absorbed/ingrained impurities.

14.Carding/Combing wool - Separating/disentangling fibres.

15.Dyeing - Coloring/enriching the color of any material or substance.

16.Spinning - Twisting fibres into a thread or twining strands into a yarn.

17.Warping - Creating the first form for the purpose of weaving.

18. Making two loops/threading heddles - Forming loops for the purpose of weaving or the making of net like materials. This is also the threading of two heddles on a loom to allow a 'shed' for the shuttlecock to pass through. According to the Rambam it is the making of net-like materials.

19.Weaving - Form fabric (or a fabric item) by interlacing long threads passing in one direction with others at a right angle to them.

20.Separating two threads - Removing/cutting fibres from their frame, loom or place.

21.Tying - Binding two pliant objects in a skilled or permanent manner via twisting.

22.Untying - The undoing of any Koshair or Toveh (see above) binding.

23.Sewing - Combining separate objects into a single entity, whether through sewing, gluing, etc.

24.Tearing - Ripping an object in two or undoing any Tofair (see above) connection.

25.Trapping - Forcible confinement of any living creature. To violate the Torah's prohibition of Trapping, two conditions must be met.

1. The animal being trapped must be a non-domesticated animal.
2. The "trapping" action must not legally confine the animal. For example, closing one's front door, thereby confining insects in one's house is not considered trapping as no difference to the insect's 'trappable' status has occurred. I.e. it's as easy or difficult to trap it now as it was when the door was open.

This creates questions in practical Halakha such as: "May one trap a fly under a cup on Shabbat?" The *Meno Netziv* says that an animal that is not normally trapped (e.g. a fly, or a lizard) is not covered under the Torah prohibition of trapping. It is however, a Rabbinic prohibition to do so, therefore one is not allowed to trap the animal. However, if one is afraid of the animal because of its venomous nature or that it might have rabies, one may trap it. If it poses a threat to life or limb, one may trap it and even kill it if *absolutely* necessary. Animals which are considered too slow moving to be 'free' are not included in this category, as trapping them doesn't change their legal status of being able to grab them in 'one hand swoop' (a term used by the Rambam to define this law). One is therefore allowed to confine a snail or tortoise, etc. as you can grab them just as easily whether they are in an enclosure or unhindered in the wild. For these purposes trapping them serves no change to their legal status regarding their *ease of capture*, and they are termed legally pre-trapped due to their nature. Trapping is therefore seen not as a 'removal of liberty', which caging even such a slow moving creature would be, but rather the confining of a creature to make it easier to capture in one's hand. Laying traps violates a Rabbinic prohibition regardless of what the trap is, as this is a normal method of trapping a creature.

26.Slaughtering - Ending the life of a creature, whether through slaughter or any other method.

27.Flaying/Skinning - Removing the hide from the body of a dead animal. Removing skin from a live creature would fall under Shearing/Gozez.

28.Curing/Preserving - Preserving any item to prevent spoiling. The list of activities in the Mishna includes salting hides and curing as separate categories of activity; the Gemara (Tractate Shabbat 75b) amends this to consider them the same activity and to include "tracing lines", also involved in the production of leather, as the thirty-ninth category of activity. This activity extends rabbinically to the creative act of salting/pickling of foods for non-immediate use on the Sabbath.

29.Smoothing - Scraping/sanding a surface to achieve smoothness.

30.Scoring - Scoring/drawing a cutting guideline.

31.Measured Cutting - Cutting any object to a specific size.

32.Writing - Writing/forming a meaningful character or design. Rabbinically, even writing with one's weaker hand is forbidden. The Rabbis also forbade any commercial activities, which often lead to writing.

33.Erasing - Cleaning/preparing a surface to render it suitable for writing. Erasing in order to write two or more letters is an example of erasing.

34.Building - Contributing to the forming of any permanent structure. Building can take two forms. First, there was the action of actually joining the different pieces together to make the mishcan. Inserting the handle of an axe into the socket is a derived form of this *melakha*. It is held by some that the act of Halakhic "building" is not actually performed (and therefore, the prohibition not violated) if the construction is not completed. From this, some authorities derive that it is prohibited to use electricity because, by turning on a switch, a circuit is completed and thus "built." (See "igniting a fire" below.) Also, any make of a "tent" is forbidden. Therefore, umbrellas may not be opened (or closed), and a board may not be placed on crates to form a bench. Either of these forms is only forbidden if done in a permanent fashion, though not necessarily with permanent intent.

For example, closing and locking a door is permitted, regardless of how long one intends to keep the door closed. Making a pop-up tent is considered permanent (since it can stay up for a long time), even if one intends to take it down soon afterwards.

35.Demolition - Demolishing for any constructive purpose. For example, knocking down a wall in order to make space for an extension or repair of the wall would be demolition for a constructive purpose. Combing a wig to set it correctly and pulling out hairs during the procedure with a metal toothed brush or comb would be constructive 'demolition', as each hair that's removed in the process of the wig (a utensil) is progressing its state towards a completion which is desired. Each hair's removal is a partial demolition of the wig (for these legal purposes) and is considered constructive when viewed in context of the desired goal. Of interest, this would include bowling, as the pins are knocked down, hopefully, during play. However, even if only gutterballs are thrown, the mere intention of knocking down pins is a violation of the prohibition against demolition. It is a matter of rabbinic debate as to whether intentionally throwing gutterballs during Shobbos is subject to the prohibition, as no demolition occurs. Commentary tends towards making this a violation as well, since the very act of bowling involves causing a machine to reconstruct the pin matrix upon each round, which action is initiated by the participating player.

36.Extinguishing a fire - Extinguishing/diminishing the intensity of a fire/flame. While extinguishing a fire is forbidden even when great property damage will result, in the event of any life-threatening fire one is *required* to extinguish the flames.

37.Igniting a fire - Igniting, fueling or spreading a fire/flame. This includes making, transferring or adding fuel to a fire. (Note, however, that transferring fire is permitted on Jewish holidays. It is one of the exceptions to the rule that activities prohibited on Shabbat are likewise prohibited on Yom Tov.) This is one of the few Shabbat prohibitions mentioned explicitly in the Torah Exodus 35:3. Many poskim ground their prohibition of operating electrical appliances in this *melakha*. Note that Judaism requires that at least one light (ordinarily candle or oil) be lit in honor of Shabbat immediately before its start. This prohibition also was (and in many circles, still is) commonly understood to disallow operating electrical switches. One reason is that, when actuating electromechanical switches that carry a live current, there is always the possibility that a small electric spark will be generated. This spark may be thought of as a kind of fire, although since it is incidental and one does not benefit from it, it may not be a Sabbath violation at all. In any case, as science became more advanced, and the properties of fire and electricity became better understood, the former reasoning broke down: fire is a chemical reaction involving the release of energy; the flow of an electric current is a physical reaction. Therefore, some hold that the proper reason it is forbidden to complete electric circuits is because it involves construction or building (i.e., the building and completion of an electric circuit—see above). For Shabbat Observant Jews who want to turn a light on and off on the sabbath the Shabbat lamp was invented. This circumvents this melocha, as the light is never turned on & off, only obscured and revealed via the design of the lamp housing.

38.Applying the finishing touch - Any initial act of completion. This *melakha* refers to an act of completing an object and bringing it into its final useful form. For example, if the pages of a newspaper were poorly separated, slicing them open would constitute "applying the finishing touch". Ribiat, *infra*. Using a stapler involves transgressing "applying the finishing touch" in regard to the staple, which is brought into its final useful form by the act. Ribiat, *infra*. Adding hot water to a pre-made 'noodle-soup-pot' type cup (a dehydrated mixture of freeze-dried seasoning and noodles) would be the final act of completion for such a food as the manufacturer desired to make the product incomplete awaiting the consumer to finish the cooking process at their convenience. This particular example would also violate (cooking) as well if hot water from a kettle/urn was directly applied.

39. Transferring between domains - Transferring something from one domain type to another domain type. This law is often referred to as *carrying*. Chapters 1 and 11 of Talmud tractate Shabbat deals with the *melakha* of transferring from one domain to another, commonly called "carrying". The tractate distinguishes four domains: private, public, semi-public and an exempt area. It holds that the transfer of an article from a private to a public domain is Biblically forbidden. Transferring an article between a semi-public to a private or public domain is Rabbinically prohibited. Transferring an article between an exempt area and any other domain is permissible. There's a special rule regarding the carrying of an article four *amos* (about 1.7 m) which may be forbidden in a public (or semi-public) domain alone, while it's permitted in a private domain or exempt area. If one's in a truly public domain from a Halachic perspective, the area around the individual is considered a small domain within the public area. So, carrying out of that encapsulated surrounding area a person is standing in is problematic as one moves into a 'new' domain every four amos. This is an in-depth area of study with many ramifications. An Eruv functions to merge areas into one encapsulated "private domain" thus allowing people to carry items within the confines of the Eruv, as the area within the Eruv is considered a private domain for these purposes, and therefore no transference is taking place.

For these purposes "transferring" means "removing and depositing", so carrying an article out of one domain type and returning to the same domain type without setting it down in the interim into a different domain type does not constitute transference from one domain type to another domain type. Although, this is rabbinically prohibited. The definition of public and private domain is related to its relative amount of enclosures, not on strict ownership. It should be noted that this is a particularly complex area of law, as the legal definitions of private and public domains are intricate, although clear. Background knowledge, and definitions, of domain types must be understood before one can fully understand the laws of transference in this context. This law is often referred to as *carrying*. This is a misnomer. Carrying within a domain type is perfectly permitted. It's the *transference* between domain types that is considered a creative activity for the purposes of Sabbath observance. Indeed, all an Eruv accomplishes is a merger of different domain types into one domain type, making carrying within the area enclosed by the Eruv no different from carrying within a room of a house (i.e. one domain type, namely a private domain), which is permitted. According to traditional Jewish commentators,[10] this category of *melakha* (work) is mentioned in Exodus 16:29: "Let no man leave (go out) his place on the seventh day" Likewise according to the Talmud,[11] the account of the man who was executed for getting wood in Numbers 15:32 was because he violated this prohibition.

To order more copies of this book, please go to
www.jesusrevolutionbook.com or www.amazon.com
You are welcome to leave your comments about this book at
amazon.com too.

Other books by Billy Ng:
Witnessing To Dracula: A Memoir of Ministry in Romania.
This bestselling book on missions is available at your local church
bookstore or at **www.witnessingtodracula.com** and at
www.amazon.com

Thanks for supporting our ministry! We appreciate it very much.